CLASSIC
HIKES
of
NORTH AMERICA

Also by Peter Potterfield

IN THE ZONE

HIGH HIMALAYA

EVEREST

CLASSIC HIKES OF THE WORLD

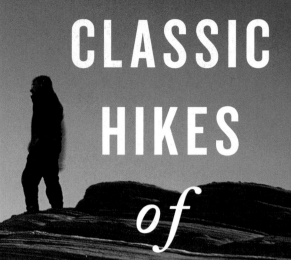

CLASSIC HIKES of NORTH AMERICA

*25 Breathtaking Treks
in the United States
and Canada*

PETER POTTERFIELD

W. W. NORTON & COMPANY

NEW YORK • LONDON

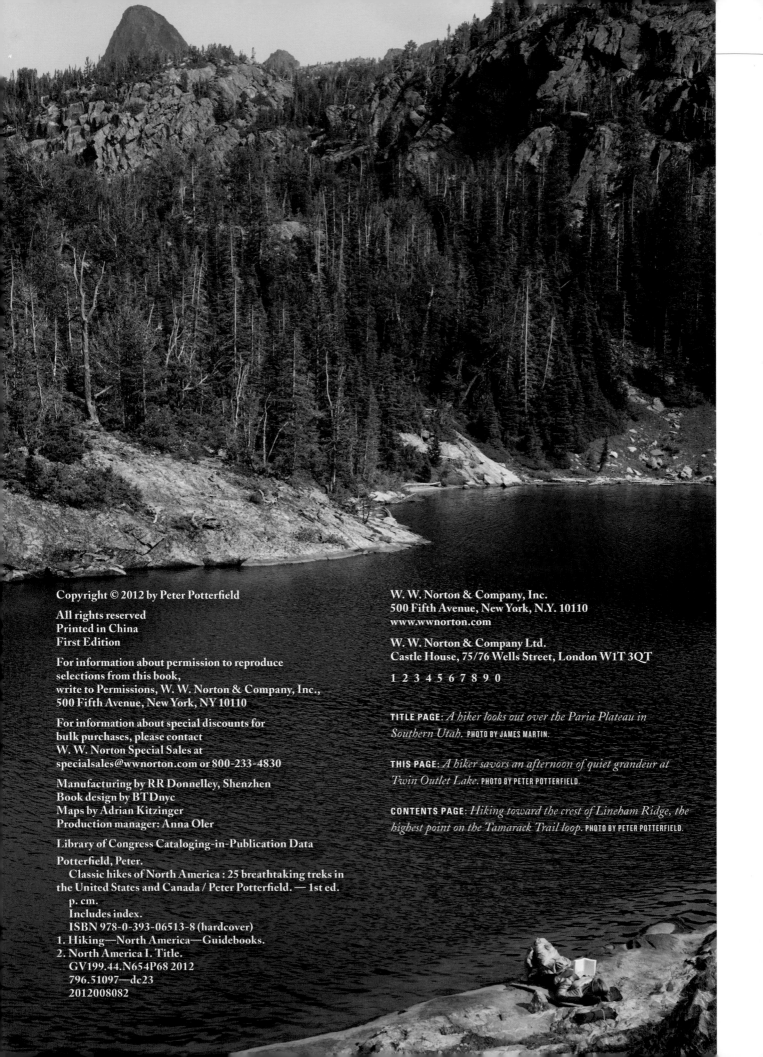

Copyright © 2012 by Peter Potterfield

All rights reserved
Printed in China
First Edition

For information about permission to reproduce
selections from this book,
write to Permissions, W. W. Norton & Company, Inc.,
500 Fifth Avenue, New York, NY 10110

For information about special discounts for
bulk purchases, please contact
W. W. Norton Special Sales at
specialsales@wwnorton.com or 800-233-4830

Manufacturing by RR Donnelley, Shenzhen
Book design by BTDnyc
Maps by Adrian Kitzinger
Production manager: Anna Oler

Library of Congress Cataloging-in-Publication Data

Potterfield, Peter.
   Classic hikes of North America : 25 breathtaking treks in
the United States and Canada / Peter Potterfield. — 1st ed.
   p. cm.
   Includes index.
   ISBN 978-0-393-06513-8 (hardcover)
1. Hiking—North America—Guidebooks.
2. North America I. Title.
   GV199.44.N654P68 2012
   796.51097—dc23
   2012008082

W. W. Norton & Company, Inc.
500 Fifth Avenue, New York, N.Y. 10110
www.wwnorton.com

W. W. Norton & Company Ltd.
Castle House, 75/76 Wells Street, London W1T 3QT

1 2 3 4 5 6 7 8 9 0

TITLE PAGE: *A hiker looks out over the Paria Plateau in Southern Utah.* PHOTO BY JAMES MARTIN.

THIS PAGE: *A hiker savors an afternoon of quiet grandeur at Twin Outlet Lake.* PHOTO BY PETER POTTERFIELD.

CONTENTS PAGE: *Hiking toward the crest of Lineham Ridge, the highest point on the Tamarack Trail loop.* PHOTO BY PETER POTTERFIELD.

This volume is dedicated to the people who work to preserve what's left of wilderness in North America—and actively resist those who would sully or exploit it.

The author takes in the beauty of Skoki Lakes. PHOTO BY REBECKAH HORNUNG.

CONTENTS

ACKNOWLEDGMENTS

Many people who assisted me with this project gave encouragement, material help, photographs, companionship, and sage advice, some going truly beyond the call of duty—or even friendship. I offer my thanks to: James Martin, Bob Farrington, Scott Williams, Star Lawrence, Joel Rogers, Beth Tondreau, Anna Oler, Melody Conroy, Michael Shnayerson, Anna Olsen, Debbie Harrington, Richard Bangs, Ed Viesturs, Maria Coffey, Ed English, Keith Payne, Gillian Marx, Monica Campbell-Hoppe, Heather Dolan, Andrea Peddle, Judy Love Rondeau, Leigh Albra, Charlie Locke, Rebeckah Hornung, Valerie Haig Brown, Carey Tetzlaff, Bard Nordby, Claude Beaudoin, John-Philippe Chartrand, Carla Bechard, Amy McInnis, Karen Hill, Mike Harrelson, Becky Edwards, Robin Hoover, Donnie Sexton, Kellie Kluksdal, Kirk Bachman, Joey Hockett, Buddy Seiner, Julie Jones, Stefan Wackerhagen, Keith Gunnar, Cameron Martindell, Randall Hodges, Craig Romano, Ethan Welty, Dave Schiefelbein, Seth Pollack, Jim Nelson, Elizabeth Wales, Lace Thornberg, Ted Evans, Cooper Atkinson, Moe Witschard, Michael Wald, Jerry Monkman, Frits Meyst, Anton Foltin, Allegra Huston, Angela Salzl, Randy Brooks, Paula Pawlovich, Torsten Eder, Mika Ryan, Carla Mont, Cindy Burr, Mandy Rutkowski, Ian Elman, Laura Steinbach, Nancy Harrison, Shelley Smith, Megan Mayo, Deirdre Skillman, Art Wolfe, and Adrian Kitzinger.

INTRODUCTION

Almost three decades have passed since I first succumbed to the irresistible appeal of wilderness. An early hike took me to a windswept ridge in Colorado's Sangre de Cristo Range. From camp, I looked south across September slopes golden with autumn aspen and ridgetops painted blood-red by a setting sun. It was a transforming vision. At that moment I made a promise to myself to see more of these pristine places, to experience as many of the highlights of the natural world as possible—while they remain beautiful.

So far, I've managed to keep that promise, but it's been a long road with a steep learning curve. In the beginning, my first backcountry forays were made to places close to home. Into the mountains of Shenandoah National Park, the hills of western Massachusetts, and finally into the bigger wilderness of the Rockies and the Sierra, I trudged in too-heavy hiking boots under the backbreaking load of my bulging external-frame pack. It was hard work, but I loved backcountry from the beginning, despite the self-inflicted agonies resulting from my rookie decisions on what to carry and how to go.

But the more you do something, the better you get. After an adult lifetime spent loving wilderness travel, I'm pretty good at it by now. I can move through the backcountry with some ease, with lighter loads but greater comfort. If there is a surprise, it's this: I enjoy backcountry travel now more than ever. And, more importantly, I've gotten better at figuring out where to go. That's the critical skill. When I realized early

on that there were more great wilderness places than one could see in a lifetime, I understood the need to prioritize. The urgency I felt was to find the places and the routes that bring the greatest return on time and effort and expense applied.

That was the idea behind *Classic Hikes of North America*, a book that reflects thirty years of searching for the best routes to the most enchanting places on the continent. The hikes contained here are some of my favorites—at least so far. I'm still looking, and hope I always will be.

People ask me: what are your favorite hikes? I used to struggle with a reply until I realized the truth: they are all my favorites. How does one compare, say, flying to Las Vegas, driving for four hours to the Grand Canyon, and spending four days in the embrace of that earthly wonder with, say, driving to Mount Rainier to spend four days on the wild north side? Can one rate a trip to Newfoundland's pristine Long Range Traverse ahead, or behind, a journey to the incomparable Coyote Gulch tucked away in southern Utah's Escalante Canyon system? I don't see how.

What I can see, however, is that getting out in any of these wild places, whether close to home or far away, is one of the best things we can do with the time we are given. I'm no wilderness snob. If you can't do one of these hikes, do one of the local favorites near your place. The payoff for me is to inspire people, to motivate them to get off the couch and "get out," and reap the joys of wilderness. Because of that, I have worked to make this book not just a collection of appealing destinations, but a utilitarian one, a resource that enables real results. Inspiration is great, but I've learned from long experience that good information can make any wilderness excursion easier, and more fun, and that's what I've tried to supply.

Sometimes reliable information can be hard to come by, so I urge you to benefit from my experience: take the routes and tips compiled here and go see for yourself. I hope to achieve just a couple of things in this volume: to share my enthusiasm for these wonderful hikes, and to provide practical and useful information about how to go about doing them. It is my intention that any fit hiker can do any of the routes in *Classic Hikes of North America* with nothing more than this book and a decent topo map. So now, there's no excuse.

HOW TO USE THIS BOOK

While the hiking routes described in *Classic Hikes of North America* have a tremendous variety of terrain and character, each chapter in the book has uniform elements that make it easy to compare one hike with another.

Each write-up begins with a short, **bold-faced block** of pertinent information. This, at a glance, provides a thumbnail overview for each hike: distance, average number of days required to complete the route, a subjective rating of the physical effort required and psychological challenge encountered on the hike, and, finally, the best location from which to stage for the route.

The number of days recommended for each hike represents a range that reflects the likely time spent on the trail. The low end of the range is the number of days usually required by a fit hiker moving reasonably fast; the high end of the range is what's required for a hiker of average fitness taking time to relish the experience.

Physical challenge is presented on a scale of one to five. Hikes at the low end of the scale, such as the Black Elk Wilderness trek, are there because the time spent each day on the trail is less than six hours, and elevation gain, trail condition, and other factors are moderate. Hikes at the high end of the scale, such as the route along Washington's Olympic Peninsula coast or Newfoundland's Long Range Traverse, are rated high because of long days, dangerous tides, problematic weather conditions, fog and rain, and extremely difficult trail conditions.

The rating for psychological challenge, also on a scale of one to five, reflects the more subtle measures of a given hike that nonetheless can have a significant impact on one's experience. For instance, hiking in North Carolina is relaxing and enjoyable. There are no carnivorous animals to worry about, the track is well-marked, and, being in the East, one is never more than half a day from a road. For these reasons, the Art Loeb Trail deserves as low a rating for psychological challenge as it is high for appeal. Hiking the Tamarack Trail in Waterton National Park, on the other hand, comes with unusual elements, such as unpredictable grizzly bears. Realities like that add stress and uncertainty, which calls for a higher rating for psychological challenge. A trek in the Brooks Range of Alaska can be similarly trying to one's psyche: dependence on light aircraft, the presence of unpredictable predators, and long, hard days in an unforgiving environment can weigh on one's spirit far beyond whatever physical effort is required to get there. For that reason, the Brooks Range trek receives a five on the scale of psychological challenge.

Staging city is meant to be a helpful suggestion, based on my experience, for the best place to prepare for the route in question. Some are obvious: Escalante, Utah, is best for Coyote Gulch; Rapid City, South Dakota, the best choice for the Black Elk Wilderness. In some cases, I've provided a choice: for the Olympic Peninsula hike, Port Angeles is best if you've come from afar and need to stock up on stove fuel and food, but Neah Bay is best for those already well provisioned and equipped.

Beyond the bold-faced copy block, all of the hike descriptions have common elements:

Each chapter begins with a brief **overview** of the hike, noting its appeal and unique features, along with some historical notes. This describes succinctly the appeal of the route, its character, and special considerations.

The overview is followed by a more thorough discussion of **logistics and strategy** that helps provide a feel for how to get where you need to go, where to buy what you need in the way of food or fuel, where to start a given route, and how to incorporate available variations, if any, into your plans. Every hike has its own unique circumstances; some are complicated, some are not. For the Grand Canyon, is it better to descend the Hermit Creek Trail or the Bright Angel? On the Teton Crest Trail, is it better to descend Paintbrush Canyon or Cascade Canyon? On the Chilkoot Pass Trail, how does one get from its terminus at Bennett Lake to Whitehorse? Or even to

Skagway? For Newfoundland's Long Range Traverse, how does one get from the airport in Deer Lake to the start of the hike? These kinds of practical considerations of transport, supply, and accommodation are discussed in this section.

Following the discussion of logistics and strategy comes a brief section on the **hazards**, if any, one might expect to encounter, or should take preparations against. Another short section provides information on the best **time of year** to do the route, which can be more complicated than you might at first expect. For instance, it may be that July and August have statistically the best weather for a hike of the Canadian Rockies' Slate Range. But that, predictably, is also when the backcountry sees its heaviest use, so there is increased competition for campsites and hiking permits. For those reasons, hiking in early or late season may turn out to be the smart choice.

Below these short sections comes the **route description**. Rather than a cryptic or abbreviated note on where the route goes, these descriptions are meant to be useful, advising you in some detail on the correct route, potential trouble spots, recommended camps, detours around predictable obstacles, and particularly strenuous or potentially dangerous sections of trail.

Each chapter concludes with practical information on how to plan for the hike: current address, telephone and Web information on the appropriate management agency or permit issuer, suggestions on sources for trip planning, and, where applicable, information on guide services and shuttle services.

But the really important information on how best to use this book is simply to do it. Use it, as a practical reference or as inspiration. Take a walk in the wilderness. See the quality of light in the evening, get your heart rate up on the steep sections, feel the wind against your face. Look out over that canyon, or that mountain, or that coastline, and remember again how a landscape with nothing in it but the earth can revitalize you.

BELOW: *Crossing Fox Creek Pass on the Teton Crest Trail.* PHOTO BY SCOTT WILLIAMS.

FOLLOWING SPREAD: *Hiking along the magical headwaters of the Merced, with its countless waterfalls and pools, is a highlight of the Yosemite Grand Traverse.* PHOTO BY PETER POTTERFIELD.

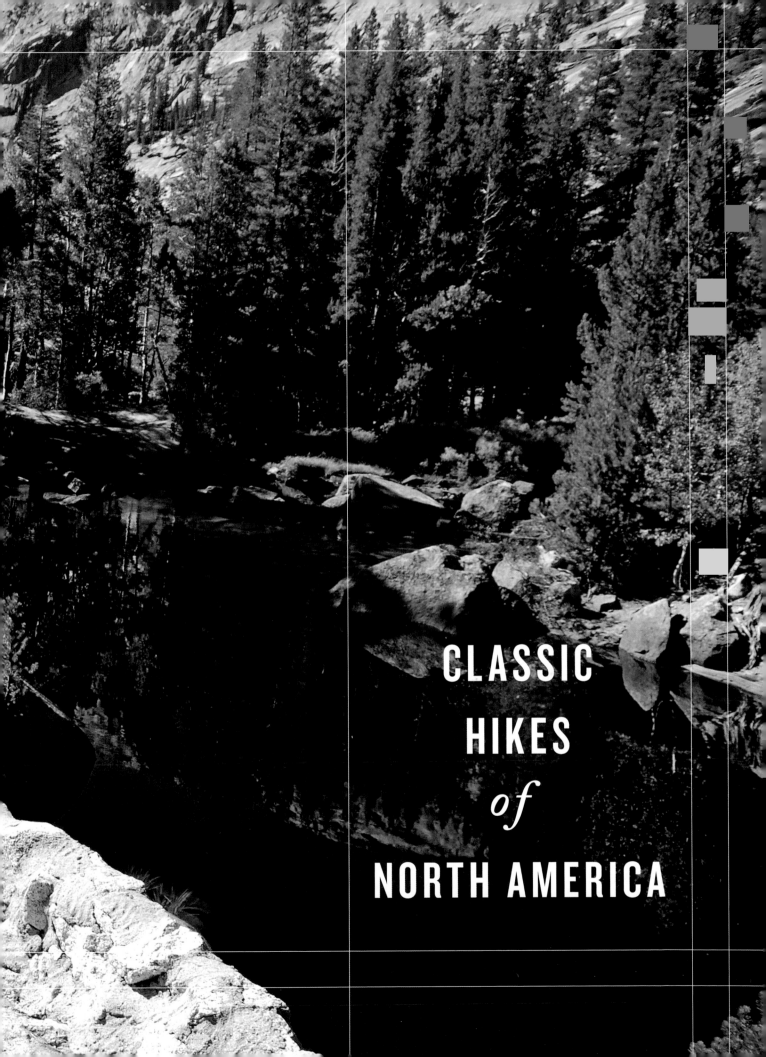

CLASSIC

HIKES

of

NORTH AMERICA

TAMARACK TRAIL
Waterton Lakes National Park, Waterton-Glacier International Peace Park

Alberta, Canada, and Montana, United States

DISTANCE: 23 miles (37 km) one-way
TIME: 2–3 days
PHYSICAL CHALLENGE: 1 2 3 4 5
PSYCHOLOGICAL CHALLENGE: 1 2 3 4 5
STAGING: Waterton Park, Alberta

Waterton is one of those places—Grindelwald is another—where when you finally arrive you could kick yourself for not having come sooner. The immediate question is: what was I thinking? How could I have been so dumb? The hamlet of Waterton itself, relaxed and low-key even in the heart of a mid-August summer, stands in marked contrast to its busier Rocky Mountain sister cities of Kalispell and Banff. This place is truly end-of-the-road laid-back, organically friendly, perversely uncrowded. And when you at last hit the trail for that first foray into the stunning mountain landscape rising all around the town, your appreciation for this out-of-the-way jewel goes off the scale.

The day hiking is so good here that people forget to go backpacking. Signature, full-day classics like the Carthew-Alderson Trail, the Akamina Ridge walk or the unique Crypt Lake Trail and its legendary natural tunnel can reset your threshold for what constitutes world-class alpine hiking. These are

The rugged and remote Lineham Lakes, to which no trail exists. PHOTO BY PETER POTTERFIELD.

A hiker enjoys the view from the spectacular summit of Lineham Ridge. PHOTO BY PETER POTTERFIELD.

beautiful and challenging routes, a good way to get acclimated to the wildness and steepness of the impressive Lewis Range that runs from Waterton down into Glacier National Park, just across the international border. But to really steep yourself in the unique landscape of this, the narrowest part of the Rockies, where the mountains just pop up out of the plain without bothering with foothills, you've got to cycle through a couple of sunrises and sunsets. And the best way to do that is to hike the Tamarack Trail on an overnight trip.

Gird your loins, because this is grizzly bear city. No other park I have visited, not even Denali, comes with bear mojo this intense. Waterton is a place where at the end of the day, you can say, "Hey, let's go see some bears," and within a 15-minute drive enjoy a handful of sightings. Those close encounters feel a little different, a little scarier, when you're out in the backcountry, miles from the safety of the car. But you have to deal with it because the fact is: in Waterton, bears come with the territory.

The bears are here, along with sheep, moose, elk, mule deer, cougar, wolf, and coyote, because Waterton sits on a one-of-a-kind pinch point in the Rocky Mountains, a waist if you will, that creates a natural wildlife corridor. And because the mountains rise so abruptly from the plain, blurring the line between peak and prairie, an incredibly diverse range of flora and fauna exists here. Almost 50 different ecozones converge in just a few miles, from grassland to aspen forest, from wetland to alpine zone, from tundra to subalpine meadow. A coastal influence blowing in from British Columbia adds yet another environmental element to the equation. The result is a place so biologically diverse and abundant that there are more species of wildflowers in Waterton than in Banff and Jasper national parks combined.

The park is unusual in other respects, including the fact that it, and Glacier National Park on the other side of the US–Canadian border, were joined in 1932 to create the first International Peace Park. This collaboration of adjacent parks is not just window-dressing, but a practical way to protect the exceptionally diverse habitat within its boundaries. Parks Canada and the US Park Service work together to manage the unique environment in both parks, along with the wildlife and the humans who come to visit. The two parks are managed as one, so you can actually hike from Canada into the United States and back again, or vice versa. A standard feature to any visit here is the day-long voyage on the venerable *M.V. International* (in service since 1927) down Waterton Lake, the deepest in the Rockies, from the townsite of Waterton to the landing in Glacier National Park at historic Goat Haunt.

The distinctive mountain–prairie interface protected by these parks, and the innovative international management of them, resulted in the Peace Park's designation as a UNESCO World Heritage Site in 1995. It's yet another external accolade for a truly exceptional landscape, but what's more important is how much fun it is to hike here. The Tamarack Trail is not a long hike, just a weekend, less than 24 miles (37 km). But the route will show you wonders, from the alpine gem of Rowe Lake in its perfect basin, to the breathtaking view from Lineham Ridge, to the wild, lonely camp at Lone Lake. This walk is a crash course in the beauty of the mountains around Waterton. And maybe, if you're lucky, you might even see a bear or two.

LOGISTICS & STRATEGY

Look at a map and it's a tough call whether to come to Waterton via Kalispell and Glacier National Park, or Calgary. But learn from my experience and arrive through Calgary. The three-hour high-speed run down Canada Route 2 through the canola fields and small towns of southern Alberta beats the pants off the alternative: the all-day creep up through Missoula or Kalispell, over Going-to-the-Sun Road behind all those RVs, and on to the unknown wait at the tiny, seasonal, closes-at-night Big Chief border station.

So Calgary it is. From the airport, head south on Highway 2 for a couple of hours, turning right, west, on Highway 3 to Pincher Creek (go through Pincher Creek, not Cardston, that saves an hour). Stop in the thriving burg of Pincher Creek for the big grocery shop, enter the park on Highway 6 and finish off the 10-mile (16-km) run into the hamlet of Waterton Park (everybody calls it just Waterton). Except for a big supermarket, everything you need is right here, including lodgings ranging from campgrounds to comfortable hotels and motels, to a surprising variety of restaurants, and a good espresso shop. Outdoor gear shops, shuttle services, and guide services make hiking here easy to organize. Even the hotels dare you to get off the couch and go hiking by presenting you on check-in with the challenge of completing the Waterton Triple Crown, a trio of classic day hikes.

A rental car is useful in Waterton Lakes National Park. Shuttle services do operate, and prove useful for the Tamarack Trail and other hikes, but having your own vehicle makes it much easier to get here, and to explore the park and look for wildlife. Even though the park is small by Rocky Mountain standards at 325,000 acres, it's got a lot of odd geography that calls for exploration. Two main roads leave from the Waterton townsite to the features and trailheads in the park, the Red Rock Parkway and the Akamina Parkway.

The Tamarack Trail loop described here leaves from the end of the Red Rock and finishes halfway down the Akamina. The route is not particularly difficult or long: pretty much a basic weekend trip at two nights and three days, but lots of hikers do it in one

Hikers leave Twin Lakes on their way up the Tamarack Valley to Lone Lake. PHOTO BY FRITS MEYST/ADVENTURE4EVER.COM.

night and two days. The whole point of doing the Tamarack is to see the scenery and to enjoy the Waterton vibe over multiple days in the backcountry. It can be done in either direction but in my opinion the counterclockwise route is best as it saves the longest and most strenuous effort for the final day, when you'll finish at your car and so head back to town instead of making camp.

First, leave your car (or one car) at the Rowe Creek Trailhead on the Akamina Parkway, and take the trailhead shuttle back to town (or catch a ride). The next morning, take the first trailhead shuttle out to the end of the Red Rock Parkway. From the parking lot, you have two options.

The obvious route might seem to be the one to do: taking the Snowshoe Trail to Snowshoe Camp, and then hike on to camp at Twin Lakes, for a 6- to 8-mile (11- to 12-km) day. This option is not recommended. The Snowshoe Trail, an abandoned road, is unaesthetic and slightly boring, and it's open to mountain bikes. Some people don't mind hiking with mountain bikes, but I do. Why choose a trail like that in one of the prettiest parks in the world? For me the decision to do this hike via the Blakiston Creek Trail is a no-brainer, despite a short backtrack required on day two. The Blakiston has less traffic and better views, and follows an exceptionally scenic creek in the early going.

For the recommended option, find the trailhead for the Blakiston Creek Trail at the end of the Red Rock Parkway. Follow the trail west to the intersec-tion with the Tamarack Trail. Turn right on the Tamarack and follow it north over the Bauerman Divide to the first night's camp at Twin Lakes. From the trailhead to Twin Lakes Camp is about 8 miles (12 km). For day two, leave Twin Lakes Camp, backtrack to the Blakiston Trail intersection, and continue south on the Tamarack Trail. The next and final camp is at Lone Lake, just 2.5 miles (4 km) from the intersection. This short day allows ample time for exploring, or side trips to Sage Pass in the morning or South Kootenay Pass at midday.

The other strategy is to choose the one-night, two-day itinerary by hiking directly to Lone Lake on day one, and make that your only overnight location. Hike the Blakiston Trail and then turn south on the Tamarack Trail to Lone Lake on the first day. The distance involved is about the same as hiking to Twin Lakes, just over 8 miles (13 km). You'll miss the scenery on the Bauerman Divide and at pretty Twin Lakes, but you'll eliminate the middle day. This two-day option is about as popular as the three-day option. It's merely a question of how much time you have.

From Lone Lake, there's one more day to go. The final day takes you on a 2,000-foot (650-m) climb 6 miles (9 km) up to spectacular Lineham Ridge, perhaps the most scenic spot in all of the park. Linger here at 8,400 feet (2,600 m) to enjoy lunch and the 360-degree view, including a glimpse down into the remote basin holding Lineham Lake. From the ridge it's an easy 6 miles (9 km) down from the alpine zone into pretty Rowe Lakes basin and down through the forest to where you left your car at the Rowe Creek Trailhead on the Akamina Parkway.

HAZARDS

This is grizzly bear country, and some of the most frequently used trails in the park traverse excellent bear habitat. Bears often use the same trails that humans do. Bear attacks are rare, but they do happen, so you must know proper techniques when hiking in Waterton. Park wardens close trails when aggressive bears are present, but it is incumbent on all hikers to behave properly to prevent avoidable bear–human encounters and unnecessary trail closures. Educate yourself about how to travel and camp safely in bear country. The basics include making noise so you do not surprise a bear; talk, sing, or clap your hands to make your presence known, as most experts think bear bells are not effective. Carry bear spray and

The view of Upper Waterton Lake from the historic Prince of Wales Hotel. PHOTO BY PETER POTTERFIELD.

The deep valley of Blakiston Creek: Lone Lake nestles at its north end. From there, the Tamarack Trail climbs into the high country.
PHOTO BY PETER POTTERFIELD.

know how to use it. Camp carefully by cooking at a 100-yard (100-meter) remove from your tent, and storing all food out of the reach of bears and other wildlife (bring 30 feet or 10 meters of utility cord for this purpose). Ask at the warden station about bear activity when you pick up your permit.

Weather can and does change rapidly in this high but very narrow stretch of mountains. It can snow suddenly any month of the year, including August. Be prepared with proper clothing and camping equipment. Treat or filter all your water.

SEASON

Despite that fact that Waterton is a Rocky Mountain park, the season is just slightly longer here than it is a bit farther north in Banff because the heights of the peaks are slightly lower, and the range is quite narrow at this location. Access to the best hiking remains dependent on the previous year's snowfall, but generally the hiking season ranges from early June to early

October. Early season hikes may warrant the use of an ice ax, as significant snow can linger in the high country. Late season hikes can be particularly rewarding here, as the tamarack trees, which in fact are mountain larches, turn a brilliant gold in the autumn.

A large population of deer lives right in the hamlet of Waterton, sometimes causing injuries and creating problems for humans and pets. PHOTO BY PETER POTTERFIELD.

ROUTE

If you don't have two vehicles, you will need to spot a car at the end of the hike, or arrange for a pickup. From the townsite, drive north on the park entrance road to the landmark Prince of Wales Hotel, reinforced by cables to keep it upright in the fearsome wind. Turn left, west, onto the Akamina Parkway here. Drive 4.5 miles (8 km) to the Rowe Creek Trailhead, and park your car. Hitchhike and arrange for a shuttle back to town, then drive or arrange for the shuttle to the end of the Red Rock Canyon Parkway for the start of your hike.

From the parking lot, find the trailhead for the Blakiston Creek Trail at 5,000 feet (1,500 m). Just a mile or so in, just beyond the falls, look for the spectacular rock pools in the creek. From there, follow the Blakiston Creek Trail west for almost 6 miles (9.2 km) to the intersection with the Tamarack Trail. Turn right there and follow the trail north over the Bauerman Divide (6,700 feet, 2,070 m). This part of the trail is steep for much of the way, but takes you to the first night's camp at scenic Twin Lakes, less than 2 miles (3 km) from the trail intersection. Camp in the tent sites between the two lakes.

On day two, leave your camp at Twin Lakes Camp, and hike back up and over Bauerman Divide, backtrack to the Blakiston Trail intersection and continue south on the Tamarack Trail. The next and final camp is at Lone Lake, just 2.5 miles (4 km) from the intersection via an undulating trail with several creek crossings and a section through the broken timber of an avalanche path. This short day allows some time for exploring along the way, or side trips to Sage Pass in the morning or South Kootenay Pass at midday.

If you opt for the two-day itinerary, hike directly to Lone Lake on day one. Take the Blakiston Trail from the end of the Red Rock Canyon Parkway and then turn south on the Tamarack Trail to Lone Lake on the first day. The distance involved is about the same as hiking to Twin Lakes, 8 miles (13 km). You'll miss the scenery on the Bauerman Divide and at Twin Lakes, but you'll eliminate the middle day: a pity, but it's a good option if you only have a weekend.

From Lone Lake, the final day is a long one, but the highlight of the trip. The route leaves Lone Lake, climbs steeply out of the basin, over a subsidiary ridge (the shoulder of Festubert Mountain) and on up the big valley toward the big climb up to Lineham Ridge. That big wall to your right all day is the Continental Divide, and also the ridge that marks the border between Alberta and British Columbia. This is a big elevation day, more than 2,000 feet (650 m) in the 6 miles (9 km) from Lone Lake to the Lineham Ridge.

A long U-shaped sidehill loop, like a giant switchback, takes you inexorably but ever so gradually out of the Tamarack's deep valley to the top of Lineham Ridge. The spectacular ridge is perhaps the most scenic spot in all of the park. Linger here to enjoy lunch and the 360-degree view, including down into the remote basin holding Lineham Lake, where no trail or approved route exists.

From the ridgetop, follow the trail around as it sidehills dramatically around the upper basin in another big loop before reaching the intersection with the Rowe Lakes Trail. The Rowe Lakes Trail descends gradually into the emerald green sub-alpine basin holding Lower Rowe Lake, an easy 3 miles (5 km) from the high point on the ridge. A herd of bighorn sheep often feeds on the hillside here.

From the lake, it's an easy, descending 2.5-mile (4-km) hike down through the trees to where you have left your car at the Rowe Creek Trailhead on the Akamina Parkway. From here, the drive back to town is less than 15 minutes.

INFORMATION

A wilderness permit is required for overnight stays in the backcountry. Permits are available from the visitor center in Waterton, or you can reserve in advance, which is recommended, especially for overnight trips. Reservations for backcountry trips may be made 90 days in advance begin-

CLOCKWISE FROM TOP LEFT: *wild prickly rose, an icon of Alberta; sky pilot; Indian Paintbrush; Mariposa lily.*
PHOTOS BY PETER POTTERFIELD

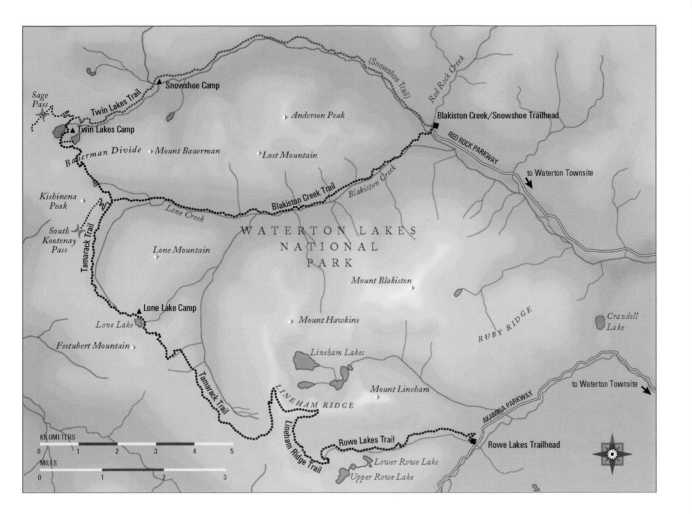

ning April 1 of each year, and must be paid for at the time the reservation is made.

To make reservations, call the backcountry warden office at: 403-859-5140 from April 1 through mid-May, or 403-859-5133 after mid-May.

Your reserved permit must be picked up at the visitor center in Waterton no sooner than 24 hours in advance of the start date of the trip.

For more information, contact park headquarters:

WATERTON LAKES NATIONAL PARK
Box 200
Waterton Park, AB T0K 2M0
403-859-5133
E-mail: waterton.info@pc.gc.ca
www.pc.gc.ca/eng/pn-np/ab/waterton/index.aspx

Shuttle Services and Hiking Guides

Tamarack Outfitters in the townsite of Waterton has a wide range of outdoor gear and clothing; its affiliate, Waterton Outdoor Adventures, offers shuttle services and guiding services to hikers. The Trail of the Great Bear also offers guide services in Waterton.

TAMARACK OUTDOOR OUTFITTERS
403-859-2378
E-mail: tamarackwaterton@mac.com
www.watertonvisitorservices.com

WATERTON OUTDOOR ADVENTURES
403-859-2378
E-mail: watertonshuttle@mac.com
www.watertonvisitorservices.com

THE TRAIL OF THE GREAT BEAR
114 Waterton Avenue
Waterton Park, AB T0K 2M0
403-859-2663
E-mail: tgbear@telusplanet.net
www.trailofthegreatbear.com

Planning a Trip

For more information on planning a trip to Alberta, see the Travel Alberta Web site:
www.travelalberta.com

COYOTE GULCH
Canyons of the Escalante
Grand Staircase Escalante
National Monument

Southern Utah, United States

DISTANCE: **28 miles (45 km) round-trip**
TIME: **3–4 days**
PHYSICAL CHALLENGE: **1 2 3 4 5**
PSYCHOLOGICAL CHALLENGE: **1 2 3 4 5**
STAGING: **Escalante, Utah**

Even old desert hands, already well seduced by the allure of the American Southwest's canyon country, are blown away by this pretty little canyon as it flows from the desert of Scorpion Flat toward the mighty and enigmatic Escalante River. As if the ineffably beautiful Coyote Bridge, the only natural arch I've seen that still has water running under it, wasn't enough, there's Jacob Hamblin Arch, Anasazi ruins, and a litany of other amazing features. I can't stay away from Coyote Gulch, and so now just refine my strategy to give myself the best experience there.

The attraction of Coyote Gulch lies in its broad spectrum of temptations. Lots of minor canyons are pretty, but few have water; some have arches and bridges, but few have both those *and* Puebloan ruins; and, finally, the most interesting canyons seldom have good camping. Coyote Gulch has all of those elements, and for a desert walk this rich in experience comes with fairly easy access during much of the year. Ask any hiker who has been there, and what they all take home is how pretty this canyon is. Leave camp and start down toward the Escalante, past the waterfalls and hanging gardens, and the ineffable beauty of the place takes your breath away.

Coyote Gulch is situated on the edge of the nearly 2-million-acre Grand Staircase Escalante National Monument, a controversial but epic piece of conservation that finally adds genuine protection to a stunning desert landscape that includes many of the Escalante River canyons. If it did nothing else, saving the Escalante canyon system itself makes the relatively new monument a success, as this is a stunning landscape even by Utah standards. And none of the Escalante canyons has more appeal than Coyote Gulch, which, ironically, lies mostly within the Glen Canyon Recreation Area.

The fact that you get to Coyote Gulch via the famous Hole-in-the-Rock Road, a route of historical importance to the Mormons of Utah, adds both interest and difficulties to getting here. The route was discovered in the late 1800s, and then improved, to allow wagon traffic from the west side of the Colorado River to the east, down the steep walls of Glen Canyon. The "hole" in Hole-in-the-Rock is more accurately a natural notch that was deepened by blasting powder and made less steep by picks, chisels, and human labor, eventually creating a route to Mormon communities in southeastern Utah.

Today, the historic 62-mile Hole-in-the-Rock Road provides access not just to Coyote Gulch but to a number of Utah's most interesting slot canyons, and even to the Escalante River itself, where it empties into Lake Powell. The access, however, is problematic, with much of the road requiring a four-wheel drive vehicle, and even then in wet conditions it routinely becomes impassable. The road figures heavily in approach strategies.

But Coyote Gulch can be entered in varying ways, and in most conditions there's a way in. The classic

A hiker approaches the stunning formation known as Coyote Bridge. PHOTO BY PETER POTTERFIELD.

route is to start at its west end, and follow the gulch past its high points: Hamblin Arch, then Coyote Bridge, and eventually past Anasazi ruins and Cliff Arch to its confluence with the Escalante a few miles upstream from where the Escalante flows into Lake Powell. Reliable water, good campsites, and fascinating natural features make Coyote Gulch an increasingly powerful draw for canyon hikers.

As this once obscure canyon is discovered by more hikers, a confusing number of access options have arisen in the past few years that potentially can be dangerous. As with any hike in the deep desert, be careful how you go, but do your research and go. This is a canyon you do not want to miss.

LOGISTICS & STRATEGY

There are half a dozen ways to do this hike, all appealing, but many with serious potential desert-travel dangers or problematic transportation issues. My recommendation is to do it as suggested below, which maximizes enjoyment, minimizes danger and psychological stress, and gives you two passes in opposite directions through this amazing canyon.

The hike is best staged from Escalante, Utah, a small town with a long, rich history that dates back to 1776, when Franciscan missionaries first arrived here. Its more contemporary heritage as a ranching center has given way in recent years to that of an important tourist town. Surrounded by wilderness, Escalante's laid-back cluster of cafes, grocery stores, and motels makes it a comfortable base for exploring the region. Its position at the very start of the Hole-in-the-Rock Road makes it the logical staging point for a hike in Coyote Gulch. Expect to drive six hours from Salt Lake City, or about five hours from Las Vegas, to reach Escalante.

From town, your strategy takes shape. The entrance to Hole-in-the-Rock Road lies a few miles

23

east of Escalante on Highway 12. The road itself is a big part of the equation. For much of the year, and for most of the first 40 miles (64 km), the unpaved road is pretty much passable in an ordinary car. But rain can change that in a moment's notice, and road conditions can deteriorate so that a section that last week was no problem, now requires a high-clearance four-wheel-drive vehicle to pass. In wet conditions, sometimes nobody gets through. I have been chased out of Coyote Gulch to beat a forecast downpour more than once, so be aware that the road has to be factored in to your plans.

The farther you go on the road, the more problematic it gets, so it's best to keep the distance as short as possible. For decades, two access points to Coyote Gulch were used: Red Well, about 31 miles (50 km) down the road, with a 2-mile (3-km) spur road; and Hurricane Wash, for years the *voi normal*, and still the most popular access, about 34 miles (55 km) down the road. Either of these trailheads works well, distances are very close to being equal, and both are recommended.

In the past few years, adventurous hikers have begun using two other access routes, both leaving from Fortymile Ridge Road, which intersects the Hole-in-the-Rock Road at approximately 37 miles (60 km). The Crack-in-the-Wall Route leaves from the end of the rough Fortymile Ridge Road and travels cross-country to a narrow notch in a rock wall, which leads to a long descent into Coyote Gulch via a humongous sand dune down toward its confluence with the Escalante. The other new route leads from midway on the Fortymile Ridge Road, traverses a desert flat cross-country (map and compass necessary) to a descent requiring technical climbing skills that leads to the canyon floor near Hamblin Arch.

Neither of these new routes is recommended except for experienced desert navigators and practiced rock climbers, who will find their own way. These approaches involve navigational problems and dead reckoning, off-trail travel in an inhospitable environment, and in the end do not materially add to the Coyote Gulch experience. In theory, the Crack-in-the-Wall Route could be used in conjunction with a vehicle shuttle to make a one-way trip out of a hike through Coyote Gulch, but then you'd have to take two cars down the Hole-in-the-Rock Road, and also forgo the return hike back up the gulch.

Hikers won't keep their boots dry for long as they head down-gulch below Coyote Bridge toward the Escalante River.
PHOTO BY PETER POTTERFIELD.

The elusive Coyote Gulch rock art, from the Fremont culture, which can be found only by the careful observer in the lower section of the gulch. PHOTO BY RANDALL HODGES.

I recommend starting the hike from either Red Well Trailhead or Hurricane Wash Trailhead. Driving mileage and hiking mileage are virtually the same for either route, with a slight hiking-distance advantage going to Hurricane Wash. From Red Well, it's about 14 miles (23 km) to the Escalante River; from Hurricane Wash, about 13 miles (21 km). Whichever trailhead you start from, the recommended strategy remains the same: do a three-day, two-night hike in Coyote Gulch. The itinerary is this: hike into the gulch, set up your camp in the upper canyon or midway in the gulch, day hike down to the mouth of Coyote Gulch at the confluence with the Escalante on the second day, return to your camp that night, and hike out the third day. This gives you plenty of time to see this remarkable canyon, and to do so in both directions. If you have more time, spend more time.

From the trailhead at Red Well, hike down into the upper part of the gulch and continue to the confluence with Hurricane Wash, about 6 miles (10 km) and three hours down canyon. (One factor to consider is that the Red Well start gets you to reliable water quicker, in about an hour.) From the trailhead at Hurricane Wash, right on the Hole-in-the-Rock

Road, hike the 5 miles (8 km) and three hours down the wash into the gulch. This is not an aesthetic approach, but a bit of a sandy slog, and it can be unpleasantly hot in the afternoon. Its appeal is that it is direct and straightforward, and gets you right to the good stuff.

Whichever trailhead you choose, you have the option to make camp near the confluence of Coyote Gulch with Hurricane Gulch, or continue downstream a few miles for your base camp. Many good campsites can be found in the Hurricane Gulch–Coyote Gulch confluence area, and this is the place where I usually make camp. Other hikers prefer to go a bit farther, to continue down canyon to campsites near Coyote Bridge, and establish base camp there in mid-gulch.

There are campsites near Hamblin Arch, but they are usually occupied, and too close to the trail, so the best strategy is to camp near the confluence with Hurricane Wash, or continue to the campsites near Coyote Bridge. One thing to remember is that once you are in the gulch, the day hike down to the Escalante and back is not an arduous day, so pick your campsite with privacy and quiet in mind. Proximity to the Escalante is secondary. Coyote Gulch grows ever more popular each year so find an out-of-the-way camp.

From almost any camping location, the confluence with the Escalante is easily reached in a day hike, allowing for fascinating exploration and a return to camp that evening. On the third day, hike out to your car. Whether you approach via Red Well or Hurricane Wash, your experience will be much the same. Camp on benches above the creek in the event of forecast rain and its potential for flash floods.

From the confluence of Hurricane Wash and Coyote Gulch, it's about 10 miles (16 km) to the Escalante, a few miles less if you camp near Coyote Bridge. The imposing Jacob Hamblin Arch is reached in about 2 miles (3 km); Coyote Bridge about 2 miles (3 km) farther on. The hike down-canyon is a joy, a reason to come here. You have to make frequent crossings of the creek, and you can keep your boots dry for a while, but you'll be wading in water over your boot tops by the time you get below Coyote Bridge.

Beyond the bridge, watch for pictographs and ruins high on the canyon walls, and take time to enjoy the waterfalls spilling toward the Escalante. The farther you go, the wetter it gets down here. The lower canyon, with its waterfalls, is as lush, cool, and green as any canyon in the southwest. Watch for a glimpse of Cliff Arch, above the north rim, about halfway to the river. You'll have to find your way around a waterfall in this section, and about half a mile before reaching the Escalante, you'll have to scramble up and over a bench to reach the Escalante.

In most conditions, it's possible to walk across the Escalante for a better view of Stevens Arch on the opposite side of the river. But if you have time, before you reach the Escalante (or on your way back), clamber up the big sand dune toward the rim near the start of the Crack-in-the-Wall Route, for better views of stunning Stevens Arch, across the Escalante. If you have an extra day, think about hiking up to Stevens Arch.

You do need a backcountry permit to hike in Coyote Gulch, but there's no need to stop at a ranger station as these are free and can be self-issued at the trailheads.

The combination of red rock walls and lush vegetation makes Coyote Gulch a favorite hike among the canyons in the Escalante Canyon system. PHOTO BY PETER POTTERFIELD.

HAZARDS

The primary hazard here is the desert terrain, and somehow getting lost between the gulch, and its water, and your car. Navigate carefully, and keep extra food and water in your car should you become stuck by road conditions or break down on the Hole-in-the-Rock Road. Treat or filter all water carefully. Remember, there's always water in Coyote Gulch.

My partner and I made a wrong turn in Hurricane Wash, and when we backtracked to correct our mistake, we found a line of big, unmistakable mountain lion paw prints in the sand over ours, made just minutes before. We had been stalked by a cougar. It happens. Be aware. Be vigilant.

SEASON

Everybody comes here in spring, March to late May, and fall, September and October, and those times are optimum for weather. But you're likely to have lots of

company, so think about coming in February or November to give yourself a better chance for solitude. Summer is just too hot, and it comes with flash-flood danger from thunderstorms, and lots of bugs.

ROUTE

About two miles east of Escalante, between mileposts 65 and 66, turn south on the Hole-in-the-Rock Road. The distance markers on the Hole-in-the-Rock Road are in kilometers, so don't be confused.

For Red Well Trailhead: drive 31 miles (50 km) down the Hole-in-the-Rock Road to a left-hand turnoff, signed for Red Well; drive for a little less than a mile, bear left at the fork, and drive a little less than a mile to the trailhead. A sandy wash takes you down into Coyote Gulch near its confluence with Big Hollow Wash (not labeled on some maps), past the confluence with Dry Fork Coyote, and on to the confluence with Hurricane Wash in about three hours and about 6 miles (10 km).

For the Hurricane Wash Trailhead: Drive 34 miles (55 km) down the Hole-in-the-Rock Road, watch for a location where the road dips into a dry, sandy wash, with a parking area visible on the right side of the road. This is Hurricane Wash. Simply start hiking east in the shallow, sandy wash; in approximately 2 miles (3.2 km), the wash narrows a bit and canyon walls begin to rise; in the next couple of miles the canyon deepens, offering some welcome shade, and water appears in the bottom of the gulch. The wash reaches its confluence with Coyote Gulch in about 5 miles (8 km) and less than three hours.

The confluence of Coyote Gulch and Hurricane Wash marks the beginning of the best part of Coyote Gulch. Navigation in Coyote Gulch is no problem, just walk downstream. I suggest making your base camp just downstream of the confluence on several big benches above the creek. Some people like to hike 2 or 3 miles (4–5 km) farther to camp near Coyote Bridge, which shortens the day hike to the Escalante but adds distance to your backpacking.

Spend the next day exploring the gulch. Look for pictographs and Anasazi ruins high on the canyon walls below Coyote Bridge. The route will cross the creek dozens of times, and once you are below Coyote Bridge you will want to change into river shoes. The route downstream is straightforward, but with several problems. A waterfall below Cliff Arch will force you high onto the south wall of the canyon. And very near the confluence with the Escalante, a boulder jam will force you up on a steep slick rock bench that can be tricky to descend.

The normal approach into Coyote Gulch follows the shallow Hurricane Wash from Hole-in-the-Rock Road. PHOTO BY PETER POTTERFIELD.

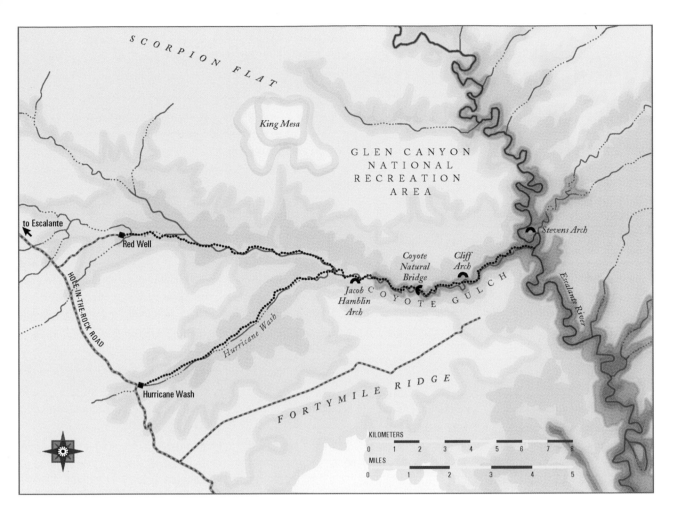

Stevens Arch comes into view before you arrive at the Escalante. If you have the time, clamber up the big sand dune on the south wall for a spectacular view from the rim, and consider crossing the Escalante and scrambling up to Stevens Arch.

Leave yourself enough time to retrace your steps back to your camp before dark. The gulch takes on a subtly different character on the hike back, and you get to see all the highlights from this new perspective. If you are on the two-night, three-day schedule, hike out to your car the next day.

Note that it is possible to get off route coming out via Hurricane Wash. Epic tales of survival have been told of people who mistake the Red Well route for Hurricane Wash, and end up in a world of hurt, hiking out to the wrong trailhead. If you get started on the correct route out via Hurricane Wash, you can still take an erroneous route, but your mistake becomes obvious in a few hundred yards. A useful tip is to bear right if presented with two equally appealing options while hiking west in the wash out to your car. The Red Well exit is much more straightforward.

A backpackers' camp in the western section of Coyote Gulch, on a bench well above the stream. PHOTO BY PETER POTTERFIELD.

INFORMATION

Permits are required to hike and camp in Coyote Gulch, but there is no charge. Permits can be self-issued at the trailheads for both Red Well and Hurricane Wash, and at the interagency visitor center in Escalante.

ESCALANTE INTERAGENCY VISITOR CENTER
P.O. Box 511
Escalante, UT 84726
435-826-5499

LONG RANGE TRAVERSE
Gros Morne National Park

Newfoundland, Canada

DISTANCE: 23 miles (37 km) one-way
TIME: 4–5 days
PHYSICAL CHALLENGE: 1 2 3 4 5
PSYCHOLOGICAL CHALLENGE: 1 2 3 4 5
STAGING: Deer Lake, Newfoundland

Newfoundland's Long Range Traverse is a unique 23-mile (37-km) backcountry route of growing reputation among wilderness cognoscenti. The storied traverse follows the ridgelines and valleys of Newfoundland's highest peaks where they rise abruptly 2,500 feet (765 m) above the island's west coast along the Gulf of St. Lawrence. The landscape here in Gros Morne National Park is as dramatic as it is remote, carved by glaciers from massive, uplifted blocks of granite that form the plateau. Huge, landlocked fjord-like bodies of water, locally called "ponds," dominate the views seaward toward the gulf.

Only in quirky, sparsely populated Newfoundland would features this dramatic be called ponds, but this place is full of understatement, and surprises. A full five time zones from my home in Seattle, the island is actually closer to London than it is to the west coast of North America. Canada's most out-there province is rapidly gaining worldwide traction as the place to come for wilderness outings. (For the record: Newfoundland is an island, Newfoundland and Labrador together make a province.)

Newfoundland has been drawing adventurous types from both Europe and North America in increasing numbers, winter and summer, and one big reason is the Long Range Traverse. This wilderness route through the mountains in Gros Morne National Park requires a water taxi to begin, and excellent map-and-compass skills to complete. Beware, there is no trail here, so your backcountry navigation needs to be sharp. In fact, the park war-dens here make you take along a locator beacon, what they call a "caribou collar," before they'll even give you a hiking permit. The idea is that if you get lost, they can find you with the transmitter much more quickly than searching through the vast expanse of mountains that follows the spine of the Great Northern Peninsula.

You know you're in for something special as soon as the boat drops you off at the head of Western Brook Pond to begin the five-day Long Range Traverse. A steep gorge leads up from the pond in a complicated, overgrown bushwhack, with waterfalls

Once out of the long gully, a hiker stops to get his bearings above spectacular Western Brook Pond before setting a course to continue the traverse. PHOTO BY PETER POTTERFIELD.

casting spray that settles on your outerwear like rain. When you finally get out of the weeds, that first view back down to the majestic inland fjord, cut off from the sea eons ago by a huge glacial moraine, beggars description. The long, narrow body of water is defined by thousand-foot-high rock walls, capped the day I was there by a low layer of cloud that emphasized its wild mood. Long, wispy waterfalls pour off high cliffs of exfoliated granite in a way that evokes memories of Yosemite Valley.

The top of the gorge offers the first look at what you're in for: a verdant landscape of mountain mead-ows, rolling peaks and shimmering lakes stretching out as far as one can see. It is a striking and slightly sobering expanse of wilderness, and one can't help but note that everything sort of looks alike. Navigating up the gorge is a piece of cake compared to what comes next: a cross-country venture through rugged terrain with few reliable landmarks but a lot of the dense alpine vegetation Newfoundlanders call "tuck-amore," better known to me as alpine krummholz. The stuff is so thick it's impossible to force a route through it, so you have to go around it, and that com-plicates navigation big time.

Caribou roam through the Long Range Mountains in significant numbers, seemingly unafraid of hikers nearby.
PHOTO BY PETER POTTERFIELD.

LOGISTICS & STRATEGY

The Long Range Traverse in Newfoundland's Gros Morne National Park is probably best staged from the city of Corner Brook, Newfoundland, served by the nearby airport in the smaller town of Deer Lake. Deer Lake is the gateway to both the Great Northern Peninsula and Gros Morne National Park, but the larger city of Corner Brook, less than an hour away, offers more in the way of accommodations, restaurants, guide services, and other essentials. Corner Brook and Deer Lake are almost a full day's drive from St. John's, capital city of the province of Newfoundland and Labrador, so it's way better to fly directly to Deer Lake, which is surprisingly easy to do. Good connections abound from Toronto and Montreal, or from Boston and Newark, and even other cities in the northeastern United States.

Corner Brook is actually farther away from Gros Morne National Park than Deer Lake, but its array of services makes it the logical starting point. However, if you arrive at the airport at Deer Lake with everything you need, and are not meeting an operator or guide service, an argument can be made for another strategy: pick up your rental car and make the one-hour drive directly to the hamlet of Rocky Harbour, which is in Gros Morne National Park, and stage your hike from there (or from one of the car campgrounds in Gros Morne National Park). No matter whether you stage in Corner Brook or Rocky Harbour, make sure you have hotel reservations in advance, particularly during the summer months. And be sure to reserve your hiking permit in advance.

You'll need to pick up the hiking permit at Gros Morne National Park Visitor Centre, 45 minutes from the airport at Deer Lake. Once there, you will be instructed to watch a video about hiking the Long Range Traverse, which warns of bad weather and the difficulties of navigation. The chief concern is bad visibility. Since you're navigating without the aid of a trail, cloud and whiteout can force your party to hunker down until the weather improves enough to see where you are going. The visitor center is also where you can buy a map, and trace the correct route (off a master map) on a light table purpose-built for that task. This is where you pick up your "caribou collar" (a locator beacon in the form of a VHF telemetry unit or radio-locator beacon), which is mandatory, along with your permit.

An experienced hiking party would have little trouble doing the Long Range Traverse on its own,

---

Welcome to hiking in the Long Range Mountains. The next four to five days is an engaging combination of map reading, compass bearings, dead reckoning and GPS observations. There's no time for daydreaming on this jaunt. But the biggest surprise is the sheer scale of this backcountry. My partner and I would carefully navigate from lake to peak to ridge, only to finally peer over and see that the lake we thought would be *right there* was instead *way over there*. When in the Long Range Mountains, the wildlife—including moose and caribou in abundance—rivals the terrain for wonder, and makes this perhaps the premier wilderness jaunt in eastern Canada.

The upside of that vast scale and authentic challenge is that it keeps the crowds down: my party and I had this amazing route nearly to ourselves the whole way. And this is a hike that never lets up. Near the final days, beyond Green Island Pond, the geography squeezed us between a series of high ridges and the dropoff above Ten Mile Pond, giving us the perfect perspective on the fjord-like lake. This was a vantage point my partner, a native Newfoundlander, had always wanted to see, even as a kid, so I was glad to be there with when he finally got that view. "What an amazing route," was all he could say, shaking his head, as we gazed at the pond and the Gulf of St. Lawrence beyond. We had been saying that to each other the whole way. It's easy to see why Gros Morne National Park has been a UNESCO World Heritage Site for more than two decades.

but logistics make the option of going with a local guide service easier. Trailhead transportation is definitely an issue, and it's one factor in your decision whether to do the hike on your own or go with an outfitter or guide service. Whatever option you chose, you will need to get a ride to, or leave one vehicle at, the Gros Morne Trailhead (which is the end of the route and also serves as the trailhead for those climbing Gros Morne Mountain, probably the most popular hike in the park), and then somehow get up to the trailhead for Western Brook Pond, an approximately 30-minute drive farther north. Guide services can help arrange transportation, and permits, and food, and fuel, all of which makes arriving from afar quicker and easier than trying to do it all yourself.

Since this was my first visit to Newfoundland, local expertise was needed. I asked Ed English of Linkum Tours in Corner Brook to help me organize the logistics for my traverse of the Long Range Mountains. He picked me up from the airport in Deer Lake, handled my accommodations on arrival in Corner Brook (and Rocky Harbour), took care of the permits and trailhead transportation, and set me up with Keith Payne, an educator and wilderness guide who grew up along this coast, who proved immensely informative. As a journalist, I know there is no substitute for local knowledge. I could have done it all on my own, but it might have added a day or two to my trip, as well as extra expense (to rent a car, for instance) and a few headaches.

On the day you begin, leave one car at the Gros Morne Trailhead, where the Long Range Traverse ends, and arrange transportation to the trailhead for Western Brook Pond farther north, where the traverse begins. A long gravel and boardwalk trail leads to the dock area for the water taxis/sightseeing vessels that make the run up Western Brook Pond. The boat will be full of people, but only a handful will disembark with hiking gear at the stop at the head of the pond, about two hours from the dock. The tourists look on with exclamations of wonder as the bold backpackers leave the safety of the boat and disembark for the wilderness.

From the landing place, hikers head up the steep gorge at the head of Western Brook Pond. You'd think navigating up the gorge would be dead easy, but it's not. There are lots of dead ends, lots of ways to expend energy getting nowhere or backtracking. Eventually, everybody finds the way, gaining the crest of the ridge at the top of the gorge. That's when the first views of

Ten Mile Pond is a striking inland fjord cut off from the sea eons ago by a huge glacial moraine. The Gulf of St. Lawrence is in the distance. PHOTO BY PETER POTTERFIELD.

Hikers drop into Ferry Gulch near the terminus of the traverse only to encounter several large moose. Welcome to hiking in Newfoundland. PHOTO BY PETER POTTERFIELD.

this expansive wilderness come, and when the hiker realizes the navigational challenges that lie ahead. Green ridges (even in August), lakes, and peaks stretch to the horizon. It is beautiful, but it all kind of looks alike. Which way to go? It's time to get out the map, the compass, and the GPS device, and don't even think about doing this route without all three.

Most guided parties take five days (six for those parties that hike the shoreline trail of Western Brook Pond instead of taking the water taxi) to do the traverse, and in my opinion that is pretty good timing, if perhaps a day longer than necessary. But, pressed for time, and being in a small, fit party, Keith and I did the whole thing in three days, two nights on the trail. I don't necessarily recommend that, but it can be done. The point is: this is not a place to hurry through. Four days is probably the best.

The route is often described as a 37 km route, or about 23 miles. But that's measured as the crow flies, and the actual distance walked will be much longer, the result of detours mandated by terrain and the thick patches of tuckamore. A typical party, guided or otherwise, usually follows this five-day, four-night itinerary: leave the head of Western Brook Pond in late morning and camp at Little Island Pond; hike the next day to Marks Pond; hike the next day to Hardings Pond; hike the next day to Green Island Pond; then hike out to the Gros Morne Trailhead.

But that itinerary can be shortened. Keith and I wanted to shave several days off the usual travel time, so we hiked the first day all the way from the boat landing to Marks Pond. On arrival there, I was amazed to find a lakeside campsite of pristine quality, in glorious solitude. This was exactly the sort of wilderness experience I had hoped to find here in Newfoundland, and it's a reason to come here. For our final camp we hiked beyond Green Island Pond,

passing a small herd of caribou, who paid us no mind at all, and made camp on an open alpine plateau within sight of Gros Morne Mountain. The mountain for which the park is named misses being the highest peak on the island of Newfoundland by 8 meters (about 25 feet), but it is an impressive sight nonetheless. Once again, we camped in solitude, if you don't count the family of ptarmigans running around, seemingly unconcerned by us.

Given the variations possible, this, clearly, is a route that can be done at one's own pace. Take two nights or four, just be careful when navigating around the thick alpine vegetation. The tuckamore is cut through with clear trails, called caribou leads, created by the constant passage of the animals, and they are tempting. But they can lead you astray. Our only misstep came beyond Hardings Pond, in rugged terrain called the Middle Barrens, where we cleverly thought we'd go around a peak on a caribou lead instead of over it. This technique had served us well a few times before but it was a mistake here. By the time we realized we had been lured off the route, we had to undertake a brutal bushwhack to get back on course. After that, we made sure to stay closer to the little black line drawn on our map.

We thankfully avoided the infamous fog and bad visibility that is a standard feature of this hike. It's serious business. In a cloud, there's no recourse but to stay put until the weather clears. It's just not prudent to try to travel in a wilderness like this when you can't see where you are going. But we did get a taste of the world-famous wildlife of the region on our final day. After dropping down into Ferry Gulch, we were met by the biggest bull moose Keith had ever seen, and that's saying something. I was fascinated, but Keith showed wise caution, and we made a big detour around the huge beast to join the popular trail coming off the summit of Gros Morne.

We hiked out via the trail coming off Gros Morne Mountain down to the truck we had stashed at the trailhead parking lot several days before. From there, it's an hour's drive back to Corner Brook. Since we were not completely sure when we would be hiking out, I had arranged to stay in Rocky Harbour for a night before getting a lift back to Corner Brook. Keith and I made the 20-minute drive from the trailhead into Rocky Harbour. There, we enjoyed a big breakfast of the local specialty, fish cakes, and I settled in at a local inn for a long shower and a day of catching up on notes before heading back to Corner Brook the next day.

HAZARDS

Perched right on the edge of the Gulf of St. Lawrence, right in the path of major weather systems, it is the fog, storm, and whiteout that poses the greatest risk to hikers on the Long Range Traverse. Since every hiker must find his own way by map, compass, and GPS device, it's just not prudent to travel when you can't see where you are going. So take extra food, and take beefy camping gear and outerwear to prepare for this potential danger. Large animals, such as moose and caribou, can present a danger as well, but that can be mitigated by paying attention to your surroundings and avoiding the wildlife when they pose a threat. Finally, navigation is the third danger, because you won't end up at the end of the traverse if you don't stay on course. Most people do fine, although almost everyone makes a few mistakes that result in backtracking or bushwhacking. One thing is for certain: you'll be a better wilderness navigator when you get back than when you left.

SEASON

Given the likelihood of bad weather, the Long Range Traverse must be considered an alpine route, even though its highest point is under 3,000 feet (1,000 m). For that reason, summer is the time to come here, but it's a longer season than other alpine areas. Mid-May to mid-September is considered prime time, but most hikers come in July or August. The advantage of off-season travel is fewer bugs; the downside is the greater potential for bad weather.

ROUTE

The Long Range Traverse begins at the trailhead for Western Brook Pond. From the parking lot, a busy, landscaped gravel trail leads approximately .5 mile (1 km) to the docks on Western Brook Pond itself. Here, hikers buy their tickets and wait to embark on the boats that are filled mostly with tourists. Backcountry travelers are easy to spot (their packs give them away). The trip is unbelievably scenic, as the pond is nestled between towering walls of exfoliated granite, with waterfalls pouring off in wet weather. It takes about two hours to reach the head of the pond, where the boat docks, the hikers disembark, and the tourists get a close-up look at the scenery.

The Long Range Traverse proper begins with one of the toughest sections of the whole 23-mile (37-km) route: from the pond up to the ridge via a wet, overgrown, narrow gully. This can be trying, and it's almost impossible to avoid inevitable dead ends, with the ensuing backtracking. Remember, there's no trail on this route. Here's the best advice for the gully: stay in the creek bed where you can, don't be lured out of the middle of the gorge, and go to the right of the big waterfall midway up. The crux is a creek crossing .5 mile (1 km) below the big waterfall; that's what puts you on the right side of the creek and positions you for the clamber up on the muddy trail, hanging onto roots and small trees, up the right side of the waterfall.

Soon, you emerge on to big flat rocks on top of the waterfall, a good place to take a moment to catch your breath, get a bite, and enjoy the view back down Western Brook Pond. From here it's a long but more leisurely meander up to the top of the ridge, about 3 miles (5 km) in, where the expanse of wilderness you'll soon be traveling through presents itself. It's big and pretty, but it's confusing: a lot of peaks, lakes, and ridges look the same.

Everybody gets out the map here and plots a course south toward Little Island Pond. Since there is no trail, there are no reliable hiking distances for this route. In the end, you will walk far longer than the 23-mile (37-km) straight-line distance usually given for the route. What follows is my best estimate of actual distance traveled on foot through the varied terrain. The GPS-derived UTM coordinates were taken by Keith Payne and me as we hiked the route.

From the top of the gorge, the route skirts one unnamed pond on the west side, then skirts Little Island Pond on the west side of the pond. This is the first legal camp on the traverse, and almost all backpackers camp here about 1.8 miles (3 km) from the top of Western Brook Pond gorge (UTM: 21U 455400 5503600).

The following day, continue in a southerly direction another 2.5–3 miles (4–5 km) over more level and much

Pondering the map and checking it against landmarks and compass bearings is par for the course as hikers work to navigate across the trail-less wild plateau on the crest of the Long Range Mountains. PHOTO BY PETER POTTERFIELD.

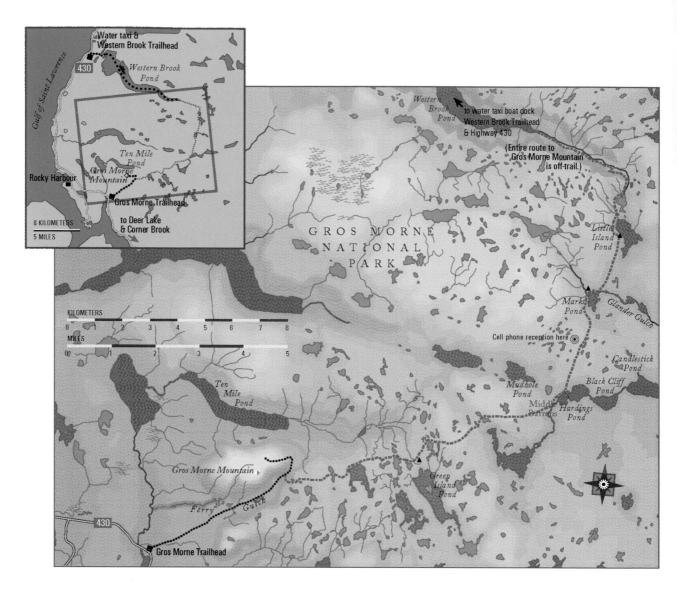

easier ground to the west side of Marks Pond, with outstanding camping on its western shore (UTM: 21U 454600 5501200). A word to the wise here: don't make the common mistake of going east down Glander Gulch, an inviting little valley just north of Marks Pond. It's easy to be led astray, but will cost you hours before you figure it out.

Marks Pond is a delight, and this is where I made my first camp. It took about seven hours of hiking to get here from the boat. This is a quintessential camp on the Long Range Traverse: green meadows, mountain peaks, and a big lake, with loons providing the soundtrack.

The trick on the Long Range Traverse is to navigate by compass bearing from lake to lake, using the peaks as secondary checkpoints to confirm you are on the right route. The hard part is figuring out which lake is which, as a lot of smaller lakes can confuse you into thinking they are the bigger, key lakes. Pretty soon, you get the hang of it.

From Marks Pond, continue heading south just east of a small knob, an important landmark as this is one of the few reliable places on the route where you can pick up a cell phone signal. In an emergency, that can be life-saving. From

there, continue slightly southwesterly and begin the descent to one of the prettiest places on the route, Hardings Pond. The route follows its western shore. Most hikers camp here by the lake, about 4 miles (7 km) from Marks Pond (UTM: 21U 453800 5497200).

This camp has outstanding exploratory possibilities. Mudhole Pond is just to the west, and the grand Black Cliff Pond and Candlestick Pond lie to the east. From Hardings Pond, the route enters the section of the traverse known as the Middle Barrens, a place where careful navigation is required. This is the one place where my party was lured off route by a tempting caribou lead through the tuckamore on the high peak south of Hardings Pond. (We went east around the peak on the caribou lead, but we should have stayed west of the mountaintop.) A brutal bushwhack was required to get us back on route at the distinctive but unnamed double lakes south of the peak.

From Hardings Pond, the route trends west-southwesterly for about 5 miles (8 km) to the fourth legal camp on the east side of a small unnamed pond north of large Green Island Pond (UTM: 21U 449000 5494500). This is another strikingly scenic area with great potential for afternoon roaming after camp is set up.

Beyond Green Island Pond, there's a troublesome river crossing, but the remaining section to the southwest may take the cake for scenery on this stunning route. The topography here squeezes you between a series of lakes and high cliffs to the east and to the west the dropoff down to Ten Mile Pond, another of those stunning landlocked fjords to rival Western Brook Pond for beauty. From the route, you get a perfect perspective on the fjord-like lake, a vantage famous here in Newfoundland. It's beautiful, with the pond below and the Gulf of St. Lawrence stretching beyond into the west.

Most hikers camp the last night at Green Island Pond, then hike out the following day. My party made a very long, even arduous, second day, hiking all the way from Marks Pond about 9 miles (15 km) to a high plateau within sight of Gros Morne Mountain for our second and final camp. We did so because we were pressed for time, and because a "mackerel sky" indicated the weather was changing so we wanted a short final day in the bad weather to come. That last day on the Long Range Traverse can be a tough one.

The fact is, the Long Range Traverse never lets up. Without a doubt, one of the most challenging parts of the route is the descent off the high plateau down to the Gros Morne Mountain Trail in Ferry Gulch. You've got to navigate to the top of the descent precisely, that's critical, then deal with a precipitous descent to the trail in the valley bottom. You'll be hanging onto roots and rocks as you lower yourself down the wet, muddy descent carved out by hikers in recent years. In wet weather, the steep drops, sodden vegetation, and slick rocks make the final descent to the trail even more challenging. It's a place to take great care.

Once into the welcome bottom of Ferry Gulch you will find a final wilderness camp, but most hikers simply continue out to the parking lot, about three hours away. The final few miles descend an endless line of gravel and timber steps to the trailhead.

INFORMATION

Permits are required and should be booked in advance. To obtain a permit in advance, contact:

GROS MORNE NATIONAL PARK
P.O. Box 130
Rocky Harbour, NL A0K 4N0
709-458-2417
Fax: 709-458-2059
E-mail: grosmorne.info@pc.gc.ca

Long Range Traverse permits and information:
www.pc.gc.ca/eng/pn-np/nl/grosmorne/activ/
activ2e.aspx#longrange

General park information:
www.pc.gc.ca/eng/pn-np/nl/grosmorne/index.aspx

Planning a Trip

Newfoundland is about as far east as you can get without bumping into Greenland. For help in planning a trip, the Newfoundland and Labrador tourist office is a good place to start.
www.newfoundlandlabrador.com

Guide Services

Check with Parks Canada for an up-to-date list of accredited guide services.

LINKUM TOURS
For help with trip logistics, lodging, and guided hiking.
Corner Brook, NL
877-254-6586
www.linkumtours.com/site

GROS MORNE ADVENTURES
Norris Point, NL
709-458-2722
www.grosmorneadventures.com

LONG RANGE ADVENTURES
Sallys Cove, NL
877-458-2828
www.longrangeadventures.com

One reason to come to Newfoundland is to enjoy pristine campsites, such as this one at Marks Pond on the Long Range Traverse. PHOTO BY PETER POTTERFIELD.

TETON CREST TRAIL
Grand Teton National Park

Wyoming, United States

DISTANCE: **39 miles (63 km) for full route**
TIME: **3–5 days**
PHYSICAL CHALLENGE: **1 2 3 4 5**
PSYCHOLOGICAL CHALLENGE: **1 2 3 4 5**
STAGING: **Jackson Hole, Wyoming**

That first glimpse of the Grand Tetons, rising toward the sky out of the Wyoming plain with startling abruptness, is a sublime experience, if slightly discomfiting. You rub your eyes, look again, and think: can they be real? And if the mere view is scarcely believable, imagine the reality of living it, of hiking right through that iconic landscape, wandering for days up among those storied peaks: the Grand, the Middle, the South Teton, and Mount Owen. It is an irresistible backcountry journey, but one that's surprisingly easy to do.

For many visitors on a motor tour of the American West, the Tetons are an afterthought to the rich allure of Yellowstone, just to the north. But a drive-by visit here misses the best of what the Tetons offer. For lovers of wilderness, the ability to explore this dramatic range from the inside is the reason to come. While thousands of visitors exclaim from the lowland viewpoints at the majesty of the 13,770-foot (4,197-m) Grand Teton rising above Jenny Lake, it is the backcountry traveler taking on this route who will experience the place intimately.

The Teton Crest Trail, truly one of the great backcountry routes on the continent, makes it possible to do just that: walk for three days or five, for 25 miles or 40 (40 km or 64), under the shadow of these famous mountains, seldom dropping below 8,000 feet (2,438 m) on the entire route. In fact, for such an epic hike,

The Grand Teton at sunset from Death Canyon Shelf.
PHOTO BY PETER POTTERFIELD.

the Teton Crest Trail presents unparalleled flexibility. The geographic nature of the range—a huge monolithic uplift cut by deep canyons—provides multiple options for getting onto the route and for getting off. You can tailor your stroll among these impressive peaks to fit personal whim or time constraints.

I loved the variety of this wilderness excursion, from the relaxed civility of the starting point, Jackson Hole, to the grandeur of the scenery, the rich wildlife, and even the quirky elements that make the route unique. The new aerial tram at Teton Village can whisk you up into the high country in minutes, and many people shave the final 2 miles (3 km) off the route by taking the shuttle boat across Jenny Lake back to the trailhead. Or you can do it the old-fashioned way, and go by foot all the way from Teton Pass to Paintbrush Canyon.

However you plan it, this route will take you through the signature features of the Grand Teton landscape: wild little Marion Lake, unique Death Canyon Shelf—an odd, wide bench hanging below the crest but above the canyon—scenic Hurricane Pass and its close-up views of the Teton summits, and lovely Lake Solitude nestled in its high cirque. You'll almost certainly see moose, antelope, and elk along the way, and have marmots for company at every camp. Midway through the trek, drop down into the rolling, expansive Alaska Basin, and spend a few days in this classic high-country bowl where grizzly bears roam. If you're lucky on timing, outrageous wildflower displays turn the meadows into gardens. This is a route that shows so much to those who venture on it, it can stand as a potent symbol of America's Rocky Mountain wilderness.

LOGISTICS & STRATEGY

The extensive visitor infrastructure and good-time vibe of the Jackson Hole area and Grand Teton National Park make a trek along the Teton Crest Trail relatively easy to organize. Hikers can fly right into Jackson Hole Airport, the only major airport fully contained within the boundaries of a national park, or into Idaho Falls, approximately an hour and a half's drive away (often a less expensive air fare). A rental car can make trailhead logistics easier, but this is a route that can be done without a vehicle, if you're creative. The Jackson Hole ("hole" is descriptive of this long, deep, epic valley) neighborhood is more complicated than one might think, made up of the communities of Jackson, Moran Junction, Wilson, Teton Village, and Moose, all connected by a series of highways and roads that come and go across the borders of Grand Teton National Park.

The classic Teton Crest trekking route starts just east of Teton Pass, 10 miles (16 km) from Jackson on Wyoming Route 22, where it follows the Crest Trail to Cascade Canyon, picks up the Solitude Lake Trail and finally exits the crest via Paintbrush Canyon out to String Lake, just north of Jenny Lake. That's about 40 miles (64 km), and four to six days (this is not a landscape you want to hurry through) for most backpackers.

TOP: *On the Teton Crest Trail below Marion Lake.* PHOTO BY PETER POTTERFIELD.

BOTTOM: *The route from the Top of the Tram joins the Teton Crest Trail several miles below Marion Lake in Grand Teton National Park.* PHOTO BY PETER POTTERFIELD.

OPPOSITE: *From a high camp midway on Death Canyon Shelf, a hiker heads toward Alaska Basin and Hurricane Pass.* PHOTO BY PETER POTTERFIELD.

Looking into Death Canyon, one of several exit routes off the Teton Crest Trail. PHOTO BY PETER POTTERFIELD.

In recent years, however, most hikers have started the hike via Granite Canyon, much closer to town, an approach which joins the traditional Teton Crest Trail at Marion Lake. And the most popular exit off the crest has become the hike down scenic Cascade Canyon to Jenny Lake, where you can hike out to the highway or wait in line for the shuttle boat to save a couple of trail miles. That shortens the hike to 32 miles (51 km), making for a great two- or three-night backpack. The completion of the Jackson Hole Mountain Resort's aerial tram in 2009 added yet another option: a cable car ride to the top of Rendezvous Mountain, 7 miles (11 km) from Marion Lake, shaving a few miles (but not as much as you'd think) off the Granite Canyon start.

The route I recommend can be described as the "new" classic three- to five-night trip: up to Marion Lake via the tram or Granite Canyon, and out via Paintbrush Canyon if you have time, Cascade Canyon if you don't, with camps at Marion Lake, Death Canyon Shelf, Sunset Lake, and Lake Solitude (actually, just below it). If you can build in an extra night to allow for exploring Alaska Basin or a side trip to Snowdrift Lake, that will enhance the whole package.

The small, comfortable, resort-oriented Teton Village is perfectly situated as a staging point to start the route. Hikers who stay in the village can simply walk over to the new tram and ride in comfort to the 10,000-foot (3,048 m) level, or save a few bucks by walking to the Granite Canyon trailhead and hiking up from there. Stash your rental car at the String Lake trailhead if you're coming out via Paintbrush Canyon, or at the Jenny Lake Visitor Center if you're coming out via Cascade Canyon.

But there are multiple options to this trek, as you can combine the entry and exit points in creative ways. For instance, if trailhead transport is an issue, you can backtrack: a satisfying two- or three-night backpack on the Crest begins and ends in Teton Village: Ride up on the tram, camp at Marion Lake, hike to Death Canyon Shelf for a second night's camp, day hike to Alaska Basin, return to camp for a final night and hike back to the tram the next day.

Be creative. In fact, you might *need* to be flexible as obtaining the necessary permits for the Teton Crest can be problematic. Grand Teton National Park is quite strict on its backcountry regulation. Each permit is good for a given night in a given backcountry zone (or, as is the case with Marion Lake, a specific location). If you are not able to get the campsite you want, you may have to change your itinerary to match what you can get. There's usually a good alternative on a route this rich in options, and the rangers at the Moose Visitor Center and the Jenny Lake ranger station can help you figure out a solution.

HAZARDS

Grand Teton National Park is home to both black bears and grizzly bears, so it is essential that hikers who come to the Crest Trail are "bear aware" and know correct behavior in bear habitat. Bear-proof food containers are required in the park; rangers will issue you one when you pick up your hiking permit if you don't have one. Many hikers don't believe it, but moose, too, present a danger to people equal to that of bears. When I did the Teton Crest Trail in 2009, my partner and I heard a wild thrashing in the brush just before a big bull moose came tearing out of the forest to cross the trail at a full gallop just in front of us. Had we been 10 feet farther up the trail, we would have been badly injured. Wildlife is definitely an issue on this hike, so pay attention. With all of the tourists and visitors to Jackson Hole, it's easy to forget that the Tetons are still in a wild part of North America.

Weather, too, can present problems, at any time of the hiking season. A sunny summer day can turn into a cold, soggy whiteout with alarming speed, and thunderstorms can roll in quickly on a hot afternoon. Both situations can present problems to hikers traveling near 10,000 feet (3,048 m). Use common sense, navigate carefully, and come equipped for the usual hazards of mountain travel.

SEASON

The Teton Crest Trail is aggressively alpine, most of it is over 9,000 feet (2,743 m), which makes for a short season and one that is absolutely determined by the previous winter's snowfall. In some years, this route can be done as early as late June, although steep snow slopes may make an ice ax advisable. In heavy snow seasons, the trail might not be passable until mid-July. Expect a snow-free trail from mid-July until early October. September journeys along the route are most often quite reasonable, pleasant, and bug-free, if quite cold up high. Beware, an early snowstorm can put an end to your plans. By early October, you have to face the fact of serious cold in any event, and a greater likelihood of show-stopping snow. So watch the weather when you push the length of the season, but remember the advantages of doing the route in early or late season may be worth it: less company on the trail, and a greater ease of getting the permits you want. The best reason to go in mid-season are the wildflower blooms, which follow the snowmelt in the high meadows, usually late July into early August.

ROUTE

For the full 39 miles (63 km) of the Teton Crest Trail (actual mileage will be higher as side trips and roaming from scenic camps will add distance), begin at the Jackson Hole Mountain Resort's new tram in Teton Village. Lots of tourists, day hikers, paragliders, and other visitors to Jackson Hole ride the new tram up into the alpine zone. The tram can allow even disabled travelers a mindblowing perspective on the impressive Grand Tetons from up high. Choosing the tram turns what would otherwise be a steep four-hour hike up through the ski runs from Teton Village on the trail into a 20-minute thrill ride.

The upper end of the aerial tram (known as Top of the Tram) is at 10,450 feet (3,186 m) on the ridgetop of Rendezvous Mountain, with 360-degree views of the mountains and adjacent valley. The hike begins here, where a side trail takes you 2 miles (3 km) to the intersection with the Teton Crest

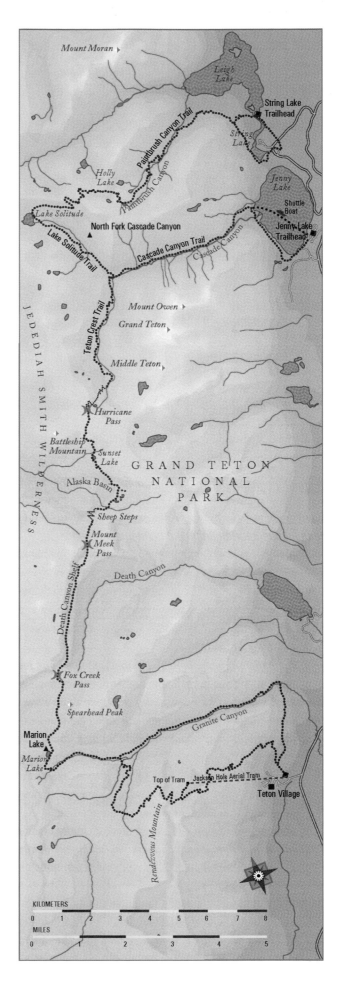

The Grand Tetons viewed from the Snake River Overlook, where Ansel Adams made his famous image of the range. PHOTO BY PETER POTTERFIELD.

Trail. But just because you saved 3,000 feet (915 m) of elevation gain from the village by riding the tram, don't expect an easy walk to the first campsite. The route loses and gains more than 2,000 feet (610 m) through glorious alpine high country in the 7 miles (11 km) from Top of the Tram to Marion Lake, where most hikers try to spend the first night.

Not every hiker will get a permit for the limited spaces at Marion Lake. The permitting process is rigorous in Grand Teton National Park, limiting backcountry camping to designated areas. Marion Lake is the most restricted of all these areas. Only a handful of well-used tent platforms are available to backpackers each night.

If you can't get a Marion Lake permit, get one in upper North Fork Granite Canyon. These campsites are only a few miles from Marion Lake, although you will lose some elevation. Some hikers actually choose to hike up Granite Canyon, accessible from the trailhead on Wyoming Route 390, or from Teton Village via the Valley Trail, instead of taking the aerial tram. This route follows lower Granite Canyon for 8 miles (13 km) up to the upper canyon campsites, joining the Teton Crest Trail a few miles below Marion Lake.

From Marion Lake, the route meanders north on the Teton Crest Trail past striking Spearhead Peak, over gentle Fox Creek Pass (9,650 feet, 2,941 m) and down onto an unusual feature known as Death Canyon Shelf. This is a highlight of the route, a broad ledge hard up against the ridge above Death Canyon, with stunning views north to the Grand Teton and down a thousand feet into the green depths of Death Canyon. Good campsites are plentiful all along the shelf; anyplace you choose to camp here is going to make a reasonably short day from Marion Lake, between 5 and 7 miles (8–11 km), but the shelf is so scenic it would be tragic to walk by it and not to spend the night here.

The Teton Crest Trail ascends from Death Canyon Shelf by meandering up heather slopes to Mount Meek Pass (9,726 feet, 2,965 m), a vague divide that marks a high point of the trail before it descends toward the cliffs on the edge of Alaska Basin. The sprawling green expanse of Alaska Basin's big bowl comes as a surprise, rising gently up out of the Idaho side of the Tetons above the Grand Targhee ski area. Alaska Basin is not in Grand Teton National Park, but in the Jedediah Smith Wilderness, which means fewer camping restrictions on the backcountry traveler. Permits are not an issue in Alaska Basin, so it's a natural place to camp.

The trail drops into Alaska Basin and on toward the famous lakes above it via a steep descent known as Sheep Steps. Campsites are plentiful here in the basin, and if you have an extra night it makes a good campsite. If time is precious, I recommend hiking across the basin to its northern edges and grinding up the switchbacks to camp at Sunset Lake at 9,605 feet (2,928 m) approximately 5 to 6 miles (8–10 km) from Death Canyon Shelf, depending on the location of your previous camp. The lake is one of the most scenic places near Alaska Basin, and a camp up here puts you in a good position for the strenuous ascent up to Hurricane Pass the next day.

From Sunset Lake, hike north back into the park, and climb steeply up the final 900 feet (274 m) of elevation gain to austere Hurricane Pass, with Battleship Mountain looming above. From the pass, hike down on the South Fork Cascade Creek Trail into upper Cascade Canyon and into the South Fork Cascade Canyon camping zone. At the intersection with the North Fork Cascade Canyon Trail, 6 miles (10 km) from Sunset Lake, you reach a major decision point: hike out via Cascade Canyon, or continue north to Lake Solitude and the Paintbrush Divide for a hike out Paintbrush Canyon.

If you are hiking out to Jenny Lake via Cascade Canyon, one of the prettiest valleys in the park, turn right on the Cascade Canyon Trail and hike 5 miles (8 km) to Jenny Lake. When you reach the lake, you can take the shuttle boat across to the Jenny Lake Visitor Center, or (if the line for the boat is long) hike around the lake the final 2 miles (3 km).

If your plan is to hike out via Paintbrush Canyon, continue north on the North Fork Cascade Canyon Trail to Lake Solitude (9,035 feet, 2,754 m), 9 miles (15 km) from Sunset Lake, one of the most scenic spots on the Teton Crest. The Grand positively towers above this small lake nestled in its high cirque. Camping is not allowed at the lake itself, but designated campsites are situated just a half mile (1 km) below in the North Fork Cascade Canyon camping zone.

From Lake Solitude, the final day climbs steeply from the lake on one of the toughest sections of the trail to Paintbrush Divide at 10,700 feet (3,261 m). It's a physical challenge working up more than 1,500 feet of switchbacks with a pack at this altitude, but this part of the route is one of the most scenic backcountry trails anywhere in the world. The impressive bulk of the Grand Teton virtually fills the view to the south. Once at the crest of the divide, it's Mount Owen that steals the show. This is the heart of the Teton Crest, and being here makes choosing the Paintbrush Canyon exit worth the extra effort, and time. From the divide, it's 10 scenic miles (16 km) down alpine meadows, past Holly Lake and into Paintbrush Canyon. Wildlife and wildflowers are abundant in this classic canyon. Camping is allowed here as well, if you wish to spend another night before hiking out to the String Lake Trailhead, 12 miles (19 km) from Lake Solitude.

INFORMATION

Permits are required for any and all backcountry hiking in Grand Teton National Park. Reservations for summer backcountry permits may be made from January 5 through May 15. One-third of all backcountry permits may be reserved, the rest are available first come, first served one day prior to starting the hike. After May 15, you have to take your chances, but I had no trouble getting a permit the day before my 2009 hike.

Mail reservation form to:
GRAND TETON NATIONAL PARK
Backcountry Permits
P.O. Drawer 170
Moose, WY 83012

Fax reservation form to:
307-739-3443

For more information:
GRAND TETON NATIONAL PARK
P.O. Drawer 170
Moose, WY 83012
307-739-3300
www.nps.gov/grte/index.htm

Visitor Center and Ranger Station

CRAIG THOMAS (MOOSE) DISCOVERY
AND VISITOR CENTER
307-739-3399

JENNY LAKE RANGER STATION
307-739-3343

Backpackers' camp on Death Canyon Shelf.
PHOTO BY PETER POTTERFIELD.

YOSEMITE GRAND TRAVERSE
Sierra Nevada Mountains
Ansel Adams Wilderness Area and Yosemite National Park
California, United States

DISTANCE: 60 miles (97 km) one-way
TIME: 7–8 days
PHYSICAL CHALLENGE: 1 2 3 4 5
PSYCHOLOGICAL CHALLENGE: 1 2 3 4 5
STAGING: Fresno, California

The Yosemite Grand Traverse is a 60-mile (97-km) backcountry journey that takes the hiker through the Ansel Adams Wilderness, over Post Peak Pass, and into Yosemite National Park on the way to its climax in wthe Tuolumne high country. This route covers a lot of ground, and takes in awe-inspiring Sierra scenery along the way. Starting on obscure trails with unexpected views of landmark Sierra Nevada peaks, the traverse soon enters Yosemite to follow the unique drainage of the Merced River before joining the iconic John Muir Trail for a spectacular finish.

Here's a hike that touches more than a few of the real high points of the Sierra in just a week, and offers the hiker a compressed experience that still manages to provide an authentic sample of multi-day travel in these irresistible mountains. It's hard to say "Sierra in summer" without thinking of granite spires thrusting above sparkling high-country lakes into deep blue skies. You can surely get hailed on and blown around, but most hikes in the Sierra, even long ones, are remembered for long sections of hiking in shorts above 10,000 feet (3,048 m) under the California sun.

You know you're in for something special when you work up the south side of Post Peak Pass, a 3,000-foot (914-m) day made more challenging when carrying a pack with six days' worth of food. After a stop for lunch beside a pretty alpine tarn nestled in its rocky bowl, the route continues up to finish off the last thousand feet of elevation gain to the pass. When you finally scramble up to the top of the ridge, there it is, the kind of payoff that reminds us all why we hike: the imposing broadside of Banner, Ritter, and the Minarets is *right there*, creating an unforgettable tableau of iconic Sierra peaks standing shoulder to shoulder that makes all the hard work more than worth the effort.

Ritter, Banner, and the Minarets looming over there at 13,000 feet (3,962 m) used to be the centerpiece of the Minarets Wilderness. But the California Wilderness Act of 1984 doubled the size of the preserve and renamed it after the famous Sierra Club photographer whose artistic images provided the impetus to save it. Now the 231,000-acre Ansel Adams Wilderness is sandwiched between the John Muir Wilderness to the south and Yosemite National Park to the north. The act preserved a precious, pristine piece of the Sierra that when put together with its contiguous parks and wilderness areas is larger than some states.

OPPOSITE: *It's another perfect day in the Sierra as the sun sets on Cathedral Peak.* PHOTO BY PETER POTTERFIELD.

The iconic Sierra Nevada peaks of Ritter, Banner, and the Minarets as seen from Post Peak Pass. PHOTO BY PETER POTTERFIELD.

This week-long immersion in classic Sierra backcountry manages to avoid most of the crowds that are inevitably drawn here, even as the traverse enters Yosemite. The route soon descends from the peaks into the extensive drainage of the Merced River, the lifeblood of Yosemite Valley, where the route traces the headwaters through granite basins and channels, interspersed with subalpine meadows with stands of massive red fir.

The journey is something like the *CliffsNotes* of Yosemite backcountry as it follows the river down toward the valley along hundreds of small waterfalls, shallow ponds, and big lakes. The route even takes a day for an early morning ascent of Half Dome (from the back side, so avoiding the crowds), or to the sublime viewpoint of Clouds Rest. With a finish that drops down to Cathedral Pass and into the meadows and smooth granite domes of Tuolumne, the Yosemite Grand Traverse offers more Sierra mojo in a week than some 100-mile hikes. When you have lunch near Columbia Finger near the end of the trip, and look back at Post Peak and the 60 miles (97 km) of wilderness you've covered in a week, the scale of this traverse comes home.

Any fit party of hikers will have little trouble doing the route, but this is one moderate backcountry journey that becomes a little easier when done as a guided trip. In fact, this hike is a modern invention: it is actually the brainchild of Ian Elman, founder of Southern Yosemite Mountain Guides. He scouted the route and began offering it on his menu of backcountry trips in 2008, when the hike won *National Geographic Adventure* magazine's trip-of-the-year honors. It's well worthy of the accolades, and made easier when done with the guide service, which handles everything from hiking permits, trailhead transportation problems, and even food.

There's no substitute for the real thing, but this extraordinary traverse gives you a taste of what it's like to hike the John Muir Trail or the Pacific Crest Trail along the spine of the Sierra but in a small fraction of the time and distance. At a week and 60 miles (97 km), however, it's no pushover. A week's worth of food is about the limit most backpackers can carry, but not having to resupply is an upside. Time and effort are required to do the traverse, but this route pays a big return as it wends its way through remote and classic Sierra touchpoints.

LOGISTICS & STRATEGY

Fresno, California, is the classic gateway to Yosemite National Park and the trailheads for this hike. The air terminal is large and uncrowded, with car rentals onsite. The drive to the trailheads requires between three and four hours. Some hikers will arrive via Reno, Nevada, which has better connections and sometimes less expensive fares, and also boasts an easy airport with onsite rental cars. The drive from Reno to the exit trailhead in Yosemite takes between four and five hours, and it's six or seven to the starting trailhead in the Ansel Adams Wilderness.

It's possible to do this hike in either direction, but

it works far better and builds to the proper climax if done from south to north. Hiking permits are easier to obtain for that direction as well, so that is how the route is described here. If you do the Yosemite Grand Traverse on your own, the trailhead transportation issues are similar to other classic traverses in this volume, including the Beartooth Traverse and the Long Range Traverse: you need two vehicles.

Leave one car at the terminus of the hike on the Tioga Pass Road in Tuolumne Meadows, Yosemite National Park, at the trailhead for Cathedral Lakes Trail, a few miles west of the Tuolumne visitor center and small store. Park on the shoulder of the road, and stash any extra food in your car in the bear-proof food lockers nearby to avoid a nasty surprise—a car ripped opened by bears—when you hike out. Then, in the other vehicle, drive back down to Yosemite Valley and out of the park to the Fernandez Trailhead above Bass Lake, California, off Highway 41. If starting from Fresno, this vehicle shuttle will take you approximately six to seven hours but a one-way drive from Fresno to the start is only three hours. If you wish to camp near the trailhead the night before the hike, campgrounds are nearby.

This is a trip that is easier logistically when done as a guided hike. Southern Yosemite Mountain Guides operates the trip several times per summer. On the guided program, you simply fly to Fresno, overnight at an airport hotel provided, meet your group and your guides for dinner, and the next morning you are delivered to the Fernandez Trailhead. Hiking permits are arranged in advance, guides lead the way and prepare the meals on the hike. On completion of the route, a van will be waiting at the Cathedral Lakes Trailhead on the Tioga Pass Road, replete with cold beer and a picnic, to take you on a tour of Yosemite Valley and back to Fresno.

If you go on your own, be aware that hiking permits are required for this route, and those take some advance planning. But since you are starting from the Ansel Adams Wilderness, the process is a little easier than if you were starting in Yosemite National Park. Simply reserve your permit in advance through the Sierra National Forest, and take your permit with you as you enter Yosemite National Park. With that permit you are legal all the way through to the terminus at Cathedral Lakes Trailhead, but when in the park you must follow the somewhat more restrictive park regulations, such as no dogs and no guns.

The farther you go on this hike, the more deeply you enter black bear country. Bears are not the problem they were a decade ago, thanks to aggressive measures and new rules to prevent bears from having access to human food, and therefore seeing campers and hikers as a food source. Regulations demand that all your food be carried and stored in bear-proof food containers. That's going to add a little bit of weight and bulk to your pack, but it's going to keep you safer. Under no circumstances should you try to subvert these bear safety precautions. The rangers check that you have the proper equipment and follow backpacking regulations.

From the Fernandez Trailhead, above 7,000 feet (2,134 m), the route climbs a bit up into the high country, and then descends to Post Creek and its reliable water for the first night's camp. Day two is a big one. The route climbs steadily up toward the peaks of the Triple Divide, and then up and over Post Peak Pass, almost 3,000 feet (914 m) of elevation gain, before leaving the Ansel Adams Wilderness and dropping down into Yosemite National Park and the next night's camp at Lake 10K. This is a scenic camp with views of Isberg, Forester, and other surrounding peaks. From there, the route drops down into the pretty headwaters of the Merced River. The trail often runs right next to the river as it drops down into big timber and open meadows to a camp near Washburn Lake, an area with lots of camping options near the river.

Columbia Finger rises from its ridgetop above Cathedral Pass.
PHOTO BY PETER POTTERFIELD.

49

A long day takes you past the High Sierra Camp at Merced Lake and gradually up out of Echo Valley to the intersection with the John Muir Trail, and a camp near Sunrise Creek. The classic traverse calls for two nights here, with the extra day spent on an early morning ascent of Half Dome, via the Cable Route, which is steep and exposed but does not require climbing skills. Or, take the half-day hike up to Clouds Rest. The following day on the traverse takes you steeply up and over Sunrise Moun-

A backpackers' camp near Cathedral Lakes.
PHOTO BY PETER POTTERFIELD.

tain, and then winds along some of the most dramatic scenery of the trip, through Long Meadow, past Columbia Finger, over Cathedral Pass and down to Cathedral Lakes for the final night's camp. From there, it's a half-day hike out to your car on the Tioga Pass Road in Tuolumne Meadows, at about 10,000 feet (3,048 m).

Consider spending another night or two at the Tuolumne campground for a day or two of day hiking the expansive meadows before your drive back down to Yosemite Valley and back to your car at Fernandez Trailhead, about three hours away.

HAZARDS

Bears can be troublesome and potentially dangerous in this part of the Sierra, particularly in the Yosemite National Park section. Store all food in approved bear-resistant food canisters and keep a clean camp.

Much of this hike is above 9,000 feet (2,743 m), where rapid changes in weather present a danger of hypothermia, so take precautions and use adequate clothing and gear. It's frankly appalling how quickly a sunny afternoon turns into a radical storm. Be prepared. Conversely, the bright sun of the Sierra can burn quickly at high altitudes, so use hats and sunscreen, and drink adequate water. Water must be filtered or treated on this route.

SEASON

Given the altitude on the Yosemite Grand Traverse, the previous winter's snowfall determines the opening of the hiking season. In most years the route is passable from mid- or late June through the end of September. Late season hikes can be particularly appealing, with stable, cool weather and fewer bugs. Check with rangers regarding trail conditions if you go early or late in the season.

ROUTE

From Fresno, drive north on Highway 41 approximately 80 miles (129 km) to Yosemite National Park. (Stop in Oakhurst for your hiking permit, if necessary.) Once in the park, turn onto Highway 120, the Tioga Pass Road, and continue north and east up to Tenaya Lake and Tuolumne Meadows. Leave one vehicle at the Cathedral Lakes Trailhead, 2

A party of hikers crests Post Peak Pass and catches a glimpse of the rocky peaks of the Tuolumne high country, with Isberg Peak on the right. PHOTO BY PETER POTTERFIELD.

miles (3 km) west of the visitor center and store. Drive back through the park and onto Highway 41 toward Oakhurst.

Twelve miles (19 km) south of Yosemite, and 4 miles (7 km) north of Oakhurst, turn east on County Road 222 toward Bass Lake. Follow this road around the lake, turn left onto Beasore Road (Forest Service Road 7, or the Sierra Vista Highway). The narrow winding road continues 27 miles (44 km) past Globe Rock, passing Jackass Trailhead and Bowler Group Campground. Continue less than a mile (approx. 1.5 km) to a junction with a dirt road departing to the left to Norris Creek and Fernandez trailheads. Drive 2 more miles (3 km), crossing Norris Creek, and take the right fork northeast 1 mile (2 km) to Fernandez Trailhead.

From the trailhead at 7,200 feet (2,195 m), follow a complicated network of trails north to cross Madera Creek, then northeast toward Lillian Lake, but bear right before reaching Lillian Lake and hike north. In approximately 8.5 miles (14 km) and five hours from the trailhead, the route crosses Post Creek at 9,000 feet (2,743 m), where reliable water makes for good camping.

Day two follows the trail north with two 800-foot (245-m) sections that climb steeply uphill for approximately 5 miles (8 km) to the odd Porphyry Lake and its striking giraffe-spotted granite boulders, a good spot for lunch. From there, work up the final 1,000 feet (305 m) of trail to Post Peak Pass and stunning views of the Triple Divide peaks and Ritter, Banner, and the Minarets. Continue north along the crest of the ridge until the trail descends westward to leave the Ansel Adams Wilderness and enter Yosemite National Park. Follow the trail until it forks in .5 mile (1 km), take the left fork and descend to Lake 10K, unnamed on most maps, and a scenic campsite beneath Isberg Peak, approximately 10 miles (16 km) from your camp on Post Creek.

From Lake 10K, the route continues north, turning left at the first intersection north of Lake 10K and traveling steeply downhill along the Triple Peak Fork to where it joins the upper Merced River above the footbridge, approximately 5.5 miles (9 km) from Lake 10K. From the footbridge, follow the trail as it descends, steeply in sections, alongside rocky pools of the Merced toward Washburn Lake, 3 miles (5 km) farther, and look for appealing campsites by the lake or along the river.

From your camp above Washburn Lake, the trail descends past the Merced Lake ranger station, past a trail intersection at a major footbridge, 5 miles (8 km) from camp. The trail continues west past the High Sierra tent camp and Merced Lake.

The monumental flank of Matthes Crest, with the peaks of the Merced Range behind. PHOTO BY PETER POTTERFIELD.

Isberg Peak reflected in the waters of Lake 10K. PHOTO BY PETER POTTERFIELD.

Continue 3 miles (5 km) past Merced Lake to another footbridge across the Merced, and another trail intersection. Do not turn left, toward Yosemite Valley, but ascend steeply for 2 miles (3 km) above the footbridge to another trail intersection. Go left here, and traverse at about 7,500 feet (2,286 m) for 4 miles (7 km) to the intersection with the John Muir Trail. Turn north on the John Muir Trail for approximately .3 miles (just a few hundred meters) to well-used campsites at 8,200 feet (2,499 m) along Sunrise Creek, and reliable water, just over a berm from the John Muir Trail.

The classic Yosemite Grand Traverse calls for two nights here, with the day off spent hiking to Half Dome, and climbing to its summit via the Cable Route, a 9-mile (15-km) round trip from camp. Another good day hike option is to hike up to Clouds Rest, a 9.5-mile (16-km) round trip with almost 2,000 feet (610 m) of elevation gain.

From your camp on Sunrise Creek, follow the John Muir Trail due north up and over the shoulder of Sunrise Mountain, about 9,700 feet (2,960 m) and 3 miles (5 km) from camp. The trail descends toward Sunrise High Sierra Camp, then continues north through Long Meadow before climbing once again to the shoulder of Columbia Finger, a good spot for lunch, about 6.5 miles (10 km) from camp. From here the route descends through some of the best scenery of the trip to Cathedral Pass and down to Cathedral Lakes and the final camp at 9,200 feet (2,800 m), 8.5 miles (14 km) from camp.

The final day is a short, downhill 4.5-mile (8-km) trek on the John Muir Trail to Highway 120, the Tioga Pass Road, and the Cathedral Lakes Trailhead. If you plan on spending the night here, the campground is 2 miles (3 km) east on the Tioga Pass Road.

INFORMATION

Hiking permits can be a troublesome detail for hikes in Yosemite National Park, but they are a little easier by starting in the Ansel Adams Wilderness instead of in the park itself.

Get a permit for the Fernandez Trailhead at any of the Sierra National Forest offices, either in North Fork (near Bass Lake), Oakhurst, or Mariposa. Once you have your permit for entry, you are legal to walk out of the Ansel Adams

Backcountry cookery need not be boring. This morning the menu is polenta with Monterey jack and sun–dried tomatoes, with ham. PHOTO BY PETER POTTERFIELD.

Wilderness, finish the traverse as described above, and exit via the Cathedral Lakes Trail. Just be sure to keep your permit on your person, and follow the national park rules, such as no dogs and no guns.

See the Sierra National Forest Web page on wilderness permits to reserve your permit:
www.fs.fed.us/r5/sierra/passes/getwildpermit.shtml

Or call these ranger stations:
SIERRA NATIONAL FOREST HEADQUARTERS
1600 Tollhouse Road
Clovis, CA 93611
559-297-0706

BASS LAKE RANGER DISTRICT
57003 Road 225
North Fork, CA 93643
559-877-2218

YOSEMITE SIERRA VISITOR BUREAU
41969 Highway 41
Oakhurst, CA 93644
559-683-4636

MARIPOSA INTERAGENCY VISITOR CENTER
5158 Highway 140
Mariposa, CA 95338
209-966-7081

If you wish to do this hike in reverse, which is not recommended, you'll need to get a permit from Yosemite National Park for the Cathedral Lakes Trailhead. For information on getting a permit for that trailhead, see the park backpacking permit page:
www.nps.gov/yose/planyourvisit/wildpermits.htm
There, reserve your permit in advance. If an advance reservation is not available, consider taking a chance and going for the walk-in permits that are issued each day on a first come, first served basis. For more information, call Yosemite National Park at 209-372-0740.

Guide Services
Check out the Web site for Southern Yosemite Mountain Guides, which developed the route.

SOUTHERN YOSEMITE MOUNTAIN GUIDES, INC.
621 Highland Avenue
Santa Cruz, CA 95060
800-231-4575
www.symg.com

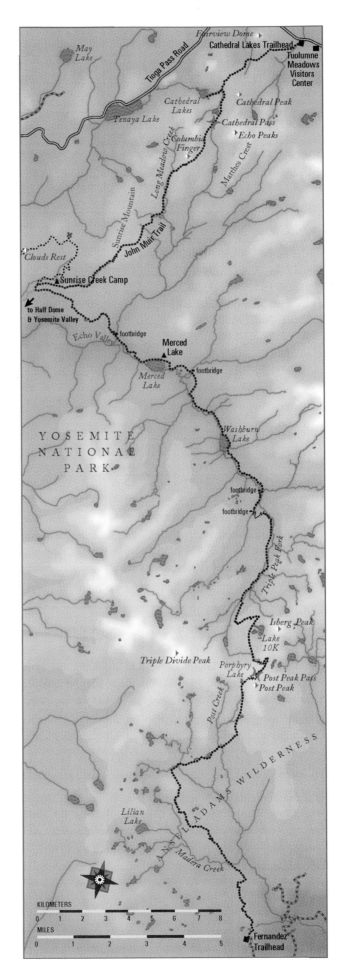

TONQUIN VALLEY
Canadian Rockies
Jasper National Park

Alberta and British Columbia,
Canada

DISTANCE: 27 miles (43 km) one-way
TIME: 3–5 days
PHYSICAL CHALLENGE: 1 2 3 4 5
PSYCHOLOGICAL CHALLENGE: 1 2 3 4 5
STAGING: Jasper, Alberta

Watching sunrise light up the enormous broadside of the Ramparts, throwing golden reflections into the waters of Amethyst Lakes, is an experience worthy of any time or effort expended to get in to this wild valley. First photographed in 1915, the unrelenting beauty of the Tonquin Valley, nestled deep in the heart of the Canadian Rockies, has drawn pilgrims ever since—including Ansel Adams, whose very first trip as Sierra Club photographer was right here. The scenic allure of this place cannot be overstated. And though legendary to the cognoscenti, this is a journey that can be enjoyed with surprising solitude when you apply thoughtful strategy and take an unconventional route.

I was tipped off to the Tonquin (the valley is named after one of John Jacob Astor's ships, as Astor's scouts ventured far afield, even here, to find exploitable natural resources) by a Parks Canada naturalist who lives in Lake Louise. But Jasper National Park lies far north of busy Banff. It is the largest of the country's Rocky Mountain parks. The backcountry within it has an out-there feel, a sense of remoteness that's hard to equal in North America outside of Alaska. That's a two-sided sword, as the genuine wildness of the place is emphasized by the rich wildlife of the area, including caribou, cougar, and bear.

The flip side is the fact that fatal grizzly bear attacks have occurred on trails into the Tonquin in recent decades. Humans are not at the top of the food chain here in Jasper. Most hikers will never see a bear in the valley, but everyone who ventures into it should accept that the reality of its wildlife is part of its beauty.

The feature called the Ramparts is actually a subrange of almost a dozen 9,000- and 10,000-foot (2,743- and 3,048-m) peaks, dominated by Redoubt and Dungeon Peak. Pretty Amethyst Lakes (one large body of water nearly separated into two smaller lobes by a peninsula in the middle, where it narrows) lie in the broad floor of the valley, with thick forest on the east slope, the Ramparts on the west. And while the Ramparts steal the show in terms of flashy scenery, all you have to do is turn around for another cluster of peaks that would easily lord it over any other landscape. On the east side of the lake, mounts Clitheroe,

Mount Redoubt and the impressive range known as the Ramparts rise from the morning fog above Amethyst Lakes. PHOTO BY PETER POTTERFIELD.

Maccarib, and Oldhorn all reach above 9,000 feet (2,743 m) above their apron of old-growth timber. This is big country, in every sense. One of the most imposing peaks in Canada, Mount Edith Cavell, more than 11,000 feet (3,322 m) high and visible from almost everywhere in the Jasper vicinity, stands guard at the start to the Astoria River Trail.

Two trails reach the Tonquin from different directions. One comes in over 7,100-foot (2,180-m) Maccarib Pass, the other follows the drainage of the Astoria River, in the next valley to the south. The trails are nearly equal in length, and the merits of each over the other are argued eloquently, usually summarized like this: the Maccarib is more scenic, but the Astoria is shorter, and therefore a faster way to the campgrounds by the lake. On my second visit here, it became clear that the best way to experience this remarkable valley is to connect the two trails into one 27-mile (44-km)

journey. That route takes you into the Tonquin Valley from the north, over striking Maccarib Pass with its views of the Ramparts from up high, takes you through the entire valley along the shores of Amethyst Lakes, and takes you back out along the Astoria River. In that context, then, the Tonquin Valley becomes more like a 4-mile-long (7-km-long) pass connecting the two approach routes.

Doing it this way will require that you spend more time on the adventure, but that's a good thing. The Tonquin requires a few days for acclimatization to its beauty, and begs to be savored over the course of days in changing light and conditions. The in-and-out, point-to-point route suggested here also complicates trailhead transport, but that's easily solved with the resources of Jasper. The town of Jasper itself is a big part of what's good about this hike. Small, casual, and friendly, but with good food and a worldly, cos-

Mount Clitheroe and other 9,000-foot (2,745-m) peaks line the opposite shore of Amethyst Lakes. **PHOTO BY PETER POTTERFIELD.**

mopolitan vibe, it makes a pleasant and very Canadian base from which to embark into the wilderness, and even better to return to after five days in the Tonquin. Jasper has outstanding reentry qualities, softening one's return to reality with its funky character.

LOGISTICS & STRATEGY

Staging for a backcountry journey through the Tonquin Valley is done from the town of Jasper, headquarters for sprawling Jasper National Park, which sits astride the boundary between Alberta and British Columbia. Jasper is about four and half hours from Edmonton's airport, and about four and a half hours from Calgary's airport, so in terms of drive time it's a wash. But for my sensibilities, I find Edmonton the better option when going to Jasper. It's a straight shot due west from Edmonton on a fast, uncrowded highway, and the town of Edson, about halfway, makes the perfect stop for supplies. The drive is colored by the palpable aura of the province's northern tier, a

little wilder and rougher than down south. For those doing a tour of the Rocky Mountain parks, a good option is to fly to Edmonton, see Jasper, do the Tonquin, then head down to Banff via the Icefields Parkway, do the Rockwall Trail near Lake Louise, then drive to Calgary and fly home from there.

In Jasper, accommodations abound to fit any budget, with restaurants, good cafes with wi-fi, outdoor shops, and a distinctive frontier congeniality. I like to live like a local here, rent a bike and ride around town (parking can be tough), enjoying the cafes and good saloons. Trains rule in Jasper, the yard and its rumbling locomotives dominate the town, and lots of people arrive by rail, avoiding the long drive from the major airports.

The national park headquarters are here, in the historic old building across from the train station, where you can sort out your hiking and backcountry camping permits, and get the maps you need. The strong allure of the Tonquin has of late put permits for the hike in greater demand. The safe strategy is to reserve your permit early. The park's backcountry offices are open from June to September, but the Jasper Trail Office handles backcountry reservations year-round. Reservations are accepted up to three months in advance. Reservation fees are over and above the daily backcountry fee, but securing a reservation in advance means you are assured of getting the permit (called a wilderness pass) for the places you want to go.

You have to pick up your wilderness pass in person within 24 hours of starting the hike. When you do that, the rangers, called wardens by Parks Canada, can offer advice on weather and trail conditions and other urgent situations. Routes into the valley have been known to close due to bear and caribou activity, but that is rare.

The trailheads to the Tonquin are not far from town: the Maccarib Trail begins near the Marmot Ski Area, about 10 miles (16 km) from Jasper; the Astoria River Trail is at Cavell Lake, about 16 miles (26 km) from town.

I recommend starting at the Maccarib Trailhead, hiking into the Tonquin via Portal Creek and Maccarib Pass, camping in the valley for several nights, and hiking out the opposite end via the Astoria River Trail. The trail description that follows reflects that route, which is 27 miles (44 km), plus side trips, and will take

Alberta is home to at least four subspecies of grouse.
PHOTO BY PETER POTTERFIELD.

three to five days. However, for hikers who wish to shorten the trip, or wish to leave and return from the same trailhead, the best route is in and out via the Astoria River Trail. It is the shorter route at approximately six hours and 10 miles (16 km) to Clitheroe Camp on the southeast corner of Amethyst Lakes.

The Maccarib Trail–Astoria River Trail loop is 7 miles (11 km) longer, travels over a high (7,100-foot, 2,200-m) alpine pass and open meadows, and then exits by following the river. You get the whole

Hiking out alongside Amethyst Lakes, with the Ramparts as backdrop. PHOTO BY PETER POTTERFIELD.

thing, and the route will show you more than twice the country in a stunning part of the world. The Maccarib Trail follows the Portal Creek drainage from the trailhead, up to the pass and then down the west side into the Tonquin Valley with astounding views of the Ramparts. The trail reaches Maccarib Camp in 12 miles (19 km), and Amethyst Lakes at 13 miles (20 km). The first lakeside camp, Amethyst Camp, is reached at 14 miles (22.5 km).

This is the heart of the Tonquin Valley, at about 6,500 feet (1,985 m) in elevation, with the Ramparts rising majestically to more than 10,000 feet (3,050 m) across the lake. Take a few days to enjoy it. An informal network of trails around the lake can get you just about anywhere you want to go, but beware: the shores of the lake can be marshy and the trails muddy. Four legal camps are situated on the east side of Amethyst Lakes, so there is ample camping; just find the place you like the best. Many hikers prefer Amethyst for its proximity to the lake; others like Clitheroe or Surprise Point for its open views. You will need a backcountry camping permit from Parks Canada for any of the campsites. Fires are not allowed anywhere in the valley, and dogs are not permitted, in order to protect the wildlife.

From the north end of the Amethyst Lakes, the most appealing side trip is up to Moat Pass (and nearby Tonquin Hill, 7,862 feet or 2,400 m) and Moat Lake, which is reached via a spur trail to the north. This makes an interesting, day-long day hike to the boundary between Alberta and British Columbia. As you travel north in this gentle valley, you'll be amazed at how the Ramparts just go on and on, stretching far to the north beyond the imposing peak of Mount Geikie. I saw a big grizzly in the meadows near Moat Lake, along with dozens of caribou—big ones, as the animals here represent one of the largest of the species.

An oddity of the Tonquin Valley is that it actually has accommodations. A historic rustic lodge with cabins is located at the Narrows, between the lakes, and a venerable cabin camp can be found on the way to Moat Lake at the north end of Amethyst Lakes. Both cater to small group horse parties. (You may in fact see strings of horses on the trail, and even if not, you'll see evidence of them.) However, as backpacking gains in popularity, both establishments are seeing an increase in the number of backpackers who choose to stay in one of the cabins rather than camp in a tent once they reach the valley. This is a viable strategy; it's expensive, but it has its advantages. See the information section for details.

The halfway point of the recommended route is the location where the Maccarib Trail route reaches the northern end of Amethyst Lakes, so as you travel south through the Tonquin Valley beside the lake, you get ever closer to the Astoria River Trailhead and the end of the hike. A good option is to spend a night or two at the north end of the lake, at Amethyst Camp, and another night or two near the south end of the lake, at Surprise Point or Clitheroe Camp. If you have the time while camped near the south end of the lake, consider a day trip to Chrome Lake and the Eremite Valley.

From Clitheroe Camp, it's 10 miles (16 km) back on the Astoria River Trail to the trailhead. The route

A pair of backpackers reaches the crest of Maccarib Pass while hiking into the Tonquin via Portal Creek. PHOTO BY PETER POTTERFIELD.

Hiking toward Moat Pass at the northern end of the Ramparts. PHOTO BY PETER POTTERFIELD.

stays high on the slope of Oldhorn Mountain before descending steeply to join the river about 5 miles (8 km) from Cavell Lake and the parking lot.

A workable trailhead transportation plan is this: before the hike, leave your rental car at the Astoria River Trail parking lot near Cavell Lake, then hitchhike back to town (that's technically illegal but it's easy in the big parking lot there). Back in town hire a taxi or car service to take you to the start of the Maccarib Trail. As of this writing, there is no formal trailhead shuttle service in town, but if you ask around, you can find a ride; it's the Jasper way.

HAZARDS

Grizzly bears and black bears are among the abundant wildlife found in the Canadian Rockies. Grizzly bear sightings are uncommon, and attacks on hikers in Jasper National Park are rare, but they do happen. Protect yourself by being wary when hiking, making noise on the trail, avoiding areas of known recent activity, and keeping your food a safe distance from your camp. The backcountry camps on this route are equipped with bear poles and wires, which enable you to store your food and toiletries in a manner that dissuades bear activity. Talk to park wardens about bear safety and bear activity along the route.

Weather remains probably the most serious danger, as, on a route this high, it can change suddenly. Come prepared for cold and wet weather, even snow, even in summer, and be equipped to hike out in bad conditions. And even here, deep in the northern Rockies, you'll have to treat or filter water.

SEASON

Picking the right season for the Tonquin is perhaps as crucial to enjoying this hike as any route I know. This is a valley of rare beauty, but it has its challenges. Amethyst Lakes is a marvel, but it makes the valley a true bug hole, where mosquitoes and biting flies can be so thick as to rob you of joy. And given the fact that horse-packers use the same trails as hikers, the hiking routes can be stirred into muddy bogs by the stock during wet weather. It took me two tries to get the conditions I wanted, but I finally got it right: go in late season; in fact, very late season. I recommend planning to do this route between the middle of August and the middle of September (even the end of September into early October in rare years when the weather holds). Going then will give you the best chance of relatively dry, stable weather, and with vacations over and kids back in school, the best chance for uncrowded camps and trails.

ROUTE

The trailheads to the Tonquin are close to the town of Jasper. The start to the route described here, Maccarib Trail, begins near the Marmot ski area about 10 miles (16 km) from Jasper: travel south 4.5 miles (7 km) on the Icefields Parkway, then turn off on 93A toward the ski area. After 2 miles (3 km), follow the ski basin road another 4 miles (7 km) to where it crosses Portal Creek and find the trailhead parking lot.

The Astoria River Trail, the terminus of the hike as described here, is at Cavell Lake about 16 miles (26 km) from town: travel south about 4.5 miles (7.2 km) on the Icefields Parkway, turn off on 93A and drive south for 3.5 miles (5.5 km) to Edith Cavell Road. The trailhead is another 8 miles (13 km) down the road above Cavell Lake, with its big parking lot.

The Maccarib Trail–Astoria River Trail route starts at the Maccarib Trailhead, and follows the Portal Creek drainage. It's a scenic valley, with good views up to Oldhorn peak. A legal campground, Portal Camp, is located in the broad valley bottom, a good spot for lunch. The route then climbs up toward the pass, finally cresting the 7,100-foot (2,165-m) pass at 8 miles (13 km) from the trailhead before starting the long, gradual descent to the lake. The miles

down the open meadows on the west side of the pass into the Tonquin show off some the best scenery in Jasper National Park, with astounding views of the Ramparts. Finally, the trail enters the timber and reaches Maccarib Camp in 12 miles (19 km), before arriving at Amethyst Lakes at 13 miles (21 km). The first camp by the lake, Amethyst Camp, is a mile farther at 14 miles (22.5 km).

Now you are in the heart of the Tonquin Valley, with the Ramparts rising majestically across the lake. Four legal camps are situated in the Tonquin on the east side of Amethyst Lakes, from Amethyst Camp to Clitheroe or Surprise Point. There is much to explore here in the Tonquin, depending on how many nights your permit allows you to camp. From Amethyst Camp, it's less than a mile to the lodge on the north shore of the lake, another 1.5 miles (2.4 km) to Clitheroe Camp, and another 1 mile (1.6 km) to Surprise Camp.

Good day trips from any camp in the valley include the hike up to Moat Lake, at the north end of the valley, and Chrome Lake, at the south end of the valley. Moat Pass and Moat Lake can be reached via a spur trail to the north, which passes by the cabin camp on an interesting day trip to the boundary between Alberta and British Columbia. Chrome Lake is better accessed from one of the southern camps, as it's a good 5 miles (8 km) on a bad trail.

From Clitheroe Camp, it's 10 miles (16 km) out to Cavell Lake via the Astoria River Trail. The lakeshore itself is particularly marshy at the southeastern corner, so the route sidehills along the slope some distance uphill, through pretty subalpine meadows. Eventually, the route descends the steep switchbacks under Oldhorn Mountain to join the river, slow and meandering at first, then a torrent. An easy 5 miles (8 km) along the river brings you to Cavell Lake and the trailhead parking lot.

A backpacker makes a rare foray into the upper valley toward Moat Pass and the northern end of the Ramparts.
PHOTO BY PETER POTTERFIELD.

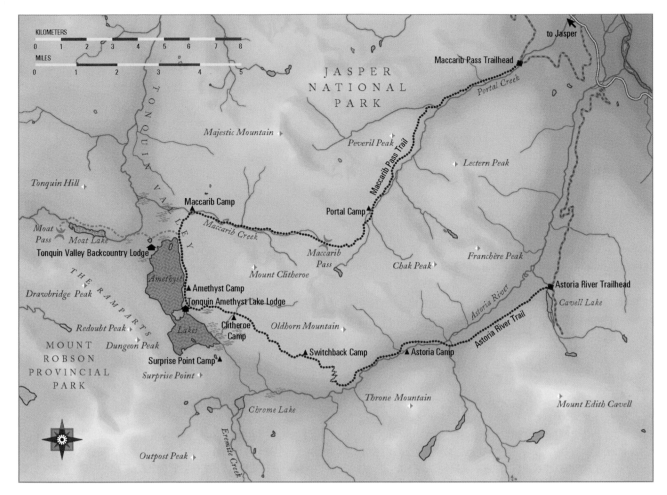

INFORMATION

JASPER NATIONAL PARK
Box 10
Jasper, AB T0E 1E0
780-852-6176
E-mail: pnj.jnp@pc.gc.ca
www.pc.gc.ca/pn-np/ab/jasper/index.aspx

JASPER BACKCOUNTRY OFFICE
PARKS CANADA TRAIL OFFICE
JASPER TOWNSITE INFORMATION CENTRE
Wilderness Pass, safety registrations (in person only),
backcountry trail reservations/information.
500 Connaught Drive
Jasper, AB T0E 1E0
780-852-6177
E-mail: jnp.info@pc.gc.ca

PARKS CANADA CALGARY SERVICE CENTRE
Visitor Services Centre
1300–635 8 Avenue SW
Calgary, AB T2P 3Z1
403-292-4401
E-mail: natlparks-ab@pc.gc.ca

Purchase of a Wilderness Pass is mandatory for any overnight backcountry visit. It specifies the area/trail and campsites you are using and the number of people and tents in your group. You must pick up your pass from a park information center within 24 hours of your departure for updates on trail conditions, closures, and other information. All Wilderness Pass fees (excluding reservation and modification fees) are entirely refundable until 10 a.m. on your proposed date of departure.

Backcountry Lodges

TONQUIN AMETHYST LAKE LODGE
Box 1795
Jasper, AB T0E 1E0
780-852-1188
Fax: 780-852-1155
E-mail: info@tonquinadventures.com
www.tonquinadventures.com

TONQUIN VALLEY BACKCOUNTRY LODGE
Box 550
Jasper, AB T0E 1E0
780-852-3909
E-mail: packtrip@telus.net
www.tonquinvalley.com

ART LOEB TRAIL
Blue Ridge Mountains
Shining Rock Wilderness
and Pisgah National Forest
North Carolina, United States

DISTANCE: **33 miles (53 km) one-way**
TIME: **3–4 days**
PHYSICAL CHALLENGE: **1 2 3 4 5**
PSYCHOLOGICAL CHALLENGE: **1 2 3 4 5**
STAGING: **Brevard, North Carolina**

Perhaps the most interesting trail in the eastern United States south of the White Mountains, the 30-plus-mile Art Loeb is an unexpected wonder. A long section of the route traverses open ridgetops above 6,000 feet (1,830 m) with absolutely stunning views out across the Shining Rock Wilderness, certainly not your average topography for a hike in the Blue Ridge. So what if these open slopes— Eastern hikers call them "balds"—are the result of last century's forest fires and over-aggressive logging, they make for invigorating backcountry travel. You still spend plenty of time under the canopy of the hardwood forest on this hike, as per usual in the Appalachians, but the scenic highlights are genuine.

Six peaks on the route reach almost to the 6,000-foot (1,830-m) level, and three actually exceed it, including Cold Mountain—yes, *that* Cold Mountain, made famous in literature and film. Even some of the waterfalls you saw in *Last of the Mohicans* can be found here. But wait, there's more, including the frankly unbelievable granite blob of Looking Glass Rock, what geologist call a pluton monolith, which not only reflects the afternoon sun like a mirror when viewed from Tennent Mountain, but its domes, slabs, and walls keep the local rock climbers busy as well. The scenery here will just win you over.

Another unique feature of the trail is the Shining Rock Wilderness, named after the 5,940-foot (1,810-m) peak of white quartzite that in the right light can stand out like patches of snow in summer. Cold Mountain is here, dramatically pointy, reaching up to 6,030 feet (1,838-m) for those who choose to take the 1.5-mile (2.5-km) side trip off the main trail to the top. I love the fact there are no signs, blazes, or other navigational aids here in the wilderness area, so be prepared to use your map and compass. The downside to all this is that the fans of Charles Frazier's Pulitzer Prize-winning novel who are drawn up here as pilgrims are not always wilderness-savvy. They get themselves into trouble, predictably, but there's something righteous about a good book driving people into the backcountry. We could use more of that.

The route itself is named after a dedicated forester who worked to protect the mountainous terrain that his namesake trail traverses. Most of what you might call Art Loeb Trail through-hikers take three or four days to do the trail, and that's about right. But this is after all the East, and the trail crosses several roads,

OPPOSITE: *Cold Mountain—yes, that Cold Mountain, the one made famous in literature and film—is a highlight of the Shining Rock Wilderness and well worth the half-day detour to reach the summit.* PHOTO BY PETER POTTERFIELD.

A hiker takes in the view of the Shining Rock Wilderness. PHOTO BY PETER POTTERFIELD.

not to mention the Blue Ridge Parkway. That means the route comes with dozens of possible options, loops, and route variations to suit your time and inclination. But if you're coming from afar, failing to do the whole thing would be tragic, because even though it has its quiet moments, the 30-mile (50-km) totality of the route is what gives it such a nice rhythm.

Just be prepared to do a little work. This is the Blue Ridge, where the high peaks are often followed by low points, some aptly named. Beware, there is not one Deep Gap on this route but two, so don't be confused. The route is strenuous, with big elevation gains the first day and even more the second. Gloucester Gap to Pilot Mountain is going to cost you a couple thousand feet, and Farlow Gap to Silvermine Bald even more. The result of such extreme topography means a lot of heavy breathing, gaining and losing elevation. But there's that long glorious ridge walk from Black Balsam all the way to the Shining Rock Wilderness to enjoy as reward for the effort.

Who can resist a mountain landscape like this? I think some visitors take offense that the Blue Ridge Parkway runs so close to the crest for almost 500 miles (805 km), and without question changes the nature of the mountain environment. But it also affords access for hikers and for those without the physical means to otherwise see the country. One could argue that the parkway—BRP to the locals—is perhaps one of the best of all public works to come out of the Great Depression recovery, even if it did take fifty years to finish.

To get here, you're going to have to fly through Asheville, and that means a chance to see not only writer Thomas Wolfe's childhood home, but the Biltmore mansion, perhaps America's greatest home. And when the sightseeing is done, you've got three five-star days of hiking one of the great trails of the Appalachians. It's wonderful in spring, with the blooms of the Catawba rhododendron and the flame azalea to brighten the way. But if you do it in fall, like I did, and hit it just right, like I did, the eloquent musing of Wolfe on this "October land" can hit home, and you'll "feel an unexpected sharpness, a thrill of nervousness and swift elation."

LOGISTICS & STRATEGY

Asheville is the gateway to the mountains of North Carolina, including its highest, Mount Mitchell. But the town of Brevard is the place to stage for the Art Loeb Trail. The airport is significantly south of Asheville, almost to Henderson, and from the rental car lots it's pretty much a straight shot down Highway 280 to Brevard, about an hour's drive. In Brevard expect to find the usual array of motel chains and fast food outlets, with a few local businesses. It's not the high life, but it's inexpensive, and easy.

A word to the wise: this is small-town North Carolina. I'd be happy to show you the ticket I got from the local constabulary while making a left turn into Looking Glass Outfitters to buy a map and some fuel canisters for my stove. It was a bogus bust, but I got the feeling I was seen as a revenue source. Learn from my experience and drive like an old lady in Brevard.

The traditional starting trailhead for the Art Loeb Trail is at the Davidson River campground, near the Pisgah National Forest ranger station, just over a half hour from Brevard on US Highway 276. The Art Loeb Trail clearly can be hiked in either direction, but for some reason the traditional way to do this route is from south to north, starting at the Davidson River and ending at the Daniel Boone Boy Scout Camp on the north end of the Shining Rock Wilderness.

That's the way I did it, and that's the way the route is described here. But if I were to do it again, I'd hike it from north to south. A lot of things would work better that way: the big elevation gain (including the ascent of Cold Mountain) comes early in the hike when you're fresh; the careful navigation required through the unmarked Shining Rock Wilderness comes at the beginning, when you're fresh; and the most scenic camps (and water) work out better that way. Definitely consider starting at the Boy Scout camp and hiking south when you do the route. But it's a rich experience either way.

Two days is a little rushed for this 33-mile (53-km) hike, especially given its strenuous nature, but three days with two nights spent on the trail is plenty. Be prepared for significant elevation gain on the first day, and even more on the second day. And you have to navigate carefully, as the Art Loeb is not one big, obvious trail, but a series of smaller trails cobbled together. To confuse matters more, part of the Mountains to Sea route follows the Art Loeb for part of the time. Navigation is even more problematic in the

Backcountry camp with a view from 6,000 feet on the Art Loeb Trail. PHOTO BY PETER POTTERFIELD.

TOP: *Yellowstone Falls in Graveyard Fields.*
PHOTO BY PETER POTTERFIELD.

BOTTOM: *A weathered trail sign is one of many on remote sections of the Art Loeb Trail, useful when a number of trails intersect the route.* PHOTO BY PETER POTTERFIELD.

Shining Rock Wilderness, where there are no blazes or trail signs. Follow the map carefully, and pay attention to the landmarks along the way.

Water sources are extremely variable. The first and last sections of the route can be both reasonable in wet weather or totally dry in late season. Inquire at the ranger stations about the availability of water. Water can often be found at Shining Rock, Butter

Gap, and at other gaps and low points for much of the year. And you can cache water by car at three locations along the trail if you want to be safe. That's actually a good, but underutilized, strategy.

From the Davidson River Trailhead, the route starts up Shut In Ridge and basically keeps climbing for most of the day, following the undulating ridge before dropping down to Butter Gap (where there is a shelter and reliable water) at about 9 miles (15 km). A lot of people camp at Butter Gap, but it's heavily used and not very pretty. Go beyond, if you can, to the vicinity of Low Gap, or Chestnut Mountain, and find a campsite a few miles farther. That positions you better for day two, which is strenuous, and may require you to carry extra water.

From Chestnut Mountain, the second day passes the intersection with US Forest Service roads 471 and 475 at Gloucester Gap, 12 miles (19 km) from the trailhead. From the gap, follow the trail as it traverses Pilot Mountain (good views from the fire tower) and descends to Deep Gap and Farlow Gap, before the long haul up Shuck Ridge to the Blue Ridge Parkway and Silvermine Bald. This begins the most scenic stretch of the entire route, but it gets busy where the trail crosses Forest Service Road 816. So keep going past Black Balsam and on to Tennent Mountain, where outstanding camps in the open are a good choice in benign weather. I camped here at 6,000 feet (1,830 m) surrounded by a riot of fall color. Don't camp on the exposed balds in marginal weather.

The final day descends past Ivestor Gap and into the Shining Rock Wilderness. The trail follows the ridge of Shining Rock Ledge for almost 4 miles (7 km), past Shining Rock, along the tricky bit of trail called the Narrows, to Deep Gap. Here you are only 3.5 miles (5.5 km) from the terminus at Daniel Boone Boy Scout Camp, but make the ascent up to the top of Cold Peak if you have the time before finishing the route down to the trailhead.

Doing the route with one camp south of Chestnut Mountain, and another north of Tennent Mountain, breaks the 31-mile (50-km) trip (not counting the ascent of Cold Mountain) into three pretty equal days. If you don't have three days, and want to see the scenery but have to do it quickly, try this strategy: day hike the route in two sections from the Blue Ridge Parkway or Forest Service Road 816. And if you have only one day, I'd do the section between Forest Service Road 816 and Daniel Boone Boy Scout Camp, clearly the highlight of the trail. But this is a route that works way better as a backpack, as that gives you an opportunity to savor the truly outstanding and varied scenery along the way.

If you have only one car, arrange to be picked up by one of a number of shuttle services that work out of Brevard. The drive back to town from the terminus at the Boy Scout camp is about an hour longer than the drive to the Davidson River Trailhead.

HAZARDS

Even in wilderness areas, the American East is pretty civilized. As this backcountry route crosses roads every 6 or 7 miles (10–11 km), you're never too far from help. Still, you are on your own, so take care. Bears are here in sufficient number that you need to take the usual precautions of cooking at some distance from your tent, and storing your food out of reach of wildlife. The greatest potential threat to hikers is the chance encounter with severe weather on the exposed ridgetops in the middle of the route, so come prepared with appropriate clothing and camping gear.

The incredible pluton monolith of Looking Glass Rock as seen from the Art Loeb Trail. PHOTO BY PETER POTTERFIELD.

SEASON

For a route that ventures above 6,000 feet (1,830 m), this hike has a long season. In fact, depending on weather, it can be done year round. There are lots of stories of the Art Loeb being done in January. And that might be a good idea. As the word about this trail leaks out, off-season travel may be the best way to avoid having a lot of company on the route. Just check the weather forecast carefully if you go anytime before April or after October. Wildflowers make the route appealing in spring and summer, and fall color makes it irresistible in autumn. I did the route in mid-October, and encountered hot days and cold nights, and a full, fat harvest moon that lingers in memory.

ROUTE

From Davidson River Campground off US Highway 274, across the street from the Pisgah National Forest ranger station, find the trailhead parking lot, gather your pack and cross the river, then turn left along the river. The trail soon starts to ascend Shut In Ridge, crosses a road near Chestnut Knob, and traverses Cedar Rock Mountain before

This plaque affixed to a rock outcrop commemorates naturalist Art Loeb, an avid local hiker who explored the area and for whom the trail is named. PHOTO BY PETER POTTERFIELD.

descending to Butter Gap at 9 miles (15 km) (reliable water here) and the first shelter. Camp here if you got a late start on the trail, but this is not a scenic camp. Continue on if you can to make day two a little more reasonable, camping near Chestnut Mountain, approximately 10 or 11 miles (16–17 km) from the trailhead. Take advantage of the fact that there are few camping restrictions on the Art Loeb Trail and look for aesthetically pleasing camps away from other hikers.

From Chestnut Mountain, the second day drops down to the intersection with US Forest Service roads 471 and 475 at Gloucester Gap, 12 miles (19 km) from the trailhead. From the gap, follow the trail as it traverses Pilot Mountain (good views from the fire tower) and descends to Deep Gap (this is the first of two, you'll see the shelter) and Farlow Gap. At this point you start the long grind up Shuck Ridge to the Blue Ridge Parkway (18 miles or 29 km from the trailhead, approximately 7 or 8 miles (12–13 km) from Chestnut Mountain). From the parkway, the trail continues uphill toward Silvermine Bald (5,978 feet, 1,822 meters) and on to the scenic climax of the route.

Carry extra water on day two as sources are unreliable. The trail turns right at Silvermine Bald and crosses Forest Service Road 816. I noticed some parties had cached water in gallon jugs where the road and trail intersect, and that's a good idea. This is a day use area and can get busy, so cross Road 816 (watch for the Art Loeb Trail markers to make sure you stay on route) and make the short, scenic hike up to Black Balsam Knob (6,214 feet, 1,895 meters). Pay attention, as a network of day use trails can be confusing here. Follow trail markers to the plaque commemorating Art Loeb, and continue on to Tennent Mountain. Outstanding camps in the open on the north side of Tennent are a good choice in benign weather, and if you have sufficient water. In bad weather, don't camp on the exposed balds. If you're out of water, you'll have to go on a few miles, past Ivestor Gap, to find more.

Going south to north, the third day is easier than the first two. From Tennent Mountain, it is the third 10-mile (16-km) day. The trail descends gradually toward Ivestor Gap where it enters the Shining Rock Wilderness, about 9 miles (15 km) from the far trailhead at Daniel Boone Boy Scout Camp. This marks the point at which your navigation has to be perfect or you'll end up having to bushwhack to stay on route, as a seeming maze of trails can create problems here. There are no blazes or signs in the wilderness area to help you, so follow the map carefully, and tick off the landmarks. Use a compass if necessary.

The trail crosses Grassy Cove Top, descends past Flower Gap and down to Shining Rock Gap and a busy intersection of four trails. The route passes Shining Rock itself, climbs Stairs Mountain (5,869 feet, 1,790 m), and works onto the ridge of Shining Rock Ledge. A surprisingly narrow section of trail called The Narrows ends at Deep Gap, 26.5 miles (43 km) from the start of the hike. Watch how you go at Deep Gap, as another confusing web of trails can throw you off.

Here you are only 3.5 miles (5.6 km) from the terminus at the Boy Scout camp, but if you have the time, take the spur trail (#141) 1.5 miles (2.5 km) up to the top of Cold Mountain (6,030 feet, 1,838 m) before finishing the route down to the trailhead. From the trailhead near the Boy Scout camp, follow Highway 215 to US Highway 276 and head east back to Brevard.

INFORMATION

At present, hiking permits and overnight backcountry permits are not required on the Art Loeb Trail in the Pisgah National Forest. Hikers are free to camp almost without restriction, except within 500 feet of a road or restricted area.

PISGAH RANGER DISTRICT
District Ranger, Randall Burgess
1001 Pisgah Highway
Pisgah Forest, NC 28768
828-877-3265

NATIONAL FORESTS IN NORTH CAROLINA
Supervisor's Office
160 Zillicoa Street, Suite A
Asheville, NC 28801
828-257-4200

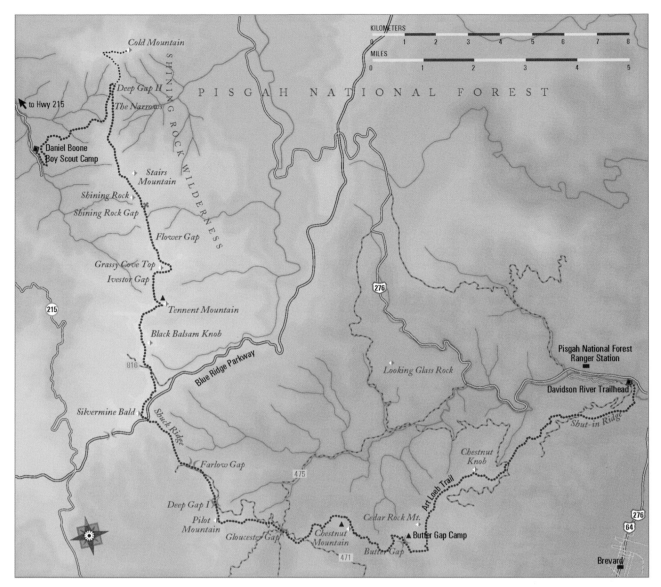

Guides and Shuttle Services

Contact Pisgah National Forest for a complete list of approved hiking guides.

PURA VIDA ADVENTURES
Offers Art Loeb Trail shuttle service as well as guide services.
772-579-0005
E-mail: contact@pvadventures.com
www.pvadventures.com

LOOKING GLASS OUTFITTERS
A good outdoor shop in Brevard that is also a reliable source of information about shuttle services and guides.
828-884-5854
E-mail: info@lookingglassoutfitters.com
www.lookingglassoutfitters.com

While the exposed balds on much of the Art Loeb Trail are what make it stand out among hikes in the Appalachian Mountains, long sections take the hiker through dense canopies of indigenous hardwood forest. PHOTO BY PETER POTTERFIELD.

LITTLE BEAVER–BIG BEAVER LOOP
North Cascades
North Cascades National Park
Washington, United States

DISTANCE: 30–35 miles (48–56 km) loop
TIME: 3–4 days
PHYSICAL CHALLENGE: 1 2 3 4 5
PSYCHOLOGICAL CHALLENGE: 1 2 3 4 5
STAGING: Seattle or Sedro Woolley, Washington;
or Vancouver, British Columbia

This enchanting wilderness walk takes you through some of the most magnificent ancient forest on the planet, with a side trip that allows a good look into what may be America's most dramatic mountain landscape. A hundred miles of jagged, ice-draped rock spires with names like Challenger, Forbidden, Fury, and Terror are hidden up here in the North Cascades behind an impenetrable moat of dense forest. Some are so remote they cannot be seen from any road. The Little Beaver–Big Beaver loop, combined with a day trip up above Beaver Pass—or even better, Whatcom Pass—offers not just a deep immersion into that magical, primeval forest, but an unforgettable close-up perspective on the dramatic climax of the rugged North Cascades.

Big Beaver Creek and Little Beaver Creek are classic, glacier-carved U-shaped valleys, perfect examples of the low-altitude river valleys of old-growth forest that separate the rocky ridges of the North Cascades. Many of these valleys are so choked with slide alder and devil's club that a mile a day is good time for anyone game enough to take them on. The going

The astounding grove of thousand-year-old western red cedar trees in the Big Beaver valley. PHOTO BY TED EVANS.

here can be so difficult that one almost mythic group of craggy summits less than 10 miles (16 km) from the North Cascades Highway—the storied Picket Range—remained virtually unvisited until the 1960s. Well protected by these long, difficult approaches, the North Cascades remain, arguably, the most pristine mountain wilderness in the lower 48 states.

But the Little Beaver–Big Beaver loop follows excellent valley-bottom trails that make for relatively easy hiking, permitting reasonable access into the hidden magnificence of this remote realm deep inside North Cascades National Park. Created in 1969 with an emphasis on wilderness preservation, the mere existence of the park is one of the most significant conservation achievements of the modern environmental movement. Snatched from the jaws of development and timber interests, the 700,000-acre park is the brightest jewel in the Pacific Northwest—a region of great parks, such as Mount Rainier.

I've been hugging trees for a long time, and would dare say that you won't find a better 30 miles (48 km) anywhere for those who love ancient forests. Mile after mile of pristine stands of Douglas fir (not, by the way, a real fir), hemlock, and fir provide a rare journey through what used to be the great temperate forest that covered western North America from Puget Sound to Alaska. But that's just background music

once you finally come upon the grove of ancient cedars in Big Beaver, a stand of living, breathing trees to rival in their own way the redwoods, trees that have been right here since the time of Charlemagne. Northwest conservation icon Harvey Manning calls this grove the "Epiphany," and who's to argue?

Thirty magnificent miles through old-growth forest would be enough to lure most backcountry lovers, but how about we throw in a day hike up into the edges of the alpine zone, and jaw-dropping views of the most reclusive peaks in the North Cascades. From the high point of the Little Beaver–Big Beaver loop, near Beaver Pass, it's possible to scramble up the western slopes of Prophet Ridge for a glimpse of snowy peaks. Even better is to hike up to lofty Whatcom Pass for views of the infamous Picket Range and peaks such as Challenger and Luna, draped with their mantles of ice. The view is worth the effort, even if it adds a few miles to the loop. The mountains here in the North Cascades harbor more than 300 glaciers, more than any other park in the lower 48 states.

The combination of old-growth forests and mountain vistas is hard to resist. And to top it all off, the trip begins and ends with a half-hour long water taxi ride up Ross Lake, first to the Little Beaver Trailhead, then down from Big Beaver at the hike's conclusion. The views from the boat ride on Ross Lake are practically worth the trip in themselves, as the narrow body of water penetrates the inner reaches of North Cascades National Park. Towering Jack Mountain and its sprawling Nohokomeen Glacier will blow you away. On the way up you can marvel at the fact that almost a century ago somebody had the vision to use this narrow valley as a giant reservoir and thus ensure a water supply for the city of Seattle. Now it's also a magic carpet ride to a beautiful wilderness excursion.

LOGISTICS & STRATEGY

North Cascades National Park is three hours from Seattle by car, and about the same from Vancouver, British Columbia. One of the reasons this area remains unspoiled is simply this: the place is remote, and difficult to get to. Virtually nowhere in the park is accessible via public transportation. You really need a car to see the park, and get to the trailhead.

For that reason, visitors from afar will arrive at either the Seattle or Vancouver airports and drive here in a rental car. As for where to stage for this extraordi-

A hiker calls for the water taxi from the Ross Lake Resort for a pre-arranged pickup. The boat ride takes just more than a half hour on the run up to the Little Beaver landing. PHOTO BY TED EVANS.

Fording Big Beaver Creek in the riot of North Cascades lowland valley vegetation. PHOTO BY SETH POLLACK.

nary loop, there are a couple of factors to consider. It comes down to this: do you want to hang out in the big city, then drive up to the North Cascades for a mid- or late-day start? Or do you want to stay in a small nearby town, or even out in the boonies at nearby campgrounds, both within a short drive of the trailhead, and get an early start? You can do either.

Since the hike starts and finishes with a water taxi run up (and down) Ross Lake, that's the key consideration in where you stay the night before. If you're exploring Seattle or Vancouver, you could leave town in the morning for the drive along Interstate 5 and Highway 20 to the park. Along the way, stop at the ranger station in Marblemount for your permit, take in the outrageous sightseeing along this famous North Cascades Highway, and arrive at Ross Lake in time for a midday shuttle up lake to the Little Beaver Creek Trailhead. Arriving late means you will make camp at the lake shore campground at Little Beaver Creek, which is pretty, or camp a few miles up the trail at one of several potential sites.

If you choose to leave Seattle or Vancouver later in the day, you can drive to Sedro Woolley (about two hours), located where Highway 20 leaves Interstate 5, spend the night there in one of many motels, or camp at a half dozen campgrounds along the North Cascades Highway between Sedro Woolley and Ross

Lake. Colonial Creek Campground, a big one, is just 5 miles (8 km) west of Ross Lake. Either of those options puts you close enough to Ross Lake for an early morning water taxi, which means an early morning start on the Little Beaver Trail, #731.

The basic situation is this: the Little Beaver–Big Beaver route forms a nearly equilateral triangle with Ross Lake. The northern leg is Little Beaver Creek, which flows into Ross Lake. There is no trail access to Little Beaver Creek, so to get here you have to take the water taxi. The route follows Little Beaver Creek eastward to Beaver Pass, which connects the drainage of Little Beaver Creek with the drainage of Big Beaver Creek. To return to Ross Lake, you cross the broad pass and hike back southeast along Big Beaver Creek to Ross Lake, reaching the lake about 12 miles (20 km) south of where you began at Little Beaver Creek. From here, you can schedule a water taxi, or hike out 7 miles (11 km) along a lakeside trail to the Ross Lake Resort, and up to your car.

You can do the hike in either direction, but I prefer moving counter clockwise by starting where Little Beaver Creek flows into Ross Lake. The reason is simple: doing it this way means you'll hike Little Beaver, go up and over Beaver Pass, down to Big Beaver, and end up where Big Beaver Creek flows into Ross Lake. You can walk out from there, so if

Some backcountry travelers choose to paddle up to Little Beaver Trailhead rather than take the water taxi. **PHOTO BY JOEL ROGERS.**

something has gone awry, or you've missed your boat pickup, or gotten it wrong, or it's rare bad weather that prevents the boat from getting to you, you can still hike back to your car on the lakeside trail. Do it the other way and you end up at Little Beaver Creek and Ross Lake. From there, you cannot walk out and are totally dependent on the boat. And finally, starting in Little Beaver puts the climax of the trip, the majestic cedar grove in Big Beaver, near the end of the hike. That's an experience you want to take home with you as a fresh memory.

The hike itself is not arduous, and for such great fun brings a high payoff considering the effort applied. Both Big Beaver and Little Beaver valleys have good trails, even with the possibility of wet creek crossings, particularly in early season. Expect to gain 2,000 feet (600 meters) going up Little Beaver to Beaver Pass, and lose about the same coming back down. A fit party could do this route without hardship in two days, with one camp midway (14 miles, 23 km) near Beaver Pass. But the whole point is to savor the majestic forest, and also take a day to enjoy unique views of the North Cascades peaks. I recommend a strategy of spending at least two nights, and possibly three. Just where you camp depends on when you reach the Little Beaver Trailhead, and whether you do the optional day hike up to Whatcom Pass. Good campsites in both valleys are never more than 5 miles (8 km) apart, and often come every few miles. Make camp when the mood strikes, as there are sufficient possibilities.

The important strategizing comes when you near the pass between the two valleys. Here, you must decide on how you want to view the North Cascades. About 10 miles (16 km) from Ross Lake, and 3 miles (5 km) before Beaver Pass, a bridge across the creek marks a junction where the Little Beaver Trail continues straight ahead for Whatcom Pass. Whatcom Pass is the best place to view the peaks of the North Cascades, but it's 2,000 feet (600 meters) and 6 hard miles (10 km) from the Little Beaver bridge. From the pass, views into mounts Whatcom and Challenger, unbelievably close, and glimpses of the Picket Range are unforgettable. If you camp nearby and do the hike up to Whatcom Pass with day packs, this is a reasonable day, and an exceptionally rewarding one. When will you be here again? This day hike to Whatcom Pass will add a day to your itinerary, but will transform a beautiful forest walk into something much more.

However, if you don't have the extra day, or plan to camp elsewhere, there is a second option for getting views of the North Cascades. At the bridge, instead of going straight, turn off the Little Beaver Trail onto the Big Beaver Trail and head for Beaver Pass, about two hours away at 3,600 feet (1,000 m) elevation. From the pass, where a popular hikers' camp is located, spend the afternoon roaming the high country to the east, on the lower western slopes of Prophet Ridge. From the shelter, climb the forested slopes to the east. In just a half hour, you will begin to catch glimpses of Luna Peak from open areas, and if you go an hour or more, your views are much better. This option is easier and quicker that hiking to Whatcom Pass, but the payoff is not quite as spectacular.

From Beaver Pass, the midpoint of the trip, it's a final 13 miles (20 km) back down Big Beaver Valley to Ross Lake. The highlight of the entire trip comes a little more than halfway downstream from Beaver Pass. This is where you enter the lower Big Beaver valley and gradually come upon the stand of ancient western red cedars that has made this hike famous. Some of the trees are more than a thousand years old. This is where you are likely to see beavers at work in the ponds as well. From the grove, it's another 5 miles (8 km) out to Ross Lake, where you have arranged the water taxi, or will begin the hike out south along the lake. Take my word for it, the boat is easier, particularly after three days on the trail, but then you're on a schedule. Also, the three-hour hike back will save a few bucks.

If you are camping another night at Ross Lake, chose between one of two options: the lakeshore camp near the Big Beaver landing, or, if that's busy with boaters, hike south across the bridge to a backpackers' camp a few minutes away.

A hiker at Whatcom Pass, a recommended side trip for this forest loop, which offers a rare glimpse into the hidden snow and rock of the North Cascades peaks. PHOTO BY ETHAN WELTY.

HAZARDS

In this wild part of the Cascades, encounters with black bears, deer, and other wildlife can be expected, but seldom present any danger. Persistent rumors of grizzly bear sightings in this area lead some biologists to think a remnant population, or visitors from Canada, may pass through these valleys.

Weather is the principal concern here in the North Cascades, a place famous for wet, cold weather, bringing the potential for hypothermia. Ensure that your camping gear and outerwear are up to the challenge. Snow may be an issue in early season at Beaver Pass. Inquire about conditions when you get your permit.

Treat or filter all your water.

SEASON

The hiking season in the North Cascades in generally a short one, but these two lowland valleys open fairly early, by mid-June, and, weather permitting, are usually passable into early October. The critical factor in terms of when you can do the loop as described here are the snow conditions at Beaver Pass, which probably won't open until late June, or Whatcom Pass, if that's your strategy, which probably won't open until early July. But don't let that stop you. If you do the hike in early season, just go as far up toward the views as snow conditions allow.

A backpackers' camp at Whatcom Pass, where wilderness travelers who make the extra effort enjoy sunset on Mount Challenger and Whatcom Peak. PHOTO BY JOEL ROGERS.

ROUTE

From Interstate Highway 5 near Burlington, WA, take the Cook Road exit (232) east to where it joins Highway 20 (the North Cascades Highway) in Sedro Woolley. Drive Highway 20 approximately 70 miles (112 km) through the town of Marblemount and past Colonial Creek campground, to the Ross Dam/Ross Lake Resort Trailhead. Park your car in the lot and hike .8 mile (1 km) down to Ross Lake (1,600 feet, 490 m, elevation) just above Ross Dam. If you've called ahead, the water taxi will pick you up at the dock.

From this point, Big Beaver Creek can be reached via a 6-mile (10-km) trail along the west shore of Ross Lake. Note that there is no trail access beyond Big Beaver up to Little Beaver Creek. The only way up to Little Beaver is the Ross Lake Resort's water taxi; reserve your up-lake boat and return trip in advance.

The scenic run from the Ross Dam up to Little Beaver Creek Trail covers about 18 miles (29 km) and takes just over 30 minutes. A lakeside campground is near the landing, a good place to camp if you've arrived late in the day. The trail veers northward a bit, switchbacking uphill with good views across Ross Lake before dropping over a shoulder and down into the Little Beaver drainage. In a matter of minutes, you're hiking through serious old-growth forest, the predictable Douglas fir, hemlock, cedar, and fir, but also wildflowers in season, and extraordinary carpets of moss and ferns and other forest vegetation. The aroma is fecund.

Five miles (8 km) down the trail you reach Perry Creek camp, with a shelter structure, where the braided channel in the stream can present a complicated crossing. The valley bottom here is marshy and thick with devil's club, so be careful not to stray off the trail. Near Mist Creek in particular, the dense underbrush can be confusing.

Cross Redoubt Creek on the logjam 9 miles (15 km) from the lake, and pass through a field of huge, moss-covered boulders. Just over 10 miles (16 km) from the lake, reach the bridge across Little Beaver Creek, which marks the intersection with the Big Beaver Trail. This is decision time: camp nearby for a day hike up to Whatcom Pass, or turn left onto the Big Beaver Trail and head for Beaver Pass.

If you are doing the hike up to Whatcom Pass for the views, stay on the Little Beaver Trail. Hike through dense forest on the valley floor, past Pass Creek flowing down the rock face, and into Twin Rocks Camp, a viable camping option. There's a grove of hemlock here that makes a good camp, or lunch spot. The trail enters a stretch of dense slide alder, then passes a stand of big cedars before working up the head of the valley in a seemingly endless series of switchbacks. Hike up onto the talus at last and up to the pass for stunning views of Challenger and its glacier. Whatcom Pass is at 5,200 feet (1,560 m), 6 miles (9.5 km), and 2000 feet (600 m) above the intersection with the Big Beaver Trail. Spectacular campsites can be found near the pass for those so inclined.

If you are not going to hike up to Whatcom Pass, or after you have gone there, turn off the Little Beaver Trail onto Big Beaver Trail, #732. Cross the creek on the bridge, and continue up the Big Beaver Trail. Hike past Stillwell Camp in about 1 mile (1.3 km) and work uphill 3 miles (5 km) on a series of switchbacks to broad, forested Beaver Pass, at 3,600 feet (1,000 m). This is the midway point of the loop, not counting side trips for mountain views. From the saddle it's 14 miles (23 km) to Ross Lake via either the Big Beaver Trail or the Little Beaver Trail. Take a few hours to scramble up the forested slopes to the east for surprisingly good views of Luna Peak. The higher you go, the better the view.

When it's time to head down Big Beaver Trail, from the saddle make a gradual descent down into the Big Beaver valley, eventually negotiating a series of switchbacks before reaching Luna Creek and Luna Camp in 4.5 miles (7.2 km). Look for views into the high peaks up the drainage. Just beyond Luna Camp are two creek crossings that can prove problematic in early season, so be prepared to take your boots off.

The trail passes an impressive gorge near McMillan Creek, about 3 miles (5 km) beyond Luna Camp, (about 7 miles, 11 km, from Ross Lake). Look for peekaboo views up to McMillan Cirque and McMillan Spires in the Picket Range. Another mile farther down valley brings you to good campsites at 39 Mile Camp.

Another mile or two below that, and you enter the magical lower valley and begin to see the big cedar trees. Take your time hiking through the valley here to savor the experience of this impressive grove of trees, and keep your eyes peeled in

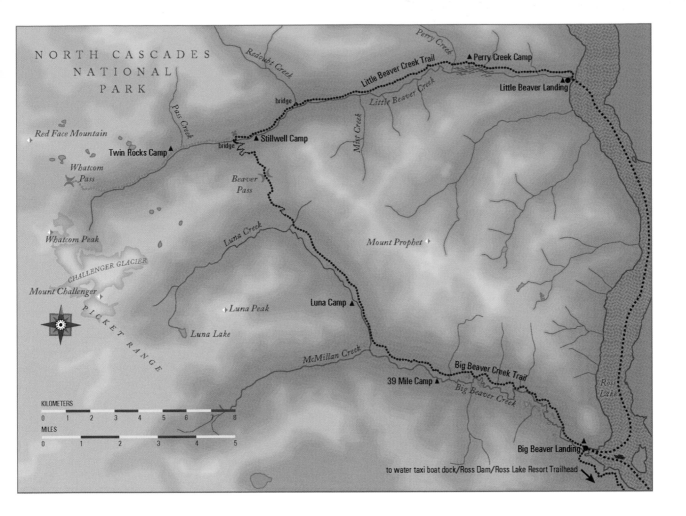

the marshy areas for beaver activity in the nearby ponds. Beyond the biggest cedars, the trail finally reaches the banks of Big Beaver Creek about 11 miles (18 km) from Beaver Pass, and 3 miles (5 km) from Ross Lake. The final miles parallel the creek to arrive at Big Beaver Landing. From here, you wait for the boat to pick you up, or begin the 6-mile (9.5-km) hike out to the resort, and the final mile up to your car.

INFORMATION

Permits are required to camp in North Cascades National Park, anytime, anywhere, but at present there is no fee. For information and current park regulations, call the North Cascades National Park ranger station in Marblemount (officially known as the Wilderness Information Center) or the National Park Service/US Forest Service ranger station in Sedro Woolley (officially known as the North Cascades National Park Headquarters/US Forest Service Mount Baker Ranger District).

WILDERNESS INFORMATION CENTER
360-854-7245

NORTH CASCADES NATIONAL PARK
HEADQUARTERS/US FOREST SERVICE
MOUNT BAKER RANGER DISTRICT
360-856-5700 or 360-854-7200

NORTH CASCADES VISITOR CENTER
Newhalem, WA
206-386-4495

ROSS LAKE WATER TAXI/
ROSS LAKE RESORT
503 Diablo Street
Rockport, WA 98283
206-386-4437
www.rosslakeresort.com

Little Beaver Creek runs through the deep forests of North Cascades National Park, eventually draining into Ross Lake. PHOTO BY SETH POLLACK.

HERMIT–TONTO–BRIGHT ANGEL LOOP
The Grand Canyon
Grand Canyon National Park
Arizona, United States

DISTANCE: **26 miles (43 km) loop**
TIME: **4–5 days**
PHYSICAL CHALLENGE: **1 2 3 4 5**
PSYCHOLOGICAL CHALLENGE: **1 2 3 4 5**
STAGING: **Grand Canyon Village, Arizona**

This often overlooked loop offers a deep immersion into the outrageous landscape of the Grand Canyon on well-trod trails past known water sources. The dramatic hiking journey descends the Hermit Trail, contours along the spectacular Tonto Platform, and reemerges at the South Rim via ascent-friendly Bright Angel Trail. While most hikers who venture below the rim choose one of the popular "corridor trails" to come and go, this road less taken delivers you in four days to the most prized viewpoints in the heart of the canyon, right down in it. Where else can you follow the rim of the *inner* gorge for two days, camp beside the Colorado at one of its most dramatic rapids, and look right into the narrowest stretch of Granite Gorge, all in just 26 miles (43 km)—and have a certified radioactive water source to boot?

Any walk in the Grand Canyon is going to rate pretty high on the Richter Scale of hikes if only because of the scenery. But to appreciate the scale of the canyon, and the forces that created it, you've got to invest some time within. This Tonto Platform circuit allows for extra days to savor the embrace of the canyon walls, and the unique ambience in its depths. Although not a

The Bright Angel Trail leads from Indian Garden up to the South Rim. PHOTO BY PETER POTTERFIELD.

true loop, because it ends at a different point on the South Rim from the place it started, this epic arc of a backcountry route shows you the best part of the canyon while eliminating the need to backtrack.

Formed at the one place on earth where it could happen, where desert and river intersect on a high plateau, the Grand Canyon may be the greatest geologic showcase on Earth. The rocks at the bottom are 2 billion years old, the ones at the top 200 million years old, creating a slice through geologic time that defies belief. To walk down through this epic historical record, stratum by stratum—through Kaibab limestone and Coconino sandstone to Bright Angel shale, right down to the Vishnu complex of the Colorado River—is to take a foot journey unlike any other.

Choose just one word for the canyon, and that's going to be "rugged." This landscape is so brutal it defeated even the hardened Spanish explorers who were the first Europeans to see it, and the first to try to get down into it, in 1550. Since then, the Grand Canyon has attracted people in ever-growing numbers. When Theodore Roosevelt saw it in 1903, he was so moved by this greatest of scenic wonders that he proclaimed it a game reserve, the best he could do at the time, to protect it temporarily. Eventually, it became a national monument, and in 1919, a national park. In the century since it was first protected, the Grand Canyon has become one of the greatest tourist attractions of all time. Five million people a year come to take a look.

Clearly, the best way to avoid the crowds in this sprawling 1.2-million-acre park is to hit the trail. Only 40,000 people hiked to any camp in the backcountry in 2010. The walk from the rim into the inner gorge brings to life the short but colorful human history of the canyon following John Wesley Powell's famous first run through it on the Colorado River in 1869. The Atchison, Topeka and Santa Fe Railroad ushered in the modern tourist era in 1901, when it completed a rail spur to the South Rim. The tourists who arrived by rail were taken down into the canyon on mules via the Bright Angel Trail, created in 1902 by Ralph Cameron and his brother by improving an ancient Havasupai route. Cameron charged a $1 toll for its use.

The railroad improved the rough Hermit Trail route in 1910 to compete with the Bright Angel Trail, and operated Hermit Camp 7 miles (11 km) below the rim until the 1930s. The current backpackers' camp lies below the ruins of the historic one, and the eye of faith can still detect the remains of a tram once used to ferry supplies down this route. Don't be put off by the moniker "unmaintained" when applied to the Hermit Trail. With sections of paved cobblestones, it has withstood the test of time. And while not a superhighway to compare with the Bright Angel, the few eroded spots are well worth the access it provides to the Tonto Platform.

The Hermit Trail, which once led down to the popular Hermit Resort, now takes hikers on the first leg of the Hermit–Tonto–Bright Angel Loop as it descends 3,000 feet (900 m) from the South Rim to the Tonto Plateau. PHOTO BY JOEL ROGERS.

As the Bright Angel Trail approaches the South Rim 5 miles (8 km) from Indian Garden, classic Grand Canyon views open up; the trail to Plateau Point, which many believe is the best viewpoint in the whole canyon, is visible. PHOTO BY PETER POTTERFIELD.

LOGISTICS & STRATEGY

The 26-mile (43-km) route recommended here takes advantage of the considerable infrastructure of Grand Canyon Village on the South Rim. The route starts at the Hermit Trailhead on the South Rim and ends just a few miles away at the Bright Angel Trailhead on the South Rim. Theoretically, this route can be done in either direction, but practically, the Hermit Trail is much better suited to descent, and the Bright Angel Trail is the best in the canyon for ascent. The route here is described from west to east, from Hermit Trail to Bright Angel.

Starting from the South Rim, the hike follows the Hermit Trail, which is in pretty good shape despite being unmaintained, into the heart of the canyon. This is a trail used daily by many on the journey down through the layer cake of the canyon to the Tonto

Platform. There the route turns east off the Hermit Trail at the intersection with the Tonto Trail, about 7 miles (11 km) down canyon. From here, the route follows the topography of the complicated Tonto Platform, at this point not the uniform ledge it is farther east, as it undulates up and down, rounds promontories and cuts back into drainages for the next 14 miles (23 km). The route passes camps at Monument Creek (with access to Granite Rapids), Cedar Spring, Salt Creek, Horn Creek, and finally Indian Garden. From there, it's a final 5 miles (8 km) back up to the South Rim on the Bright Angel Trail.

Water is the overarching concern. One of the key features of this route is the availability of potable water at these locations: at Hermit Creek (west of the route), Monument Creek, Granite Rapids, Cedar Spring (most of the year), Salt Creek (most of the year), and Indian Garden. Be sure to treat or filter all

The Tonto Trail follows the broad Tonto Platform for much of the route, only to cut sharply into the drainages encountered along the way.
PHOTO BY ANTON FOLTIN.

water. There's water in Horn Creek, but don't even think about drinking it. The Lost Orphan uranium mine of the late 1940s and 1950s made the water here radioactive. If you camp at Horn Creek, you have to carry water from Salt Creek, which some hikers find brackish, or Cedar Spring, or even Monument Creek, or fetch it from Indian Garden. The route can be done in three days, easy, but most hikers take four, and a lucky few spend five days and four nights here on the rim of the inner gorge.

The nearest city to the park, Flagstaff, is not convenient for direct air connections from most locations. Most hikers who come to the park to do this route will arrive through Las Vegas, the easiest city to reach by air, or Phoenix. Both are about five hours' drive from Grand Canyon National Park and its headquarters for visitors, the South Rim's Grand Canyon Village. This is the place from which to stage the hike. A predictable, sprawling mini-city and motel–hotel strip has developed south of the park boundary on US Highway 180, offering groceries, supplies, and lodging. Arguably a better experience is to be had by choosing accommodations within the park itself, in Grand Canyon Village.

Expect to pay a little more when staying in one of the concessionaires' hotels or motels, but the advantage of being right on the rim outweighs the greater expense. Being able to walk to the shuttle bus for trips along the rim, to the backcountry ranger station, or even to many South Rim trailheads, keeps you out of the car. Some accommodations in the village, such as the El Tovar Hotel, are quite expensive, but others, such as the Maswik Lodge, feature motel-style parking, reasonable rates, a cafeteria, and walking proximity to trailheads, administrative offices, and viewpoints.

Permits are required to hike into the inner canyon, and since permits are in high demand, advance planning is definitely required to get one for when you want to go. The park service issues permits as much as four months in advance. The technique with the best chance to get a permit for precisely the days you want is to log on to the Backcountry Information Center Web page on the first of the month four months prior to the proposed start day, download the permit request form, and submit the request via fax, including a credit card number for the fees. Three to six weeks after the application, the permit or a denial arrives in the mail.

OPPOSITE: *A hiker rounds the corner below Dana Butte, the dominant feature between Horn Creek and Salt Creek.*
PHOTO BY ANTON FOLTIN.

If you are denied an advance permit, you can reapply for different dates, or take your chances on a limited number of last-minute, walk-in permits available at the Backcountry Information Center.

For the hike recommended here, you'll need a permit for three to five nights of backcountry camping, depending on your time. Three nights is minimum, five allows for a visit to Granite Rapids and perhaps a night at Indian Garden, or extra time for exploration or unexpected weather delays.

The route works like this. From your accommodations in the village, you'll take the shuttle bus to Hermit's Rest, located west of the village on West Rim Drive. From the trailhead, follow the Hermit Trail as it descends from the rim and down through the layers of the Grand Canyon's famous geology. This is an epic 7 miles (11 km), and one that will linger in memory. The first question is, after 7 miles down to the Tonto Trail, where to camp the first night? Most people choose the Monument Creek Camp, just 1.5 miles (2.5 km) past the trail junction. Others choose

to hike down to the Colorado to a well-sheltered beach camp at Granite Rapids, 1.5 miles (2.5 km) from the Tonto Trail. The distance is nearly the same, and either makes a good camp for the first night.

From Monument Creek Camp, the Tonto Trail continues east along the spectacular rim of the inner gorge through complicated topography past Cedar Spring Camp, 1.5 miles (2.5 km) from Monument Creek, to Salt Creek Camp, 3.5 miles (7 km) from Monument Creek, or Horn Creek Camp, almost 8 miles (13 km) from Monument Creek. There's water in Horn Creek, but it is not potable. So where to camp for the second night?

One solution is to camp at Salt Creek for night two. There is water for most of the year here, but check with rangers. The camp has no shade, so it's not suitable in hot weather. From the Salt Creek Camp, it is 8 miles (13 km) to Indian Garden and the next night's camp.

Another strategy is to carry water from Cedar Spring (fairly reliable), Salt Creek (often brackish), or

even Monument Creek, and camp at Horn Creek. (Some hikers camp at Horn Creek and make the two-hour water run to Indian Garden.) From Horn Creek, it's less than 3 miles (5 km) to Indian Garden, about an hour's hike. From Indian Garden, it's 5 miles (8 km) and three hours up to the South Rim.

The trick is to use the available camps and water sources to create the three-, four-, or five-day trip you desire. One popular four-day option is to camp at Granite Rapids, then Cedar Spring, then Indian Garden. Some hikers camp at Monument Creek and Indian Garden for the reliable water, and do the route in three days. Choose the strategy that works best for you.

Expect the temperature to change radically in the course of this round-trip adventure. In November, when I last hiked the route, the South Rim (about 7,000 feet, 2,140 m) was near freezing in early morning, but the canyon floor was a balmy 80 degrees Fahrenheit (26°C). For the summer months, temperatures on the South Rim are relatively pleasant, between 50 and 80 degrees (10–26°C), but the inner canyon temperatures can be extreme, often exceeding 100 degrees (38°C) at the river. Snow can fall at either rim in early spring and late autumn.

This so-called loop offers little in the way of significant route variations, except to take more time to extend your stay. The Tonto Platform is a spectacularly scenic place, unrivalled in the canyon, and with the certainty of water you can extend your visit here to allow for bad weather, or simply more sunrises and sunsets. And more time might easily be spent at Granite Rapids to enjoy the ambience of the Colorado as it flows past one of the most dramatic rapids in the canyon. Further, you can break up your hike back to the rim by spending an additional night at Indian Garden Camp, about halfway between the river and the rim, before you hike back to the village.

HAZARDS

More than 250 hikers are rescued each year in the Grand Canyon, with most incidents resulting from heat-related problems, poor fitness, or dehydration. Temperatures in the inner canyon can take hikers by surprise because rim temperatures can be 20 or 30 degrees cooler. The uphill days for this hike will cover almost 5,000 feet (1,525 m) and 7 to 9 miles each (11 to 14 km), long days with an equivalent elevation gain to summit day on Mount Rainier. Hiking in the can-

yon, therefore, requires a good level of fitness as well as basic backcountry judgment. Avoid hiking from rim to river during the hottest summer months, and don't even consider trying a rim-to-river round trip in the same day. By planning your hike for spring or fall, you can avoid hiking out in extreme heat, and with proper nutrition, hydration, and fitness, you can make the hike an exhilarating adventure, not a grim ordeal.

Other potential problems facing hikers include lightning strikes (mainly on the rim) and falls. Black widows, tarantulas, scorpions, and rattlesnakes can cause problems, but rarely do.

SEASON

It never ceases to amaze me how many hikers choose the wrong time of year for the best walks on earth, and the Grand Canyon is no exception. The vast majority of hikers choose to come here in the summer, when conditions are at their most dangerous and crowds at their worst. But off they go, down into the 100-degree heat, ensuring that the walk back up will be a struggle. Spring and autumn are far better times to do any hike in the Grand Canyon, so try to come from March through May, or from September through November. Even if you don't have perfect sunshine, you almost certainly will have a more enjoyable hike. Winter can be appealing for hikers who aren't freaked out by cold, short days and long nights, but icy trails up near the rims can make winter trips impractical, even dangerous.

ROUTE

The park service has closed portions of the South Rim to private traffic, including Hermit's Rest, where the Hermit Trailhead is located. To get there, you'll need to catch the free shuttle bus from the Backcountry Information Center (east of the Maswik Lodge near the railroad tracks) to the trailhead, a distance of about 2 miles (3 km). I suggest taking the first bus of the morning, which for me meant a dawn start and a beautiful descent over the South Rim just as the sun blasted over the eastern horizon.

OPPOSITE: *The view from the Tonto Trail down to Granite Gorge. The popular Granite rapid camp is located on an expansive sandy beach beside the rapid.*
PHOTO BY ANTON FOLTIN.

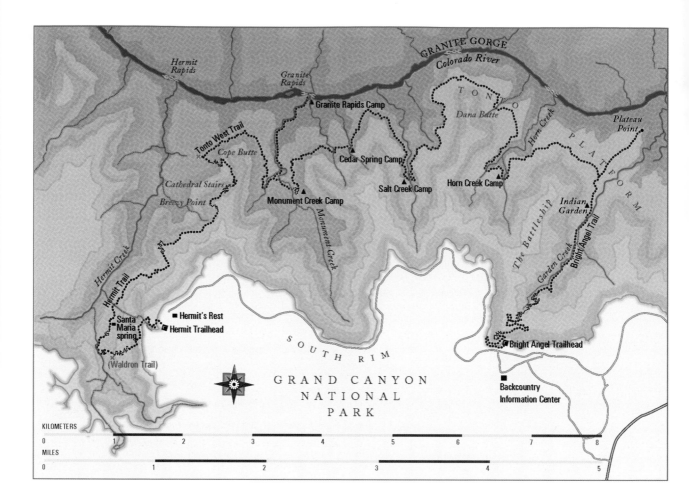

Find the trailhead for the Hermit Trail at 6,700 feet (2,040 m) just beyond the parking lot at Hermit's Rest. The trail drops down through the Kaibab limestone layer and continues steeply downhill toward Hermit Basin. The route treads some of the paved cobblestone path laid down by the Santa Fe Railroad a century ago as it reaches the intersection with the Waldron Trail. Bear right at the junction to continue downhill on the Hermit Trail, and some of the toughest hiking of the day. This is the Supai Traverse, which has seen some of the worst erosion on the trail in the past decades. Take care on this 2-mile (3-km) section as you drop past the Santa Maria Shelter. Watch for trail markers on this part of the trail, and navigate carefully.

The way gets a little easier near Breezy Point, where the first big views of the Colorado River open up. The trail descends the Cathedral Stairs before passing Cope Butte to reach the intersection with the Tonto Trail at 7 miles (11 km). Turn right, east, here and continue uphill on a moderate slope with killer views of the Colorado, now less than 1,000 feet (310 m) below. Climb over a ridge for your first views of Monument Canyon and the brilliant red cliffs rising steeply up toward the rim. A mile farther on you see the eroded desert tower, rare in the Grand Canyon, for which Monument Canyon is named.

The intersection for Granite Rapids, the riverside camp, comes up 8 miles (13 km) from the trailhead; turn left here and hike the final mile to the river if that is your destination. Or go straight for another mile to Monument Creek Camp at 9 miles (14.5 km) from the trailhead, about 3,000 feet (900 m). The pleasant camp lies directly under the huge cliffs below the rim more than 3,000 feet (900 m) above. This is the last absolutely reliable water, so carry enough to see you through the next night.

From Monument Creek Camp, climb up the Tonto Trail east toward Cedar Spring, only a mile or so away. The small camp has exceptional views, and water in the nearby creek for much of the year. Watch for glimpses of the Tower of Set and Horus Temple across the river as you hike east on the Tonto. The trail continues, with more opportunities to look down into the Colorado in narrow Granite Gorge, as it rounds a point and cuts back toward the camp in Salt Creek, 3 miles (4.8 km) from Monument Creek. There's little shade here, but the creek usually has water in it, although hikers often complain it has a mineral taste.

It's a long 5 miles (8 km) from Salt Creek to the next legal camp at Horn Creek, so ensure you have ample water. The trail climbs out of impressive Salt Creek Canyon and onto a much wider ledge as the Tonto Platform broadens. Isis Temple dominates the view across the Colorado. The trail continues along the edge of the inner gorge under Dana Butte on a long traverse before starting its descent into the Horn Creek drainage. This is one of the scenic climaxes of the hike, with views up to the South Rim, up to Dana Butte and over to the Battleship. The campsites lie near the creek. Some hikers think it's okay to bathe in the water, but do not drink it.

From the camp at Horn Creek, it's only 2.5 miles (4 km) to the piped-in water at Indian Garden. Some hikers pitch camp here at Horn Creek, and make the two-hour water run to Indian Garden. If you plan to camp here but don't have enough water, that's a viable strategy. If you are out of water, that's the only wise course of action. Some hikers plan their trip to continue on to Indian Garden for their final camp. If you've brought enough water for camp, a final night at Horn Creek positions you well to exit the next day, with a stop at Indian Garden for water on the way to the rim.

From Horn Creek the Tonto Trail rises above the impressive double drainages at Horn Creek and up onto the broad Tonto Platform. As you turn gradually right toward Indian Garden, you see the wide, obvious trail out to Plateau Point. The intersection with the Tonto Trail and the Plateau Point trail is 2 miles (3.2 km) from Horn Creek Camp. Many consider the view from Plateau Point to be among the best in the canyon. It's a vantage that is well worth the 1.5-mile (2.4-km) round trip to see it. When will you be here again? The view to Cheops Pyramid across the river makes a classic Grand Canyon tableau.

From the trail intersection, the trail becomes broad and dusty and in only a few minutes the big cottonwoods of Indian Garden come into view. A spring at Indian Garden was used for cultivation by the Havasupai Indians for hundreds of years, but the cottonwoods were planted by Ralph Cameron, the man who built Bright Angel Trail. The big trees offer welcome shade at this point in the climb, with 4.7 miles (7.5 km) remaining to the South Rim. This is the primary corridor trail in the park, and many hikers go up and down on their way from the rim to the Colorado, and down to Bright Angel Camp and Phantom Ranch. You'll have lots of company on the three-hour hike back to the South Rim.

The trail works up a set of switchbacks called Jacob's Ladder, through the Redwall and up to Three-Mile Resthouse, where the first day hikers come into evidence. The trail gets progressively busier with day hikers as it makes the final, laborious ascent up through the Coconino sandstone and Toroweap formation and, eventually, up the Bright Angel fault into the Kaibab limestone and a final tunnel before reaching the South Rim.

INFORMATION

GRAND CANYON NATIONAL PARK
P.O. Box 129
Grand Canyon, AZ 86023
928-638-7888
www.nps.gov/grca/index.htm

Permits

GRAND CANYON NATIONAL PARK
BACKCOUNTRY INFORMATION CENTER
1824 S. Thompson Street, Suite 201
Flagstaff, AZ 86001
928-638-7875
Fax: 928-638-2125
(Note: this is a very busy office, and you may have to try repeatedly to get through by telephone. If possible, use the Web and fax to communicate.)
www.nps.gov/grca/planyourvisit/backcountry-permit.htm

Fees: Cost for permits includes a nonrefundable fee plus a per person per night fee for anyone camped below the rim and yet another fee per group per night camped above the rim. Permit cancellations will incur another fee. All fees paid to the backcountry office are nonrefundable. Frequent users may wish to purchase a one-year Frequent Hiker membership that waives the initial fee for each permit.

In-Park Lodging

XANTERRA PARKS AND RESORTS
For South Rim, North Rim, and Phantom Ranch accommodations.
888-297-2757 or 303-297-2757
www.grandcanyonlodges.com

Shuttle Services

TRANS CANYON SHUTTLE
928-638-2820
www.trans-canyonshuttle.com

Guide Services

For an up-to-date list of guide services allowed to operate in the park, check:
www.nps.gov/grca/planyourvisit/guided-hikes.htm

SENTIERS INTERNATIONAL DES APPALACHES
Mont Jacques-Cartier to Mont Albert
Chic-Choc Mountains
Gaspésie National Park
Quebec, Canada

DISTANCE: **27 miles (43 km) one-way**
TIME: **2–3 days**
PHYSICAL CHALLENGE: **1 2 3 4 5**
PSYCHOLOGICAL CHALLENGE: **1 2 3 4 5**
STAGING: **Quebec City, Quebec**

Hike past the 8-foot-high cairns and come up over the last rise onto the wild, rocky summit of Mont Jacques-Cartier, and you'll find it looks more like Arctic tundra than the typical wooded mountain slopes of eastern North America. Welcome to Quebec. Well above 4,000 feet (1,250 m), this summit—highest in Gaspésie National Park—offers views not only of the entire Chic-Choc mountain range and the Gulf of St. Lawrence in the distance, but of a herd of caribou grazing for lichen among the boulders. All this makes it a little hard to believe you're actually on the Appalachian Trail.

Most hikers know that the northern terminus of the AT is found at Mount Katahdin. Indeed, the official US Appalachian Trail completes its 2,167-mile (3,490-km) journey from Springer Mountain, Georgia, there in central Maine. But just as the Appalachian Mountains continue north into Canada, the trail doesn't stop either. The International Appalachian Trail follows those mountains north, right into Quebec, a good 500 miles (805 km) north of the international border. The impressive length of Quebec's section of trail reaches its climax as it runs north onto the Gaspé Peninsula, the great finger of land that juts into the Gulf of St. Lawrence. For the local First Nation people, this was "the place where the land ends."

Here in Canada the storied AT becomes the SIA. Quebec is of course the heart of French Canada, so the International Appalachian Trail is known in the province by its French moniker: the Sentiers International des Appalaches. Its run along the crest of the spectacular Chic-Choc Mountains makes for a dramatic finish to one of the world's great hiking routes. In truth, it doesn't matter what you call this stretch of trail, it remains some of the best hiking terrain in the East, and it runs through some of the highest altitudes in the Appalachians. The SIA from Katahdin to Cap Gaspé has in fact become a new classic for long-distance hikers.

Just the drive up the Gaspé Peninsula from the small airport at Mont-Joli helps prepare you for the adventure to come. The blue expanse of the St. Lawrence stretches to the horizon, and you're quite likely to see blue whales breaching among the whitecaps. But when you turn right to travel up into the Chic-Choc

Descending off the summit plateau of Mont Jacques-Cartier toward Mont Comte. PHOTO BY PETER POTTERFIELD.

Mountains and Gaspésie National Park itself, you'll find something unexpected: this is a wild place, but it's not, strictly speaking, wilderness. Quebec has the most extensive network of parks in all of Canada, and the province manages each one carefully to better preserve them. For the hiker, that means more restrictions on where you can camp, but the upside is comfortable huts (for those who prefer them) in choice locations, a well-protected landscape free from the threat of resource exploitation, and an elaborate trail system.

The route recommended here touches the highlights of Gaspésie National Park, including some of its highest peaks and even its iconic lodge. Climbing to the summits of both Mont Jacques-Cartier and Mont Albert, not to mention Mont Xalibu, this 26-mile (42-km) route crosses Arctic tundra, penetrates thick forests, traces deep drainages, and sidehills through endless boulder fields. And if those rare wood caribou munching lichen off the rocks make it hard to believe you're on the Appalachian Trail, there are yet more surprises up here at this far end of the route.

In fact, if you've got the time, there's no need to stop when you reach Mont Albert. You might do the Grand Traverse, from Mont Jacques-Cartier to Mount Logan. That complete 62-mile (100-km) length of the SIA in Gaspésie, from one end of the park to the other, rivals any section of the Appalachian Trail, save perhaps for New Hampshire's White Mountains. But any outing through this surprisingly wild landscape at this "forgotten" end of the Appalachian Trail is going to be a good one. And a robust infrastructure, including the venerable Gîte du Mont-Albert, a historically important lodge here in the Chic-Chocs, adds a layer of civility to the adventure. Think of this as a grand tour through Quebec's backcountry crown jewel.

LOGISTICS & STRATEGY

For the route recommended here, or any hike on the Gaspé Peninsula, Quebec City makes the best staging point. Easy air connections from all over North America, or abroad, put you within a few hours of Gaspésie National Park. And the city is a place within driving distance for much of eastern Canada and the

TOP: *Diable Falls on the back side of Mont Albert.*

BOTTOM: *Descending Mont Albert toward Lac du Diable on the International Appalachian Trail, known in Quebec by its French moniker, the Sentiers International des Appalaches.* PHOTO BY PETER POTTERFIELD.

northeastern US. The considerable charms of this old city—one of the oldest in all of North America at 400 years and then some—is a reason to come. This is a place that exudes an even more intense flair for French culture than Montreal, but does so in a relaxed way without the crowds or expense of a big city.

In town, fuel for your stove and any forgotten pieces of gear can be obtained while you take a day or two to absorb the ambience. Hikers who arrive by air may choose to rent a car at the Quebec City airport for the scenic, five-to-six-hour drive up to Gaspésie National Park on Highway 132 along the western shore of the Gaspé Peninsula and the Gulf of St. Lawrence. But if you are pressed for time, catching a one-hour flight from Quebec City to the small Gaspé Peninsula airport at Mont-Joli (about three hours by highway from Quebec City), and renting a car there, shaves a full day or more off your week-long itinerary.

The airport at Mont-Joli is a few minutes from Rimouski, one of the largest cities on the Gaspé Peninsula, with the expected services. But there is really no need to backtrack, as the scenic drive toward Gaspésie National Park also takes you through Matane, with grocery stores, restaurants, and other necessities. Expect to take an hour and a half driving from Mont-Joli to Matane, and another hour and a half from there up past small seaside villages to Sainte-Anne-des-Monts.

For centuries, the residents of the Gaspé Peninsula made their living off the rich cod fishery, and each of the many villages that dot the seashore is identified by the high steeples of the big Catholic churches that are central to life here in northern Quebec. With the fishery now in trouble, however, many locals work in the fledgling but growing tourism industry, supported by visitors who come from all over the world for the pristine landscape and diverse wildlife. Just driving up the coast and into the mountains may give you a glimpse of blue whales in the St. Lawrence, or the highest densities of moose outside of Alaska, and of course the last herd of the rare wood caribou outside the Arctic.

At the town of Sainte-Anne-des-Monts, the last village of any size, turn off the coast road (Highway 132) and drive up into the mountains toward Gaspésie National Park on Highway 299. The most

OPPOSITE: *On to the vast summit plateau of Mont Jacques-Cartier.* PHOTO BY PETER POTTERFIELD.

spectacular of Quebec's national parks, Gaspésie and its surrounding reserves protects a 100-mile (168-km) stretch of the highest peaks of the Canadian Appalachians and 19,500 square miles (50,000 sq km) of untouched forest. The old growth was saved from logging because the rugged surroundings made it too difficult to reach. In fact, the First Nation moniker of Chic-Choc mountains translates as "the wall," or "the barrier," and reflects the difficulty of traveling through this terrain.

Accommodations in the park make the most sense, as that keeps you near the trails and out of the car. But staying in Sainte-Anne-des-Monts, under an hour away, is less expensive and can be more easily arranged on short notice. If you have the time, the place to stay is the landmark Gîte du Mont-Albert, the iconic lodging within the park boundaries. *Gîte* means lodge, and is perhaps something of a misnomer when applied to the impressive structure that is the classic national park lodge for Gaspésie. I recommend staying in one of the newer cabins or chalets adjacent to the lodge rather than in the lodge itself, as those offer easier access and facilitate preparations for backcountry. The Gîte du Mont-Albert is well suited for this hike as the route recommended here ends near the lodge.

Hiking permits and camping (or hut) permits must be reserved ahead of time and obtained in advance of your hike. Current conditions and camping information are available at the Discovery Centre, a part of the visitor center, where you pick up the permit you reserved before arrival. A small bistro at the visitor center provides inexpensive but surprisingly good meals and refreshments. Private cars are not allowed on some of the park roads, but bus service is provided from the park headquarters at frequent intervals.

A word about French Canadian culture: I was lucky to do my backcountry trip with one of the park naturalists. I knew that the province prizes its French heritage, but I was frankly surprised at just *how* French this remote part of Quebec is. You won't hear a lot of English spoken here. My schoolboy French was enough to get me through, but without Jean-Philippe, I would have missed out on a lot of conversation and interaction with the locals and other visitors on the trail and in camp.

Buses leave from the Discovery Centre near park headquarters, within walking distance of the lodge. Catch the first bus of the day for the 45-minute drive to the start of the route near the Mont Jacques-Cartier Campground. The bus will be full of hikers, including many Europeans, but most are day hiking to the summit and back. From the trailhead, at 2,300 feet (700 m), near the northern end of the park, the route climbs steeply up to the 4,167-foot (1,270-m) summit of Mont Jacques-Cartier, where everyone uses the lookout tower as a refuge from the wind. Trust me, the wind on the Gaspé can be frankly unbelievable. From there, most of the hikers head back down the way they came. But you continue across the summit plateau, and down the southwest corner to the valley between Mont Jacques-Cartier and Mont Comte.

After skirting the top of Mont Comte (4,032 feet,

The viewing tower on the summit of Mont Jacques-Cartier, which doubles as a refuge from the wind and cold. PHOTO BY PETER POTTERFIELD.

1,229 m), the route drops down to pretty Lac Samuel-Côté, about 7 miles (11 km) from the trailhead, where two camping options are possible: the platform tent site at La Camarine, or the hut known as Le Tétras. The huts within the park are comfortable but spartan, their chief advantage being the wood stove providing heat. Unlike many mountain huts around the world, you can't stay here without a reservation, so overcrowding is not a concern. But the campsites can be quieter, and richer in wilderness experience. Whichever option you choose, be sure to reserve accommodations or tent spaces in advance.

On the second day, the route leaves Lac Samuel-Côté, climbs up and over Mont Xalibu (3,740 feet, 1,140 m) and down to striking Lac aux Américains nestled in its bowl. A mile (2 km) beyond the lake comes the second hut, and the only overnight option in the neighborhood, the hut known as Le Roselin. As recommended, the second day is a short one, but that's by design to provide more time in the heart of this unique backcountry environment. The second full day on the trail from Le Tétras to Le Roselin is approximately 6.2 miles (10 km) with side trips. A second option is to hike out all the way to the Gîte du Mont-Albert on the second day, making it a long one at 11 miles (17 km), but that deprives you of two days and a night here in one of the most scenic stretches of the park.

The final day, for those who stay at Le Roselin, has two further options. You can make it the longest of the three by far, 17 miles (26 km) in total, by doing the final trail section followed by the 11-mile (18-km) ascent and a counterclockwise circumnavigation of Mont Albert. That option descends Mont Albert down the back side by Lac du Diable and on to the Gîte du Mont-Albert for a well-deserved feast in the dining room. Or you can break the last long day into two, stopping for night at the lodge (or park campground) first, after a 5.5-mile (9-km) hike, and doing the ascent of Mont Albert as a day hike on the fourth day.

HAZARDS

Moose, caribou, and other wild animals roam the park, but by far the greatest danger is the weather. Despite the fact that it was the height of summer during my hike—mid-August—the winds at tree line took on a frigid ferocity, cutting through our fleece with alarming force. I personally experienced windchill of 16 degrees Fahrenheit (-9°C) even in midsummer. The Gaspé is famous for weather, so be aware and come prepared with beefy outdoor equipment and adequate clothing, and a willingness to be flexible should conditions change your itinerary.

Looking back toward Mont Jacques-Cartier, across alpine Lac Samuel-Côté, from the hut Refuge Le Tétras at the end of the first day.

SEASON

Gaspésie National Park harbors mountains that are some of the highest in eastern Canada, which gives any outing here an alpine nature. Quebec's northerly position, and the fact that it is exposed to winds and weather coming off the Gulf of St. Lawrence and the Arctic, limits the hiking season to June through September. Park regulations actually close some of the trails in the park in spring and autumn, so check with park rangers when reserving your camping accommodations. From mid-June to September 30 the park's trails are open except in the rare circumstance when closure is required to protect wildlife.

ROUTE

From the trailhead for Mont Jacques-Cartier, at 2,500 feet (700 m) elevation, the route starts out on the broad, rough remains of a World War II military road, but soon becomes a rocky trail, and a steep one at that. The trail quickly gains altitude and the way becomes narrower and rougher as it winds through the trees. The stunted fir and spruce rapidly diminish in size, soon thinning out altogether.

The route skirts Lac à René in approximately two hours and 3 miles (5 km), at about 3,000 feet (1,000 m) elevation, a small body of water that was stocked with trout years ago. Now the lake has so many fish in it all you have to do is wiggle your fingers in the water to draw schools of them right to you, but there's no fishing allowed. The lake is a good place to don outerwear in advance of the windy summit plateau. The last few hundred yards follow a route in the open marked by giant cairns stacked taller than a person, a precaution that demonstrates how difficult it is to navigate up here in bad weather or low visibility.

From the frigid, windswept summit of Mont Jacques-Cartier, approximately 4 miles (7 km) from the trailhead, check out the view from the lookout tower, where everyone takes refuge from the wind. From the tower, the route follows trailside cairns, crosses a no man's land of windswept boulders, then drops down a long scree slope into the welcome lee of the mountain as it descends toward a gentle ridgeline where the stunted alpine timber reappears. The day hikers are long gone by now and this becomes one of the most enjoyable stretches of the hike, better for the solitude. You are likely to have the wild landscape to yourself as you forge eastward on the SIA toward the distant Mont Albert.

Here, 1,000 feet (300 m) below the summit, the temperature rises as the wind abates and, if you're lucky, the sun takes effect. The trail remains rough; it is not nearly as well maintained as the popular section of the route up Mont Jacques-Cartier. The way skirts the summit of Mont Comte

95

on its south side before dropping back down into deep forest. By early afternoon the route brings you to the shelter known as Le Tétras, which means grouse. (On my trip here it was fitting to be actually greeted by a mother hen with her brood of chicks trailing behind.) A nearby campground, with wooden tent platforms, offers a more economical overnight option. The hut and the camp are approximately 7 miles (11 km) and six hours from the trailhead, including side trips.

The comfortable hut (with one main room for cooking and several bedrooms with bunks) is ideally situated on the shore of Lac Samuel-Côté, and faces the rocky mountaintop of Mont Comte. For those who prefer camping, a designated tent site is only a hundred yards away. To protect its pristine environment, and the rich wildlife that calls the place home, Gaspésie National Park has stringent rules that permit camping only in designated areas. Those who want to camp where they like can do so in these mountains, but they have to venture beyond the borders of the park into the surrounding preserves. Inside the park, overnight options are limited to either the established camps or the huts.

On day two the route begins with a steep climb back into the windy alpine zone as the trail ascends to Mont Xalibu 3,740 feet (1,140 m), a striking, solitary peak, quite prominent within the wooded wilderness. A highlight is the side trail to the Belvédère de la Saillie, a high lookout platform with a sweeping view of the park. From here, the trail begins a long and abrupt descent into the forest and out of the windy, exposed alpine zone. The trail descends through bigger lowland timber down to Lac aux Américains. This impressive glacier-carved cirque, holding its namesake lake, reveals the Ice Age geologic forces that carved this impressive landscape. The lake makes a good lunch stop before the short afternoon hike through the trees to the next hut, known as Le Roselin. There is no tent camping option for overnights here.

As recommended, the second day is a short one, approximately 6 miles (10 km) from Le Tétras hut, but that's by design. This a very scenic part of the park and the idea is to savor this unique backcountry environment. One of the joys of hiking in Gaspésie is the variety of terrain.

This is one of the few places in the East where the ecozones change by the hour, where you can go from a maritime climate into the boreal forest right on up to Arctic tundra in the space of two hours.

The third day can be the tough one, or another easy one, depending on strategy, as some will opt to split the final day into two. The options are these:

OPTION 1: leave Le Roselin, hike the 5.5 miles (9 km) to the park headquarters, leave the SIA and do the Mont Albert loop 11 miles (18 km). Hike directly back to the Gîte du Mont-Albert for a well-deserved dinner in the dining room.

OPTION 2: leave Le Roselin, hike the 5.5 miles (9 km) to the park headquarters, stay at the Gîte du Mont-Albert or other overnight options near park headquarters, and make the hike up to Mont Albert on the following day.

From Le Roselin hut, the trail runs an easy 5.5 miles (9 km) to the park visitor center, much of it in the shelter of the boreal forest. From the visitor center, the best strategy is to climb Mont Albert and traverse its summit in a counterclockwise direction. To do that, leave the SIA at the well-marked intersection for Mont Albert and hike up through the trees toward the viewpoint known as La Saillie, about 2 miles (3 km) from the start. From there, the route follows the well-maintained trail up to the summit plateau near the north summit of Mont Albert, at 3,510 feet (1,070 m), well below that of Jacques-Cartier but still plenty high to be back in the cold, windy, Arctic zone. A small shelter provides relief near the summit.

From the shelter, hike due south to rejoin the SIA beyond the viewpoint of Le Versant, approximately a mile (1.5 km) from the summit shelter, then continue south to drop steeply down the backside of the mountain. The route follows a unique valley cut into the serpentine rock of the mountain, past an impressive 400-foot (135-m) waterfall on a tough boulder-strewn trail to sprawling Lac du Diable, 2.5 miles (3.2 km) from the trail intersection. One 3-mile (5-km) section of the route below the lake is nonstop

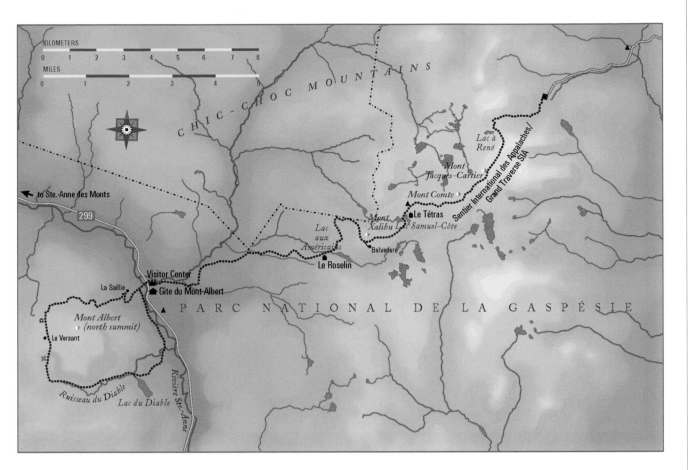

boulder-hopping, a fatiguing way to go when you're carrying a full pack. The trail follows the Diable River down into the trees, then turns north to follow along the St. Anne River and back to the visitor center in approximately 3.5 miles (6 km) from the lake. The round-trip ascent and circular tour of Mont Albert covers 11 miles (18 km), and takes six to seven hours.

INFORMATION

For hiking permits and camping reservations, contact the park:
GASPÉSIE NATIONAL PARK
1981 Route du Parc
Sainte-Anne-des-Monts, QC G4V 2E4
418-763-7494
Fax: 418-763-9492
E-mail: parc.gaspesie@sepaq.com

OPPOSITE LEFT: *Crossing the summit ridge of Mont Xalibu on the International Appalachian Trail (Sentiers International des Appalaches), with the expanse of the Chic–Choc Mountains of Gaspésie National Park beyond.* PHOTO BY PETER POTTERFIELD.

OPPOSITE RIGHT: *Working down the steep back side of Mont Albert toward the principal lodge at Gaspésie National Park, the Gîte du Mont–Albert.* PHOTO BY PETER POTTERFIELD.

For more information, visit the Gaspésie National Park Web site:
www.sepaq.com/pq/gas

And see the Sepaq site, the governing agency for all Quebec parks:
www.sepaq.com

Planning a Trip

See the Maritime Quebec Web site for information on planning a trip to the Gaspé Peninsula:
www.quebecmaritime.ca

Guide Services and Outfitters

ABSOLU ÉCOAVENTURE
418-566-5774
1118 Chemin de la Grève
Matane, QC G4W 7B1
E-mail: info@ecoaventure.com
www.ecoaventure.com

BEARTOOTH TRAVERSE
Absaroka–Beartooth Wilderness, Gallatin and Custer National Forests

Montana, United States

DISTANCE: **32 miles (51 km) with side trips**
TIME: **3–5 days**
PHYSICAL CHALLENGE: **1 2 3 4 5**
PSYCHOLOGICAL CHALLENGE: **1 2 3 4 5**
STAGING: **Bozeman, Montana**

You could drive yourself crazy trying to decide on the best hikes in Montana. The state is so rich in extraordinary wilderness that it's actually hard to choose: the trails in Glacier National Park? Yellowstone itself? The Bitterroots? The Bob Marshall Wilderness? One can hardly go wrong. But after sampling a lot of them, my favorite is this epic traverse of the Beartooth Mountains, from the heart of the range right down to the northern boundary of Yellowstone.

This is a straightforward, mindblowing, one-way trek across the heart of the Beartooths. The hike lies almost entirely in the Absaroka–Beartooth Wilderness, a land defined by rushing water, alpine lakes, and formidable peaks. One could make the argument that even in Yellowstone itself there's nothing to rival the austere beauty in this 1,500-square-mile (2,600-sq-km) preserve of classic Montana high country. The wilderness area protects two distinct mountain ranges, the Absarokas and the Beartooths. The Beartooths are the higher (including 12,799-foot, 3,900-m Mount Gardner, the highest peak in the state) and the more dramatic of the two, characterized by glacier-carved cirques above the timberline and dramatic alpine plateaus framed by rocky summits.

This route has been called the Beaten Path by some of the locals. In truth, it's no longer the well-kept secret it once was. But perhaps the most intriguing element of this wilderness excursion is the opportunity it presents for off-trail adventures. You could probably hike the entire trail in less than 27 miles (44 km) and three days. Some of my Montana friends have run the trail in a day, but even those who have done so returned for a four- or five-day backpack so they could savor a landscape with so many contrasting ecozones. And that's the reason to come; there's no need to hurry.

The trail alongside East Rosebud Creek is one of the prettiest in Montana, but rugged in the bargain as it ascends steep, rocky headwalls on its 4,000-foot (1,220-m) climb up to the Clarks Fork Divide. PHOTO BY PETER POTTERFIELD.

The way to appreciate this route is to consider it a yellow brick road, a way into the magical high and wild. We're talking classic Rocky Mountain back-country, and a lot of it. There is no better way to appreciate the scenery, the topography, and the flora and fauna of this remarkable wilderness. The Absaroka–Beartooth itself is nearly a million acres, think of it, with 700 miles (1,130 km) of trails. But together with adjoining Yellowstone National Park, it becomes part of the 20-million-acre (81,000-sq-km) Greater Yellowstone ecosystem. To say there's room to explore is an understatement.

The traverse begins at East Rosebud Lake on the edge of the wilderness, and ascends up past a series of beautiful backcountry lakes and waterfalls toward the Beartooth plateau. Even jaded local trail veterans consider the East Rosebud one of the prettiest valleys in the Beartooths, and it never lets up. For 16 scenic miles (26 km) the trail works up into the mountains before reaching the 10,000-foot (3,050-m) plateau that holds high and wild Fossil Lake. Just above that, the route crests the divide and plunges down the Clarks Fork of the Yellowstone drainage, with completely different geology, weather, even wildflowers.

Beartooth Butte, a Beartooth Range icon and just one of the amazing vistas seen along the Beartooth Highway between Cooke City and Red Lodge. PHOTO BY PETER POTTERFIELD.

The Beartooth Traverse is a journey of discovery in a magnificently varied landscape.

If you look hard, there are alpine campsites in the wilderness that compare to any. So find one of those, up high, and then consider your options for the extra day or two you've built in: bagging one of the 11,000-foot (3,353-m) walk-up summits nearby? Fishing the granite-encircled lakes? Roaming the flower-filled meadows? Exploring side trails to tantalizing features off the main route? These are the kind of choices that put a smile on the faces of serious backcountry travelers.

And just getting to the hike is going to give you an entertaining crash course in Montana culture and geography. Most people will come in through Bozeman, a growing, gentrifying metropolis ("Bozangeles" to the locals with a sense of humor) that serves as the gateway to Yellowstone. But it still retains its defining, unpretentious, laid-back Montana attitude. All the big, epic valleys that lead into the park—the Madison, the Gallatin, the Yellowstone—are accessed from town.

You'll finish the hike in Cooke City, just minutes from Yellowstone National Park's Silver Gate. A dawn start will let you take in the wildlife of the legendary Lamar Valley and still be back for breakfast. And one of the highlights of doing a hike that ends here is the drive back over the stupendous Beartooth Highway to Red Lodge. Charles Kuralt called Highway 212 the greatest road in America. The route winds for 64 miles (103 km) through the landscape, some of it above 10,000 feet (3,050 m), offering views of the Beartooths unlike any mountain view on earth accessible by a vehicle.

LOGISTICS & STRATEGY

Bozeman is the gateway to Yellowstone country, and probably the best place from which to stage the Beartooth Traverse. Trendy and civilized, Bozeman has a good airport that's easy to use, lodgings and restaurants of all sorts, and a good array of outdoor gear shops. One wrinkle to consider when coming to Montana for this route: from some places in North America it's easier and less expensive to fly into Billings. Montana's largest city, Billings also is a viable option for staging this hike. On the edge of the plains, it lacks the heavy Yellowstone vibe of Bozeman, but your drive to the trailhead will be only slightly longer. The Beartooth Traverse starts in the hamlet of Alpine on East Rosebud Lake, and the drive there will take approximately two and a half hours from Bozeman or three hours from Billings.

The route described here is a full-on traverse, and

a big one, so trailhead transportation is an essential piece of the puzzle. The route can be done in either direction, but most do it from north to south, from Alpine to Cooke City, and that's the way it's described here. For a one-way hike, you'll need to stash a car at the Clarks Fork Trailhead near Cooke City (the end of the hike) before driving to the trailhead at East Rosebud Lake (the start of the hike), or otherwise arrange transportation. This is significant as we're talking a five- or six-hour round trip to spot a car at the end and drive back to the start at Alpine.

Having done this route, I can tell you that some parties do the hike in the opposite direction from convention, beginning at Cooke City, with the intention of handing their keys off to a party of total strangers going the other way, and having those people shuttle the car to East Rosebud Lake. It happened to me, and my party was happy to oblige as we had plenty of drivers to get both our car and their vehicle back to East Rosebud Lake. This would be a good way to steal cars, and while it's not a technique I recommend, in a pinch it can work.

Be creative, and you'll find a solution to the trailhead issues. Perhaps the best is the simplest: when you reach the end at the Clarks Fork Trailhead, have a shower and a nice meal in Cooke City, and simply retrace your steps, do the whole hike again, right back to your car at East Rosebud Lake. That is an excellent strategy.

Whether you start from Billings or Bozeman to do the traverse, you'll turn off Interstate 90 at the town of Columbus. Permits are not required, so there is no reason to stop at a ranger station on your way in. From Columbus, drive one hour south on Highway 10 through the town of Absarokee (even the locals pronounce the name of this town in various ways, so enjoy that), and on to Roscoe, where you turn onto the East Rosebud Road toward the hamlet of Alpine. At this cluster of vacation cabins you'll find the elaborate trailhead, with parking lots and toilets, for the East Rosebud Trail, the start of the hike. If you wish to overnight at the trailhead, reserve one of the fourteen spots available at East Rosebud Lake Campground.

Hike up past the wilderness boundary to begin the Beartooth Traverse. Traveling up through the rocky embrace of the East Rosebud Valley, you'll tick off the first of the landmark lakes: Elk, then Rimrock and Rainbow, about 8,000 feet (2,438 m), where many people camp the first night. Rainbow Lake has good campsites but it can be busy; I prefer to camp elsewhere. The second day takes you higher and past ever more scenic lakes such as Big Park, Lake at Falls, Duggan, and a dozen waterfalls, most notably the dramatic cascades of Impasse Falls. This place is all about roaring water falling over polished rock.

You could hike the entire trail easily in three days, but this is where the landscape is most dramatic, so here is the place to spend a full day, or even two, enjoying the countryside. The most scenic camps are located above Duggan Lake, between Twin Outlet Lake and Dewey Lake. This wild, beautiful stretch makes the best location for a base camp from which to explore, so

TOP: *Ouzel Lake is just one of a dozen scenic alpine lakes that dot the upper Clarks Fork of the Yellowstone drainage.* PHOTO BY PETER POTTERFIELD.

BOTTOM: *A hiker climbs up through a wildflower garden above Dewey Lake toward the Beartooth Plateau and striking Fossil Lake.* PHOTO BY PETER POTTERFIELD.

take some time to find an exceptional spot. This is big-time grizzly bear country, so take precautions; regulations require that you hang your food bags 10 feet (3 m) off the ground and keep a clean camp.

From your camp, explore the neighborhood: hike up Mount Dewey, explore nearby cirques and basins such as Echo Lake, or even the tougher route to Oly and Cairn lakes. Just make sure any side trip is within your wilderness capabilities. My favorite outing is a long day hike up to explore outrageously beautiful Fossil Lake, an easy trip because it's on the main trail. Just be sure to do that on the best weather day you have as it can be grim up there in a storm.

Some people like to camp at Fossil Lake, and in good conditions that can be a rewarding option with unrivaled high country ambience and scenery. But above 10,000 feet (3,050 m), and on a barren plateau almost completely exposed to wind and storm, this is a place where adverse weather can drive you back down in a hurry. But taking a day to explore the area around Fossil Lake at leisure, with a safe, comfortable camp down below, is a way to savor the heart of this wild place without risk of inconvenient or even dangerous weather.

After a day or two enjoying the high country between Duggan Lake and Fossil Lake, and truly spectacular wildflower gardens in season, it's time to begin the trek out. Hike back up past Fossil Lake where the trail takes you up and over the Clarks Fork divide at 10,200 feet (3,100 m), and down into the

Clarks Fork of the Yellowstone drainage. The landscape on this side is subtly more gentle, and definitely has a different feel. While there aren't the dramatic waterfalls of the East Rosebud, the interesting backcountry travel on this side confirms the reputation of the Beartooth Traverse: the scenery never lets up.

A strong party might easily walk out the remaining 12 miles (19 km) to the trailhead, but I recommend another night in the wilderness, somewhere between Ouzel Lake and Russell Lake, 4 to 5 miles (7–8 km) from the divide, to absorb the different ambience on this side of the divide, and the lower altitude. From there it's a half-day walk out to the Clarks Fork Trailhead on Highway 212 a few miles from Cooke City.

At the trailhead you'll find another busy parking lot, as lots of day hikers use trails in the vicinity. A half dozen lodging options await a few miles away in Cooke City, and a welcome shower and extravagant dinner in one of the cafes. But there are other solutions too, such as the dude ranch, the Skyline Guest Ranch, located right at the trailhead. The smaller hamlet a few miles farther south, Silver Gate, has yet more options.

In Cooke City you are so close to the northeastern entrance, or Silver Gate, of Yellowstone, that it's wise to plan a layover day for a sightseeing foray into the park. The Lamar Valley, one of the premier wildlife viewing areas in Yellowstone, is under a half hour away. When you're ready to head back to your car in Alpine, or to Bozeman or Billings, head north on

Hikers cruise past Fossil Lake, more than 10,000 feet (3,050 m) in elevation, before cresting the divide and dropping down into the Clarks Fork of the Yellowstone drainage. PHOTO BY PETER POTTERFIELD.

Rimrock Lake shows the characteristic turquoise color from "glacier flour." PHOTO BY PETER POTTERFIELD.

Highway 212, the renowned highway through Montana's signature high country, to Red Lodge, the East Rosebud Lake Trailhead, and the interstate highway.

The drive from Cooke City over the pass on Highway 212 to Red Lodge is yet another highlight of the trip, so plan for extra time, two to three hours, to savor the views and perhaps enjoy a picnic on the broad meadows. It's hard to make decent time getting home on this highway, with vistas that include Pilot Peak and Beartooth Peak looming above the expansive meadows constantly luring you to the shoulder for a better look.

HAZARDS

Grizzly bears are abundant in the Yellowstone ecosystem, including the Beartooths, so hikers need to know and follow the rules of safe travel and camping in bear country. Techniques include hanging your food at least 10 feet off the ground, sleeping some distance from where you prepare meals, etc. The importance of bear safety on this route is underscored by a fatal bear attack in 2010 at a campground near the terminus of this route. Endangered lynx and wolf are also found here, but rarely cause problems for hikers.

Weather is a major consideration for the Beartooth Traverse as most of this route is above 9,000 feet

(2,750 m), where sudden changes in conditions can result in hypothermia and route-finding problems. Every hiker who undertakes the route should be well equipped with appropriate outerwear and backpacking gear, prepared to hunker down if necessary, or hike out in bad conditions.

SEASON

The alpine nature of the traverse means that the season start is heavily dependent on the previous winter's snowfall. Generally, the route is passable from late June through late September, although snow can fall in the higher elevations at any time. Wildflower displays usually peak in early August. Late season trips have a lot of appeal, with often cold, stable weather and way fewer bugs.

ROUTE

From Columbus, Montana, on Interstate 90, head south 10 miles (16 km) to the town of Absarokee, and on another 10 miles (16 km) to the town of Roscoe. Here, turn right, south, onto the mostly gravel East Rosebud Road for the final 8 miles (13 km) to the village of Alpine and the trailhead, at 6,200 feet (1,890 m). The dramatic peaks of the wilderness loom dead

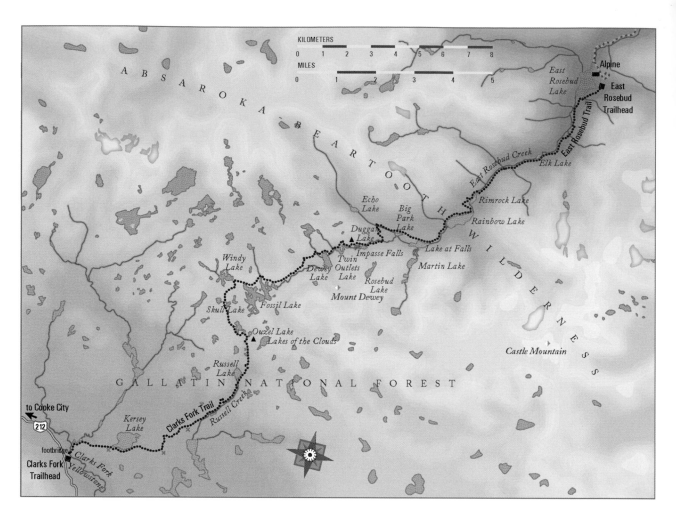

ahead, somewhat ominously, as the broad East Rosebud Trail (#15) starts out in an old burn and begins to climb right away as it enters the Absaroka–Beartooth Wilderness area. Elk Lake, 3 miles (5 km) in, makes a good lunch stop. From there, the route climbs above the roaring East Rosebud Creek to follow the granite ledges before reaching Rimrock Lake at 6 miles (10 km). If you look hard, one or two good campsites are hidden nearby, but most hikers go on to the meadows at the far end of Rainbow Lake for the first night's camp, 8 miles (13 km) and 7,700 feet (2,347 m).

The next day the trail climbs more steeply and the scenery becomes even more rugged as you work up toward Lake at Falls, Big Park Lake, and Duggan Lake with its impressive Impasse Falls, 12 miles (20 km) from the trailhead. Start looking for campsites as the trail climbs higher toward Twin Outlet and Dewey lakes, 13 and 14 miles (21 km and 22.5 km) from the trailhead, which are in perhaps the most scenic part of the upper East Rosebud Valley. Twin Outlet is at 9,200 feet (2,800 m) and Dewey at 9,350 (2,850 m), so this 2-mile (3-km) stretch is absolutely alpine but dotted with meadows and stunted timber, and quite sheltered despite the altitude. Castle Mountain and Dewey Mountain dominate the views, but the peaks of the Beartooths rise all around.

Make base camp in this vicinity, and take a day or two to explore the area. If you've brought your fly rod, success likely awaits at Twin Outlet and many of the other lakes nearby. A day of exploration will add at least 10 miles (16 km) to the 26-mile (42-km) trail distance, and another day twice that. But when will you have the opportunity again?

When it's time to move on, the trail changes dramatically as it climbs steeply above Dewey Lake up into the open tundra at Fossil Lake, 4 miles (7 km) away (approximately 16 miles, 26 km, from the trailhead). This is the most dramatic section of the route as the traverse at last enters the wild plateau holding Fossil, and works across the rocky terrain as it rises toward the top. At the highest point on the plateau, a huge cairn, more pyramid than trail marker, identifies the divide between the East Rosebud and the Clarks Fork of the Yellowstone, at 17 miles (27 km) and 10,200 feet (3,110 m). The trail number changes here to Trail 567.

The route drops down the Clarks Fork side, gradually, where there is a subtle transformation in the landscape. The wildflower displays are even more vibrant here than on the other side, and the terrain takes on a slightly softer, more benign character. The lakes start coming in rapid succession: the aptly named Windy Lake a half mile (.7 km) from the divide, and Skull Lake another half mile (.7 km) farther on. The high country lakes here are set into rocky basins, with meadows snugged up against huge granite faces.

The decision now is whether to continue on to the Clarks Fork Trailhead, 9 miles (15 km) downhill from the divide, or spend another night in the wilderness. Either is doable, but since you're still high in the wild Beartooths it makes sense to savor this part of the traverse. Both Ouzel Lake, 2 miles (3 km) from the divide, and Russell Lake, a mile (2 km) or so farther on, have decent camping, even if it's not as dramatic as the sites in the East Rosebud. Most people camp at Russell Lake the final night, at 8,700 feet (2,655 m), but Ouzel, slightly higher, can be more scenic.

From Russell Lake, the way steepens a little as the trail descends beside Russell Creek in 2 miles (3.2 km) to the Fox Lake Trail; bear right here and continue downhill past the Crazy Lakes Trail, then bear right down to Kersey Lake, 8,100 feet and 8 miles (13 km) from the divide. Bear right at the Vernon Lake Trail, cross the Clarks Fork of the Yellowstone, and continue to the Clarks Fork Trailhead at 8,000 feet (2,438 m), 26 miles (43 km) from the start, not counting side trips. A big parking lot marks the busy trailhead. Cooke City is 2.5 miles (4 km) west down Highway 212.

INFORMATION

For information on conditions and regulations in the Absaroka–Beartooth Wilderness, contact the following ranger offices in Montana:

GALLATIN NATIONAL FOREST
P.O. Box 130
Bozeman, MT 59771
406-522-2520
www.fs.fed.us/r1/gallatin

BIG TIMBER RANGER DISTRICT
P.O. Box 1130
Big Timber, MT 59011
406-932-5155

BEARTOOTH RANGER DISTRICT
HC 49, Box 3420
Red Lodge, MT 59068
406-446-2103

GARDINER RANGER DISTRICT
P.O. Box 5
Gardiner, MT 59030
406-848-7375

ROSEBUD LAKE CAMPGROUND
Beartooth Ranger District
Custer National Forest
6811 Highway 212
Red Lodge, MT 59068
406-446-2103

Planning a Trip

Montana's travel Web Site can help when planning an adventure:
www.visitmt.com

TOP: *Rock-bound lakes and stunted alpine timber define the terrain below the East Rosebud–Clarks Fork Divide.* PHOTO BY PETER POTTERFIELD.

BOTTOM: *A bull elk grazes in the Lamar Valley of Yellowstone National Park.* PHOTO BY PETER POTTERFIELD.

FISH CANYON– OWL CANYON LOOP

Cedar Mesa

Grand Gulch Primitive Area

Southern Utah, United States

DISTANCE: 17 miles (28 km) loop
TIME: 3–4 days
PHYSICAL CHALLENGE: 1 2 3 4 5
PSYCHOLOGICAL CHALLENGE: 1 2 3 4 5
STAGING: Monticello or Blanding, Utah

The three-day excursion down into Owl Canyon and back up out of Fish Canyon reveals why backcountry lovers come from as far away as Europe to hike this part of southern Utah. This is Cedar Mesa, piñon- and juniper-covered high country that soars to more than 7,000 feet (2,140 m). The entirety of this sprawling plateau in southern Utah is cut through by hidden canyons that slice deeply into the red-rock layer cake of the Colorado Plateau.

Grand Gulch and its tributary canyons—notably Kane Gulch to Bullet Canyon—has long been the signature hike here. It's a route famous for both scenic canyons and iconic ancient ruins, but, alas, its growing popularity has significantly degraded the backcountry experience in that complex of canyons. The Fish and Owl Loop offers opportunity for a more solitary journey, but one with similar allure. Reliable water, interesting slick-rock hiking, big ponderosa pines, and three classic sandstone arches—combined with Pueblo cliff dwellings and ancient rock art— make this loop a Cedar Mesa classic.

This once remote part of Utah, far from the tourist crowds of Moab and Canyonlands, has been transformed over the past decade. More hikers from North America and indeed the world have discovered the dual attractions here: interesting canyon terrain juxtaposed with the irresistible draw of relics from an ancient culture. So any hike here features not just the beauty of Utah's desert wilderness, but tantalizing signs of the long-lost Anasazi culture. These were the "ancient ones," a people who for centuries called the place home before their civilization suddenly disappeared from the mesa some 800 years ago. Granaries (small food-storage structures), rock art, and the remains of dwellings and even kivas (underground ceremonial structures) add interest and mysticism to the innate beauty of one's days on the trail.

Just ten years ago, a hike here was an off-the-beaten-path adventure. The Kane Gulch ranger station, ground zero for pilgrims to Cedar Mesa, was a ramshackle old house-trailer, not even a double-wide, tucked into the piñons next to a small, dusty parking lot. So few people visited Cedar Mesa that the rangers knew many of the hikers by name. Today, the Bureau of Land Management's expansive new solar-powered facility symbolizes the changes here. Some of the old hands view this progress with mixed emotions, a sign of growing popularity and increased use. But who can blame hikers for wanting to sample the rich backcountry experience here, which is unlike any other?

Drop down off the rim on day one of this loop and in a half hour you are greeted by a thousand-year-old dwelling in a remarkably undamaged state, mud walls and roof supports intact. Glance up at the red rock

Striking Nevills Arch on its ridge of eroded hoodoos, not far from the confluence of Fish and Owl canyons. PHOTO BY PETER POTTERFIELD.

canyon walls along the way and take in a fascinating cluster of the ever-mysterious Anasazi rock art, and still more dwellings up near the rim. Good campsites with springs and creeks make overnight trips in Fish and Owl a desert delight, with hours and hours left each day to explore the nooks and crannies of the complicated topography. And if camping in the embrace of the canyons borders on mystical, camping out in the open on the rim can be a nice foil. Save a night for this filigree, savoring views down into the canyons themselves and across Cedar Mesa to the distant Bears Ears, prominent 10,000-foot-high (3,050-m-high) geologic features to the north.

Artifacts, ruins and archeological sites on Cedar Mesa date back as far as 1500 BC. This is the era that includes the so called Basketmaker Culture, up through the more recent Pueblo I, II, and III phases of the Anasazi. The newest artifact here is almost a thousand years old. These ancient cultures suddenly disappeared from Cedar Mesa approximately 800 years ago, leaving archeologists to ponder their sudden and mysterious departure. The opportunity to go see for yourself what remains of the Puebloan cultures is unlike any other backcountry venture, and makes this hike pay off on multiple levels.

At one camp, remote and tucked out of the way of everyday traffic, my partners and I discovered two ruins, a dwelling and a granary, that to this day I'm not sure had been visited before. Where else can you do that kind of exploring? The other side of the coin is that hikers must be sensitive to antiquities, artifacts, and other cultural resources. The BLM reaches out aggressively to educate hikers on proper technique that allows for visits here and yet protects the artifacts and ruins from harm. Anyone who hikes here will tell you it is a privilege to walk through this special place, with its palpable human history. The least that we, as hikers, can do, is watch where we step.

A hiker works around a pour-off, where the canyon drainage drops steeply into a pool, in Fish Canyon. PHOTO BY PETER POTTERFIELD.

LOGISTICS & STRATEGY

Any way you approach it, getting to southern Utah is not going to be easy, and Cedar Mesa is even farther away from most airports than popular spots such as Moab and Arches National Park. Staging for this hike is best done from Monticello or Blanding. Both have motels and restaurants, but Monticello is probably better suited as a starting point because it's a bit closer to most airports, has a BLM field office for the necessary permits and information, and is a place where you can get a beer. Blanding is a bit closer to Cedar Mesa, and it boasts the outstanding Edge of the Cedars Museum, which every hiker should visit, but it is a dry community, so there's no glass of wine with dinner.

Most hikers arrive via the Salt Lake City airport, about six hours away. Las Vegas has a time advantage for some places in southern Utah, such as Zion, but not to Cedar Mesa. Salt Lake has easy connections and reasonable air fares, but for those who hate long drives before and after the hike, the answer is Grand Junction, Colorado, or Moab, Utah. Grand Junction is about three hours away, but with mainstream airline connections. Moab, just an hour away, used to be difficult and quirky, with just a handful of flights and serious car rental difficulties, but connections and services get better every year.

Whatever your airport, you'll drive south from Moab on US Highway 191. Four miles (6.5 km) south of Blanding, Highway 95 turns west and proceeds through a dramatic cut in Comb Ridge and follows the northern edge of Cedar Mesa less than an hour before turning south on Highway 261 and the final 15 minutes to the Kane Gulch ranger station. (Or, reach Highway 261 from the west, from Hanksville, in approximately one hour on Highway 95.) Backcountry permits are required for hiking on Cedar Mesa, and the best policy is to reserve one in advance, otherwise you are taking a chance that none will be available when you arrive at Kane Gulch.

Even with a reservation, you must pick up your permit at Kane Gulch ranger station the day of your hike, between 8 a.m. and noon. That's a wicked deadline, and another reason to stage in Monticello or Blanding. Otherwise, you spend hours racing to get your permit on time, and believe me, that's not fun. Most fit hikers could do this route in a two-day/one-night backpack, but that makes a rushed trip. The whole point of hiking on Cedar Mesa is to get a good feel for both the canyon terrain and the rare ancient cultural artifacts, so to speed through it misses the point. Three days and two nights is a better time frame, offering plenty of spare hours for exploration—a critical consideration, as a lot of the appeal here will be found up the side canyons. Avid canyon hikers can easily spend four or five days on this route, exploring from strategically located and comfortable base camps.

The Fish and Owl Loop can be done in either direction, but the rangers recommend starting at Owl Canyon and finishing up in Fish Canyon, and I

OPPOSITE: *The ruins of an Anasazi dwelling, one of many that can be found in the canyons of Cedar Mesa.* PHOTO BY PETER POTTERFIELD.

even waterfalls. Fish Creek Canyon is even prettier than Owl Canyon, but you have to look more closely for the cultural highlights. It's approximately 8 miles (13 km) up Fish Canyon from the confluence of Fish and Owl creeks to the head of Fish Canyon, and the exit, but don't forget to take some time to explore the side canyons along the way. On the hike out, watch carefully for the left turn up the south wall to the exit of Fish Canyon. The correct route via a small side canyon is easy to miss, as main Fish Canyon continues upstream for some distance past the exit, another good option for exploration if you have the time.

The trail up to the rim, and the exit, is steep for almost 1,000 feet (305 m), so it's a workout, and at the top expect 10 feet (3 m) of low-standard rock scrambling. Some hikers haul packs up with a rope to avoid having to climb up encumbered. This bit gets your attention, but few people have trouble with it, and I watched a dog negotiate it with no problem. From the top, and its welcome views of sky and open country, there's a couple miles yet across the plateau back to your car at the trailhead. But if you have the time, consider hiking out farther on the rim for a final camp to enjoy a desert experience under the stars with big vistas.

The entire route is only 17 miles (28 km) and just a few hundred feet of elevation gain, and many hikers can do it easily in two days. But this is an exceptional hike, and one that is worthy of your time. Two nights and three days I think is minimum, particularly if you explore side canyons; another day is not extravagant, and yet another night on the rim is strongly advised.

HAZARDS

For such a rewarding hike, the Fish and Owl Loop entails relatively few dangers. Foremost is the fact that this is an authentic backcountry route in a true wilderness, far from help and hospitals, so come prepared. The loop covers rugged terrain, and falls resulting in twisted ankles and other accidents are probably the most serious hazards The best advice is to pay attention and hike carefully, watching where you put your feet. Cedar Mesa weather is another consideration, as it can change rapidly on the plateau and present a danger of hypothermia if you are not prepared. Flash floods can result if heavy rain falls, so be prepared with fall-back plans to reach refuges above the canyon floor if necessary. Be sure to treat or filter your water, and keep a sharp eye out for rattlesnakes and scorpions.

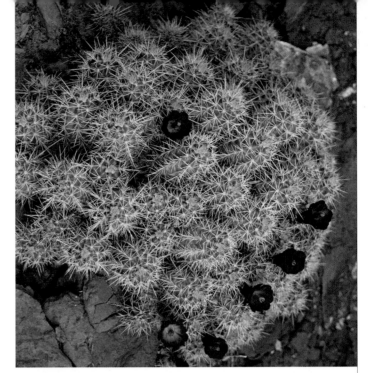

TOP: *With a perennial stream, the Fish Canyon–Owl Canyon complex supports abundant flora, like this desert cactus.* PHOTO BY PETER POTTERFIELD.

BOTTOM: *Breakfast in Fish Canyon: one of the best kitchen rocks I've encountered in decades of wilderness travel.* PHOTO BY PETER POTTERFIELD.

SEASON

Summers are hot in southern Utah, so this hike is almost always done in spring and fall. Peak times are from late March to late May, and from early September to late October. But those time frames are when all the other hikers will come here, so think about pushing the season a little earlier or a little later for a bit more solitude. And for the hardy: check the weather and go in the dead of winter if conditions are favorable. Cold, long nights and cool days are a small price to pay for having this wilderness to yourself.

A hiker works along a bench above the floor of Owl Canyon.
PHOTO BY PETER POTTERFIELD.

ROUTE

From Blanding, Utah, drive 4 miles (7 km) south on US Highway 191, and turn west on Utah Highway 95. Drive west through the cut in impressive Comb Ridge, and continue for 28 miles (48 km). At the junction with Utah Highway 261, turn south and drive 4 miles (6.5 km) to the Kane Gulch ranger station to pick up your backcountry permit. From there, proceed south on 261 about a mile (2 km) to the left turn at San Juan County Road 253. Drive 5 miles (8 km) to the end of the unpaved road and the trailhead.

From the trailhead, hike .5 mile (.7 km) in a wash across the plateau to a side canyon on the north rim, where the cairned trail leads you down. Steep drops and a few dead ends are unavoidable. Steadily, the route descends with only cairns marking the way, to the bottom of the canyon, about 2 miles (3.2 km) from the trailhead. The first dramatic ruin appears on the right, not 10 feet from the trail. Continue into the canyon with short up-and-down sections and several stream crossings. There's plenty of water here, with significant pools, making the terrace up on the left an attractive campsite, especially if you follow it down canyon a few hundred yards to get better late afternoon light.

If pressing on, continue down canyon, past more pretty pools of water and several waterfalls, another 2.5 miles (4 km) until dramatic Nevills Arch appears on the canyon rim high on the left skyline. The arch also alerts you to the end of reliable water, and the final camping opportunity before the confluence with Fish Creek. The two canyons converge at about 7 miles (11 km) from the trailhead in a broad, sandy basin with cottonwood trees surrounded by high, red rock canyon walls topped with hoodoos.

The route turns left at the confluence to follow Fish Canyon upstream, but the main canyon running to the southeast (named Fish Creek on maps) continues downstream past the confluence and is worthy of exploration. The best strategy is to stay on the Fish and Owl loop trail, turning northwest at the confluence into upper Fish Canyon as far as the next campsites (and water), about a mile or two (2–3 km) from the confluence. From a camp there you are well situated for making a foray back down to explore lower Fish Canyon and, importantly, McCloyd Canyon, well below the confluence. There's a lot to see here, including signs of the Anasazi.

From the confluence, hike up Fish Creek Canyon approximately 2 miles (3.2 km), where campsites and water sources (and more small waterfalls) can be found in the next stretch of trail. Going a bit farther, I found a campsite near a perfect desert pool with one of the best kitchen rocks I've ever seen in the backcountry. This whole area along the stream makes a good base camp for exploring the lower canyon and side canyons on the day you arrive here.

The third day takes you up scenic Fish Creek Canyon to the exit. The canyon here is wider and shallower than Owl Creek Canyon, with odd hoodoos and other rock formations along the rim. Keep a sharp eye out for ruins high on the northwest wall as you hike up canyon. There is a lot of water in Fish Creek, even beaver dams, and more opportunities for camping. Think about a third camp, well positioned to give you access to explore upper Fish Canyon where it extends beyond the exit. At approximately 6 miles (10 km) from the confluence, the canyon forks. Bear left here, and continue up canyon as it narrows dramatically.

To exit, hike through the boulders and pass a spring about a half mile (.7 km) from the fork, where cairns mark the beginning of the steep exit route. From here the way is fairly well marked as it rises approximately 800 feet (244 m) to the canyon rim. In places the going is rugged and hard to follow, but it's that last 10–15 feet (3–5 m) below the rim that requires concentration. Take care and go slow on this final pitch. Most people do fine with the final scramble, others take the time to haul up their packs with lengths of rope.

Once at the rim, enjoy the view of both canyons, the plateau, and the Bears Ears far to the north. If you have the time, hike along the rim a mile or so to enjoy a final night here camped in the open under a big sky full of stars. If not, hike south along the trail across the white, slickrock plateau approximately 2 miles (3 km) back to your car.

OPPOSITE: *A hiker climbs the final, tricky 15 feet out of Fish Canyon after three days of exploring the canyons that make up the Fish Canyon–Owl Canyon complex.* PHOTO BY PETER POTTERFIELD.

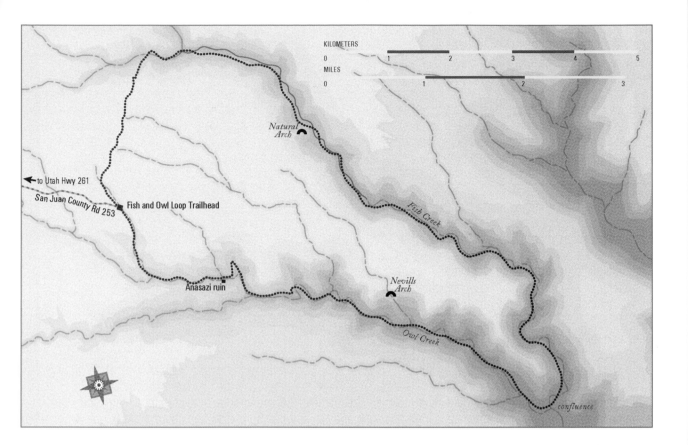

INFORMATION

Backcountry permits are required in Fish and Owl canyons, and many others in Cedar Mesa, both for day use and for overnights. Expect to pay a small fee for both during the official season, March 1 to June 15, and September 1 to October 31. It is recommended to reserve your permits in advance through the Monticello Bureau of Land Management field office, but you can sometimes pick up a walk-in permit the day of your hike at the Kane Gulch ranger station. Note that whether you reserve in advance or not, you must pick up your permit at Kane Gulch between 8 a.m. and noon on the day of your hike.

BUREAU OF LAND MANAGEMENT (BLM)
Monticello Field Office
365 North Main
Monticello, UT 84535
435-587-1500

KANE GULCH RANGER STATION
On Utah Highway 261, 4 miles south of Utah Highway 95

Check the BLM Web site for more information:
www.blm.gov/ut/st/en/fo/monticello/recreation/permits/
grand_gulch_and_cedar.html

JAGO RIVER TO AICHILIK RIVER

Romanzof Mountains, Brooks Range Arctic National Wildlife Refuge

North Slope, Alaska, United States

DISTANCE: 30 miles (48 km) one-way
TIME: 8 days
PHYSICAL CHALLENGE: 1 2 3 4 5
PSYCHOLOGICAL CHALLENGE: 1 2 3 4 5
STAGING: Fairbanks, Alaska

On one of those rare cloudless days, climb a knoll above the Aichilik River for a look around, and you will be humbled. A great wilderness stretches in all directions. Look south at the 9,000-foot (2,750-m) snowcapped peaks of the Brooks Range, high mountains hung with glaciers, and broad drainages lined with overflow ice. Then look north across the vast coastal plain to the sea ice in the Beaufort Sea. Nothing growing in the limitless expanse of tundra reaches higher than your boot top, so your view will not be obstructed. In a single day you are likely to see wolves, grizzly bears, caribou, often huge herds of them, Dall sheep, arctic fox, ground squirrels, raptors, and terrestrial birds and seabirds too numerous to count.

A hike in the Brooks Range is about as wild as you can get in North America. Stretching for more than 600 miles (almost 1,000 km), the range creates a continental divide, bisecting one of the wildest regions on the continent. The Brooks Range is one of only two major ranges that runs west to east, as opposed to north to south. On the north lies the Arctic Ocean and its polar regions, on the south, the interior of Alaska. But how best to see such wilderness? Basically, a backcountry visitor to the Brooks Range has two options: Gates of the Arctic National Park, and the Arctic National Wildlife Refuge. The appeal of the 10-million-acre wildlife refuge of late has proven irresistible. The allure of the wildlife, notably the caribou, and the scenic beauty of the coastal plain

A fact of life when hiking in the Brooks Range is the necessity of crossing rivers frequently, sometimes multiple times each day, like these hikers on the upper Jago River. PHOTO BY STEVE JONES.

between the Brooks Range and the Beaufort Sea makes it the place to go on your first trip.

All lovers of wilderness should come to the Arctic National Wildlife Refuge, but this off-trail adventure is frankly not a hike for everyone. Walking through the landscape here is hard going in the best of conditions. The plain is mostly clumps of tussock grass, and hiking on tussock has been likened to walking on basketballs. The effort is physically exhausting, and the care necessary to keep from rolling over on an ankle brings its own kind of fatigue. With luck, you'll be able to walk in the rivers—on gravel bars, on the banks, on the overflow ice, even in the water. The going here is far easier, but crossing those big Arctic rivers about once a day can be psychologically wearing as well. Five miles (8 km) a day is good time.

With 24 hours of daylight for much of the hiking season, dusk can be lengthy on the landscape of the Jago River. PHOTO BY ART WOLFE.

The only way in, or out, of the Brooks Range is by small plane. You land on a gravel bar in the Jago River, and take off from a gravel bar on the Aichilik River 30 miles (48 km) farther north. Both flying days are dependent on weather. Delays at either end can be stressful, but the rare occasions when your flight out gets scrubbed can exact a particularly painful toll. Everyone who visits remote places on the planet knows the reality of light aircraft. Better late and safe than risk flying in bad weather. A Brooks Range hike is defined by this mode of transportation.

The fact is, the only people truly at home in this wild landscape are the Inupiat Eskimo and Athabaskan people who live nearby, and the guides who run these trips every season. Experienced backcountry travelers can do this adventure on their own, but most don't. Almost every hiker who ventures up here goes with an Alaska outfitter. More than any other hike in this volume, the experience of hiking in the Brooks Range depends utterly on your guide service, and the pilots your guide chooses to work with. The Brooks Range hike as described here is one offering from Arctic Wild, a Fairbanks-based operator. Other good guide services work in the Brooks Range, but be sure to do careful research before choosing one.

Any adventure to the North Slope will be as mental as it is physical. Visitors here soon get on "Arctic time," where there's no reason to hurry, and in fact to try would just stress you out. Twenty-four-hour-a-day sunlight reinforces that mind-set. You hike when you want, pitch camp when you want, eat dinner at midnight if you want, go for a 3 a.m. walk if you want. The best advice on how to deal with a landscape this wild is to slow down and take it easy. A well-run trip to the Brooks Range is going to be relaxed and deliberate. The landscape is so vast, the wildlife so abundant, that one's place in this ecosystem is best experienced in a measured way, not a compulsive, goal-oriented one. For when the little Cessna bounces down on the gravel bar to deposit you, and then roars away, you find yourself in an environment, and in a silence, that will most definitely get your attention.

In the end, if you're a serious backcountry traveler, you have to come here. This hike through the Romanzof Mountains on the North Slope of the Brooks Range is unlike any wilderness jaunt in North America. You land at the very foot of some of the highest peaks here, then hike over a 4,000-foot (1,200-m) pass to make your way down toward the Aichilik. Here an ecotone, an overlapping of ecozones, creates a microclimate that is one of the warmest parts of the North Slope, and the perfect place to spend a week in continuous daylight absorbing the grandeur of the country and wildlife.

LOGISTICS & STRATEGY

Brooks Range adventures begin in Fairbanks, with good air connections, particularly from Seattle. Outfitters have a mandatory meeting the day before departure for a briefing and gear check, so it's best to arrive in Fairbanks a day or two earlier. That gives you time to see Alaska's second city, and ensures you'll be on time for the briefing. It's also wise to give yourself an extra day in town on your scheduled return from the Brooks, just in case weather delays your arrival back in Fairbanks.

A note on routes and guide services: The trip described here is a North Slope classic, but other hiking routes on this side of the Brooks Range are similar. Just east, for instance, is the Kongakut River, another popular Brooks Range drainage that offers an experience much like that of the Jago and the Aichilik. The North Slope is a place where the hiking experience is unique to its remote arctic Alaska location, but many routes have common elements. The differences will be largely defined by the guide service with which you choose to go. Each outfitter has favorite backcountry routes, air services, and preferred approach strategies and landing strips, which they come to know well. That's the case with this Jago and Aichilik hike described here, a favorite of Arctic Wild.

On departure day, Arctic Wild picks you up at your hotel for the run out to Wright Air Service and the flight to Arctic Village, an Athabaskan village at the edge of the boreal forest. Scheduled air service from Fairbanks to Arctic Village positions you for the final bush plane flight up to the Jago River on the North Slope, often on Coyote Air.

The flight from Arctic Village can be a mind-blowing trip in itself, usually in a three-passenger Cessna or a five-passenger DeHavilland Beaver.

From the airstrip, the flight goes upriver, into the complicated ridges of the Brooks Range, and in less than an hour into the snowcapped peaks and down to a gravel bar in the Jago River for the bumpy landing. Summer is a busy time for the bush pilots—there's lots of people and cargo to move around—so they basically kick you out, unload the gear, shake your hand, and leave you in the middle of nowhere. The moment you look around to see where you've been deposited is when you're glad to have a guide who has been here before.

The basic route for this trip leaves the Jago River drainage, climbs up over a pass to drop down into a tributary of the Aichilik River system, and then moves down to the Aichilik and the fly-out airstrip where the mountains give way to the coastal plain. With 30 miles (48 km) to cover between the airstrips, parties generally hike about 5 or 6 miles (8–10 km) per day, which is plenty in this environment, with one layover day for weather or wildlife viewing. Arctic Wild does this trek as an eight-day trip. With a full day of travel to get up to the Brooks Range, and another to get back, that leaves six days for hiking, and with one layover day, that leaves five days of travel on foot, more or less.

Purple mountain saxifrage adds color to the tundra near the Jago River on a cold morning. PHOTO BY ART WOLFE.

ABOVE: *Light aircraft are the only way in or out for hikes on the North Slope of the Brooks Range.* PHOTO BY STEVE JONES.

BELOW: *Part of the Porcupine caribou herd during its migration to the coastal plain of the Arctic National Wildlife Refuge.* PHOTO BY ART WOLFE.

Each member of the party sets up his or her own tent at camp. The guide erects a tarp shelter for the dining hall and does the cooking. Once in camp, the focus is on exploring nearby, photography and wildlife viewing. Group sizes are small, as dictated by the number of seats in a light airplane, usually three hikers and one guide. Guides carry satellite telephones for emergencies. Each member of the party can expect to carry 50 pounds or so in a backpack.

Most parties take at least one layover day, often at the pick-up airstrip at the northerly end of the route. From this camp, you can climb the ridge to the north and west of the gravel airstrip and get views down the coastal plain to the sea ice, and back to the south and the snowcapped peaks of the Brooks Range. If you're lucky, you can sometimes see a line of caribou three and four wide that stretches as far as you can see in both directions, from Alaska to Canada, west to east, like a line of ants. It's easier to walk on the tussock, the mushroom-shaped clusters of grass, with light day packs, so the layover days create the opportunity for far-ranging exploration.

The ecotone on the Aichilik is the driest part of the Arctic National Wildlife Refuge, averaging about 9 inches (23 cm) per year. If your party gets rain, it probably won't be a lot. Weather can be cold and cloudy; expect a temperature range from 20 to 80 degrees Fahrenheit (7–27° C), often in the same day. Your outfitter will ensure your clothing is adequate for likely conditions. Head nets and bug suits are considered essential pieces of gear for protection from bugs.

The Porcupine caribou herd that migrates through the North Slope, and the wolves and grizzly bear those animals attract, are probably the highlight of the trip. The opportunity to photograph the wildlife and austere scenery of the Arctic National Wildlife Refuge is what draws most backcountry travelers up here to hike through it. But the North Slope is a rich spot for birding as well. Besides the raptors and seabirds you might expect, you can see peregrine and gyrfalcons, sandhill cranes and white-fronted geese, snow geese and snowy owls. More than 180 bird species visit the refuge over the course of the year.

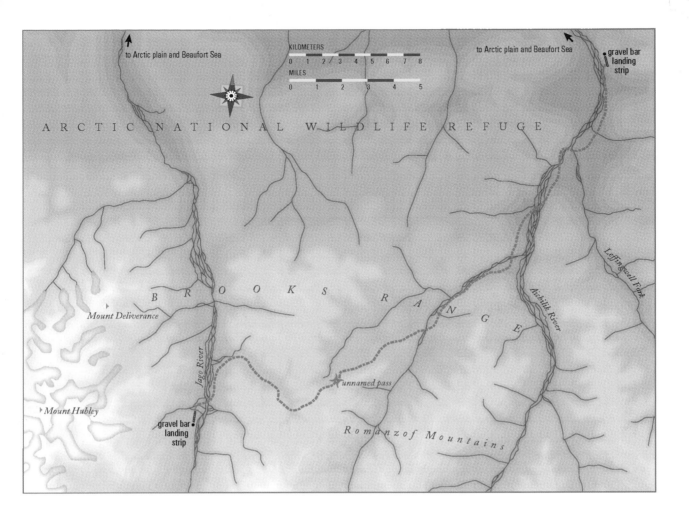

Two popular spots for layover days include the 4,000-foot (1,219-m) pass on day two or three of the route. Up on the ridges near the pass are round-topped peaks that offer broad vistas. Another is near the take-out place, where ridges to the north and west offer tremendous views and a good opportunity to spot wildlife.

INFORMATION

Your outfitter will take care of formalities such as hiking and visitation permits. For more information on hiking in the Arctic National Wildlife Refuge, contact its headquarters in Fairbanks:

ARCTIC NATIONAL WILDLIFE REFUGE
101 12th Avenue, Room 236
Fairbanks, AK 99701
907-456-0250 or 800-362-4546
E-mail: arctic_refuge@fws.gov
http://arctic.fws.gov/index.htm

Guide Services

ARCTIC WILD
Box 80562
Fairbanks, AK 99708
907-479-8203 or 888-577-8203
E-mail: info@arcticwild.com
www.arcticwild.com

SHI SHI BEACH TO LAKE OZETTE

Washington Coast
Olympic National Park

Washington, United States

DISTANCE: 15 miles (24 km) one-way
TIME: 4 days
PHYSICAL CHALLENGE: 1 2 3 4 5
PSYCHOLOGICAL CHALLENGE: 1 2 3 4 5
STAGING: Port Angeles, Washington

Often overlooked by hikers focused on the impressive peaks and volcanoes of the Cascade Range, the wild beauty of Washington state's Olympic Peninsula coastline holds equal allure. An astonishing 60 miles (97 km) of wilderness coast runs from Cape Flattery, at the northwest extremity of the United States, down the coast of the still wild Olympic Peninsula. By far the most pristine stretch of coastline left in the Lower 48, this narrow strip of beach and headland separates the ancient forest from the pummeling sea. But this is a place where the Pacific always prevails, where the power of surf and storm creates a dynamic landscape of misty, ineffable beauty.

You will find no high-rise condos here, only dramatic sea stacks beyond the surf, shipwrecks, tidal pools teeming with sea star and anemone, rugged headlands falling into the sea and wild rivers flowing into the crashing Pacific. The vibe is primeval. Seabirds call and wheel above the beaches, eagles soar and hunt, black bears emerge from the forest, gray whales swim offshore. You drift off to sleep to the barking of sea lions. Just two human settlements intrude on a length of a coastline that has otherwise remained unchanged by man for thousands of years.

Windswept beaches and rocky headlands abound on this coast, but to my mind Point of Arches is the most spectacular, in many ways more dramatic even than Big Sur, and certainly more secluded. This is a wild place, where towering sea stacks silhouette against a setting sun, and eerie coastal caves harbor at low tide fecund pools full of strange life. And best of all, it's a place you can visit, where rivers flowing out of the Olympic Mountains bring fresh water, a place where you can camp in comfort to experience an epic shore in the ever-changing variety of its moods.

Backpackers travel along the sand of Shi Shi Beach, as Point of Arches looms in the distance. **PHOTO BY KEITH GUNNAR**.

Access here is reasonable. The drive from Seattle is a long one, but the hike is relatively short, if oddly strenuous. The usual approach to Point of Arches is from the north, via the Makah Indian reservation. From the start at lovely Shi Shi Beach (pronounced "Shy Shy"), only 12 miles (19 km) of walking takes you past Point of Arches, down one of the longest arcs of beach on the coast, and across the problematic Ozette River to dramatic Cape Alava (the most western point in the Lower 48) before ending at a cape called Sand Point. Here, the exit takes you away from the beach, back into the trees and out to civilization.

Don't be fooled by the mileage. This is not a quick trip but one best done in four days or more. Linear distances mean little when hiking a coast as wild as this. One doesn't go in a straight line down the beach, but

gather in the rain-shadow communities along the Strait of Juan de Fuca's coastline, and a Native American culture dominates in the Makah village of Neah Bay and the Quileute village of La Push. A visit to this far corner of the country, quirky and unique, takes some doing. Out here Seattle seems a long way off, and it is. But you return to the city knowing you've finally had the quintessential Pacific Northwest experience.

LOGISTICS & STRATEGY

Seattle is the logical gateway to the Olympic Peninsula from afar, but it makes more sense to stage this four- to five-day adventure from the Olympic Peninsula itself. Port Angeles is best suited for that purpose, with outdoor shops, groceries, accommodations, and restaurants in abundance, in keeping with its status as the largest city on the peninsula. The necessary permits and trail information can be obtained at the Olympic National Park Wilderness Information Center in Port Angeles.

From Seattle or its airport, you'll take either the Bainbridge Island ferry (right downtown) or the Edmonds–Kingston ferry (20 minutes north of town via Highway 99) across Puget Sound to the Olympic Peninsula. Get on Highway 104 and follow it northwest across the Hood Canal Floating Bridge to its junction with US Highway 101. Head west on Highway 101, reaching Port Angeles in about three hours from Seattle, depending on your ferry timing.

Four days and three nights is ample time to enjoy this wild coast. The route can be done in either direction, but traveling from north to south, from Shi Shi Beach to Lake Ozette, is recommended. You'll need two cars to do this trip, or, optionally, arrange for one of the informal shuttle services provided by the locals.

Most people overnight in Port Angeles and start out for the hike the following morning. If you are spotting a car at the terminus of the hike at Lake Ozette, that chore will add two hours to your drive. From Port Angeles, drive west on US Highway 101 about 6 miles (10 km) from town, then turn right at Highway 112. The long but scenic drive along the Strait of Juan de Fuca ends at Neah Bay in approximately 75 miles (121 km) and two hours. However, if

through slimy, ankle-breaking rocks, around seaweed-covered boulders the size of refrigerators, up and over headlands hand over hand on the "rope assists," and back and forth between the forest. Rivers pour out of the snowcapped Olympic Mountains to create challenging crossings. Everything here is dictated by the tide: you hike when the tide allows, not when you want to hike. Your tide chart rules the itinerary on this adventure, and you will be a world expert at reading that tide chart by the time you reach Lake Ozette.

Along the way petroglyphs serve as a reminder that there is history here. This super-abundant ecosystem has been home to human beings for a long time. The hike crosses preserves for Native Americans such as the Makah and the Ozette, tribes of the ancient Salish people whose Coast Indian traditions still reverberate far up the west coast of North America. The coast culture thrived here in an ecosystem of such bounty the people had time and inclination to develop highly evolved art forms and ceremonies. The Indian culture survives on this coast, in its twenty-first-century form, becoming part of the journey's complicated appeal.

The remote Olympic Peninsula, like many places at the end of the road, comes with diverse parts. The logging culture thrives in places like Forks, retirees

you are leaving a car at Lake Ozette, turn off beyond the town of Clallam Bay (and Sekiu) south onto the Hoko–Ozette Road. It's about 26 miles (42 km) to the parking lot and ranger station at the north end of Lake Ozette.

Leave a car there and return to Highway 112 to finish the drive to Neah Bay. Primarily a fishing village, the community of Neah Bay has a few motels, campgrounds, and restaurants. If you arrive well equipped and sufficiently provisioned, staging here puts you close to the hike and allows for an early start down the coast. If you have time, be sure to check out the excellent Makah Museum for a background on the Makah culture, which evolved around whaling.

Purchase your Makah Recreational Pass in town, then drive south past Hoback beach toward the fish hatchery about 4 miles (6 km) to the trailhead. Note that this is Makah land, not Park Service land. Tradition calls for payment to the locals as a parking fee. This was once a casual affair accomplished by knocking on doors, but the process has been formalized with the introduction of the Makah Recreation Pass.

A note about safety and the unique character of this backcountry journey: before you shoulder your pack and head for the beach, be prepared for a rugged coastal hike and its inherent dangers. Tides are the primary consideration. You must have a tide table and the ability to tell day and time accurately. And you must have a good topo map. Both are crucial to navigating the coast.

Here's why: a given offshore rock or headland may be "roundable" only at a particular tide level. When you get there to find the tide is well above that, and check your map to see there is no trail over the top, you sit down to wait for the tide. Or, better yet, you have planned your itinerary to accommodate the tide. A proper map also includes specific information for each headland, such as "never round" or "round at extreme low tide only," etc. Ensure your map includes this crucial tidal height information, or you'll have to inquire at the ranger stations. I recommend Green Trails Maps sheets 98S and 130S.

Your tide chart and map is critical, as a mistake can have grave consequences. For instance, if you try to make your way around a headland but you've got the timing wrong, the tide can come in while you are rounding the headland. You will be trapped, washed out to sea and then you will die. It happens. To avoid that, simply read your tide table and check your map.

From the trailhead, Shi Shi Beach is just 3 miles (5 km) through the scrub forest on a trail that can be muddy in places. I recommend wearing an old pair of hiking boots, as the mud, sand, and saltwater will take an inevitable toll on a good pair. And bring along old sneakers or water shoes for walking in the surf or wading across rivers. While we're on the subject of

A hiker follows the beach trail around the prominent Sand Point, where the route veers off the beach to travel inland to Lake Ozette.
PHOTO BY ETHAN WELTY.

gear, the park requires that you carry bear-proof food containers. If they weren't required they would still be a good idea even if you don't encounter a bear. The raccoons and other critters on this route are wily and resourceful food thieves, so keep no food in your tent lest these pesky critters gnaw a hole in it.

At about 1.5 miles (2 km) from the trailhead, the vegetation opens up a bit, and that first dramatic view of the coast is one you won't forget. A right fork leads to the north end of the beach, if you've got extra time for exploration, otherwise stay left where the trail takes you south toward Point of Arches. Along much of this hike, a beach route is paralleled by a forest trail above the high tide mark. Your tide chart will tell you what route to take, but Shi Shi Beach is generally safe in most tides.

Point of Arches is another 2 miles (3 km) hiking south along the beach. Petroleum Creek, just north of Point of Arches, makes a good first night's camp, with reliable water. You're still close enough to explore the dramatic beachscape here if tides allow. Point of Arches is basically a headland sculpted and ruined by time and tide and storm. All that remains is an imposing line of sea stacks and craggy formations rising from a floor of weirdly ridged black rock.

After rounding the point on your journey south, the next few miles introduce you to the difficulties of coast hiking. Whether on the beach route or over the headlands, it's going to take some work. Look for the distinctive trail signs (a circle with black and orange triangles) marking the overland routes, many of which have ropes to assist in climbing up and, more importantly, clambering down the steep headlands. The ropes accommodate just one hiker at a time. This troublesome section ends on one of the longest beaches on the route.

Campsites near Seafield Creek, about 4 miles (7 km) from Petroleum Creek, are a good option for night two, with reliable water. Or you might continue hiking another 2 miles (3 km) to the Ozette River.

Good camps can be found on the north side of the river, but some hikers complain the water is discolored. This brown tint is due to naturally occurring tannic acid and does not necessarily mean the water is brackish or otherwise contaminated. But high tides can backflow salt water into the creeks to make them taste salty. In any event, filter or treat all your water.

Crossing the Ozette can be a challenge and, at high tide or after a heavy deluge in the Olympic Mountains, even dangerous. Take care here, and cross only at low tide. More campsites can be found on the south side of the Ozette River. Two miles from the river you encounter the first exit route to Lake Ozette, the Cape Alava Trail. Continue south here, past the petroglyphs at Wedding Rock and on toward Sand Point.

Make your last camp here on the coast near the low hill of Sand Point before heading back to civilization the next day. The recommended exit route is less than 3 miles (5 km) south of the Cape Alava Trail. This, the Sand Point Trail, takes you to Lake Ozette via a mostly boardwalked trail. From here, it's an hour or so back to Clallam Bay, and two hours to Port Angeles.

HAZARDS

Without question, the power of the Pacific is the greatest danger on this route. The ocean delivers a lot of wind, water, and weather to this coast, and the tides come and go inexorably without regard to your safety. Protect yourself with expert tide-chart reading, a good map, and good judgment. Weather is an important factor as well, though you might be surprised that it's not as bad as you might think. Big storms do come in, but the norm is gray and cool and cloudy, and the occasional bluebird hot summer day will blow your mind.

Wildlife is an issue, and hard-sided food containers are required for the safe storage of all food. Your biggest problem is likely not going to be bears, however, but the camp-robbing, camp-destroying, ever-so-well-habituated raccoons, so take precautions.

More dramatic hazards lurk here on the edge of

LEFT: *Rock art at the site known as Wedding Rock, south of Cape Alava.* PHOTO BY DAVE SCHIEFELBEIN.

RIGHT: *A purple sea star clings to the rocks of a tidal pool.* PHOTO BY DAVE SCHIEFELBEIN.

the Pacific's ring of fire. You cannot discount the possibility of tsunamis, as one occurred here as recently as the 1960s following an earthquake in Alaska. You'll be out of reach of the warning sirens on this hike, but if the ocean suddenly runs out to sea, head for higher ground.

Treat, boil, or filter all water on this backcountry journey.

SEASON

Due to its low elevation, this is a hike with a long season. In fact, it can be done virtually year round, as long as snowstorms or other severe weather is not predicted. A summer hike here is hard to resist, with the outside chance of an actual hot day and blue skies, but that's when you'll have the most company. My advice is to go late in the year, or early in the year, when everyone else waits for the "season" and yet the forecast calls for unseasonably good weather. Another tip on timing: schedule your trip during a time of "minus tides" (tides lower than the usual norms), which greatly simplifies navigation.

ROUTE

From the hamlet of Neah Bay, drive past the US Coast Guard station and the Makah Museum about 3 miles (4.8 km) to the fish hatchery. The Shi Shi Beach Trailhead is just 100 feet (30 m) before the hatchery. The trail heads toward the beach on boardwalked and gravel sections before hitting the muddy trail near the park boundary. A trail to the northern end of Shi Shi Beach veers right, but stay left at this juncture and continue south toward the south end of Shi Shi Beach and the Point of Arches. The trail reaches the beach proper in 2 miles (3 km). If you have time, hike back north along the beach to explore the sea caves and tide pools at the north end of Shi Shi Beach.

Point of Arches is another 2 miles (3 km) hiking south along the sandy beach. Petroleum Creek, about 4 miles (6 km) from the trailhead and a mile or so short of Point of Arches, makes a good first night's camp due to reliable water and proximity to the best scenery. The creek can usually be crossed on drift-log jams. The smaller Willoughby Creek is just south. From a camp in either location, if the tide allows, explore the ruined headland that has become dramatic Point of Arches. Any reasonably low tide will allow access to the rocks and tidepools out toward the point, which can be rounded at most low tides.

When tides allow, and the rare warm summer day comes to the Northwest coast, hikers can walk barefoot along the beach as they cover the 15 miles (24 km) of this coastal hike. PHOTO BY JOEL ROGERS.

From Point of Arches, the next 2 miles (3 km) are tough going. A low tide might allow a safe passage on the outside for at least some of the way, but that's going to be a boulder scramble, not a beach walk. If it's high tide, you will find your way to the overland routes across the headlands, marked by the round signs and colored triangles. The distinctive trail signs mark the overland routes when your way is cut off by ocean. Use the "rope assists" that are in place on some of the difficult uphill bits. These can aid in climbing up and climbing down these unstable slopes with a full pack. Once up on the headlands it's just a matter of following the trail across the top to the descent back down to the beach.

The route passes scenic offshore rocks, including Father and Son Rocks, and secluded coves that are potential private campsites if you are carrying sufficient water. Some small coves are choked with driftwood or boulders, others have big blowdowns that are difficult to circumvent. Continue south until you finally descend onto the longest beach of the hike, a 3.5-mile (5.6-km) section of open beach with relatively easy going, if not easy footing.

Campsites near Seafield Creek, about 4 miles (6 km)

from Petroleum Creek and 8 miles (13 km) from the trail-head, have reliable water and are well situated for night two. Here you might catch a glimpse of a handful of cabins that were built before the area was included in the park. South of here, big trees have toppled off the bank and may require scrambling up on shore to circumvent if the tide is up. And a final small headland just .5 mile (.8 km) north of the Ozette River can be rounded in all but a high tide.

More campsites can be found 2 miles (3 km) farther south near the Ozette River, 10 miles (16 km) from the trail-head. Good campsites in the trees are located on the north side of the river. Camping north of the river allows you to carefully plan your crossing of the Ozette, which can be problematic, and could be called the crux of the route. At high tide, the Ozette can appear positively impossible, and even at low tide it can be troublesome. Heavy rains can swell the river and present further problems. A workable strategy is to wait for the lowest tide you are going to get, then cross the river as close to the surf as possible to minimize the impact of the river's flow. Expect thigh-deep water in any event, but the river is almost always crossable if you wait for tide and conditions.

More campsites can be found on the south side of the Ozette River, but they are harder to locate. Expect to encounter more coves and headlands south of the river, but nothing like what you went through south of Point of Arches. As you move south past Tskawahyah Island the beaches eventually become easier to negotiate, although the sandy beaches become rocky and slippery as you head south and around Cape Alava.

South of Cape Alava a sign marks an intersection with the Cape Alava Trail, and the first exit option for the final 3 miles (5 km) back to Lake Ozette and your car (or your shuttle rendezvous). But the route recommended here continues south, past the petroglyphs at Wedding Rock, if the tide allows, up in the trees if not. Consider a third camp near Sand Point, almost 3 miles (5 km) south of the Cape Alava Trail. The small promontory of the point makes an excellent vantage for sunset. When it's time to leave, find the Sand Point Trail (look for the overland markers) back to Lake Ozette in a final 3 miles (5 km) of mostly boardwalked trail.

LEFT: *The section of the route between Point of Arches and Father and Son Rocks is one of the most strenuous, requiring hikers to climb up and over headlands on sandy trails using ropes fixed in place as they travel from cove to cove.* PHOTO BY JOEL ROGERS.

RIGHT: *Not for nothing is the wild Olympic coastline of Washington known as the shipwreck coast. Here, the wreck of the* USS General M. C. Meigs, *a World War II troop transport, still shows superstructure above the waves. The* Meigs *went down while under tow in 1972.* PHOTO BY JOEL ROGERS.

INFORMATION

Permits and reservations are required for all overnight trips into the Olympic National Park backcountry. Bear-proof canisters are required for food storage.

For information and wilderness permits and advance reservations, contact the Wilderness Information Center for Olympic National Park (WIC) in Port Angeles in person or by phone:

OLYMPIC NATIONAL PARK WILDERNESS INFORMATION CENTER
600 East Park Avenue
Port Angeles, WA 98362
360-565-3100
www.nps.gov/olym/index.html

Ranger Stations

CLALLAM BAY
360-963-2725

LAKE OZETTE
360-963-2725

Permits are also available through the Olympic National Park/Olympic National Forest Recreation Information Center, Forks, Washington.
360-374-7566

A Makah Recreation Pass must be purchased in Neah Bay prior to arriving at any trailheads on the Makah Indian reservation:

MAKAH TRIBAL COUNCIL
P.O. Box 115
Neah Bay, WA
360-645-2201
E-mail: makah@centurytel.net
www.makah.com

Shuttle Services and Overnight Parking

An informal network of shuttle drivers operates to the few trailheads on the Olympic Peninsula; inquire through the ranger stations for phone numbers. Overnight parking for Shi Shi Beach is only allowed at designated private parking lots.

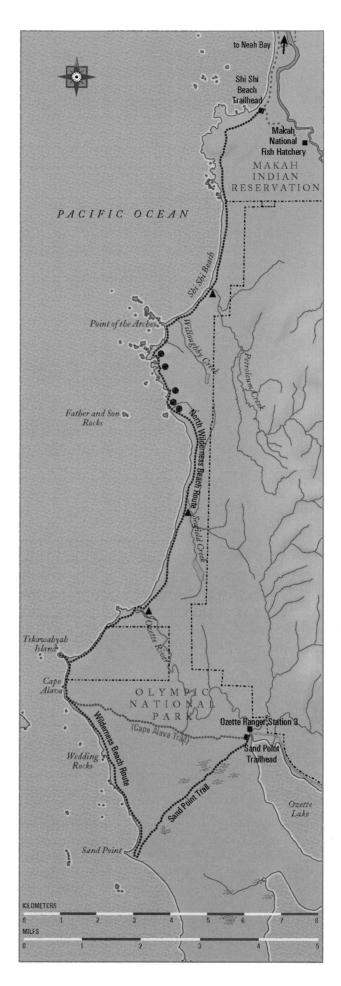

SKOKI VALLEY GRAND TOUR

Slate Range, Canadian Rockies

Banff National Park

Alberta and British Columbia, Canada

DISTANCE: 28 miles (43 km) round-trip
TIME: 3–4 days
PHYSICAL CHALLENGE: 1 2 3 4 5
PSYCHOLOGICAL CHALLENGE: 1 2 3 4 5
STAGING: Lake Louise, Alberta

Tucked away behind the sprawling Lake Louise ski area, in the heart of Alberta's Canadian Rockies, lies the impressive Slate Range. This remote collection of 10,000-foot (3,050-m) peaks harbors some of the best hiking in a part of the world renowned for great hiking. Just beyond Deception Pass and majestic Redoubt Mountain lies the pretty Skoki Valley, a worthy destination in itself but also the gateway to greater backcountry adventure farther afield. There may be no better way to sample the renowned beauty of Banff National Park than to trek through this landscape.

Just getting to Skoki Valley calls for a world-class hiking day. From the end of the Temple Lodge access road, behind the popular ski area, the route works up through the trees into a sprawling open meadow, and from there up to Boulder Pass and the first views of the impressive peaks of the Slate Range beyond. From here, Mount Richardson, Pika Peak, and Ptarmigan Peak form the impossibly dramatic climax of the Slate Range. The route follows the shore of pretty Ptarmigan Lake before climbing steeply up to Deception Pass, the high point on the approach to the valley.

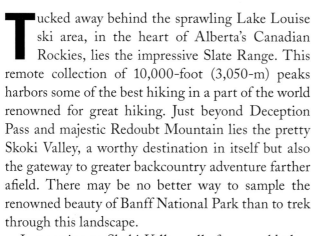

From the pass, the route offers spectacular views of the peaks beyond before dropping into the Skoki Valley. The last few miles come with tantalizing glimpses of the turquoise, glacial-silted waters in Skoki Lakes.

A three- or four-day hike into the heart of the Slate Range makes for perhaps the perfect Canadian

Beyond Deception Pass, the high point on the hike into Skoki Valley, the views open up into the heart of the Slate Range.
PHOTO BY PETER POTTERFIELD.

Rockies package, allowing for an outstanding back-country journey combined with a bigger sightseeing trip on the drive up. This excursion begins at the Calgary airport and the two-hour drive to the Rockies, which rise in the west like a great, jagged wall as you drive. Stops in laid-back Canmore and busy, precious

Banff itself set you up for the final hour up Highway 93, which becomes the storied Icefields Parkway, to Lake Louise. Call this the quiet corner of the Banff National Park milieu, one where the scenery reigns supreme, and crowds are less concentrated.

A night here in Lake Louise (in the village or a few

Hikers returning to the trailhead from Skoki Valley frequently take the scenic Packer's Pass route down. **PHOTO BY PETER POTTERFIELD.**

minutes away on the actual lakeshore) positions you for the hike into the Slate Range the following day. The outrageously scenic 9-mile (15-km) hike over two passes into the backcountry camp in Skoki Valley (or other overnight options) shows you a hidden side to this famous national park. From here you are poised for the highlight of this journey, a day hike into the Merlin Valley. Surprisingly, however, one of the best-kept secrets in this corner of Banff National Park is actually man-made: the venerable Skoki Lodge.

For those so inclined, the presence of the lodge can add a layer of civility to this backcountry experience that makes it unlike any in the Rockies. Not just one of the most professionally managed wilderness lodgings anywhere—it is, after all, run by the Lake Louise ski area—the historic log structure is steeped in Canadian history. Built in 1931 as a base for skiers, it was as popular then as it is now. Today, a half dozen years after a significant restoration, the pleasures of this unpretentious lodge are a closely guarded secret among those in the know.

No matter how you approach this trek into the remarkable Slate Range—be it a pure backcountry outing, a lodge-based hiking vacation, or a combination of the two—you're in for a classic excursion through one of the most beautiful and yet often over-looked enclaves in the Canadian Rockies. Both the campsites and the lodge are centrally positioned as base camps to explore even more rugged beauty nearby. The all-day outing to Merlin's Castle, the rarely visited tarn known as Dragon's Drink, and the ridgeline vantage point beyond, all in the shadow of Mount Richardson, may well rival any other excursion in Banff National Park.

LOGISTICS & STRATEGY

Any Slate Range adventure begins at the international airport in Calgary, where flights from around the world converge on this gateway to the Canadian Rockies. From the rental car counters, make a big loop to the north and west from the airport, and eventually south, to join Route 1, the Trans-Canada Highway. Steer west toward Canmore and Banff, stopping at one of the roadside shopping malls and suburban big box stores for groceries, stove fuel, and other essentials.

Only two hours on the highway takes you through Canmore (another shopping opportunity) and to the gate of Banff National Park. You must stop here to pay your park entrance fee, figured per person per day, which can actually get pretty steep for a week-long visit. You'll also need a backcountry permit, which can be obtained from the Banff visitor center, but which is more easily obtained in the somewhat quieter Parks Canada Lake Louise Visitor Centre another hour or so north.

The town of Banff, busy in summer and popular with Japanese and European travelers year-round, is the local center for tourism in the vicinity. Accommodations and meals can be expensive, some would say unreasonably so. For that reason, and for the sake of proximity and ease of obtaining a permit, Lake Louise makes perhaps a better staging area for the Slate Range adventure.

About 19 miles (30 km) north of Banff the Trans-Canada Highway veers west into British Columbia. Turn off at the intersection to go north on Highway 93, which continues to Lake Louise and eventually up north through the ice fields to Jasper. About 15 miles (25 km) past the intersection, exit to the village of Lake Louise.

The center of Lake Louise is, unexpectedly, dominated by an expansive strip mall with an outdoor shop, liquor store, various restaurants, and other services. The large Parks Canada visitor center and warden office is adjacent to this, the Samson Mall. A cluster of restaurants and lodgings is found nearby. Another cluster of lodgings lies a five-minute drive west, up by the lake itself, dominated by the towering landmark hotel, the Chateau Lake Louise.

Find lodgings in the village that suit your style, choosing from national park campgrounds to fancy hotels such as the Fairmont or tony Post Hotel, and most anything in between. The next day, drive to the Lake Louise ski area, just five minutes away to the east, and the parking lot and trailhead for the Slate Range hike described here. The route does not begin in a promising way, but leads up an unappealing service road past ski lift machinery for more than 2 miles (3 km) before becoming a trail.

For those who decide to stay at Skoki Lodge instead of camping out in the valley, the drill is a little different. You'll be instructed to go inside the main lodge at the ski area to check in at approximately 9 a.m., where your registration is confirmed and you are directed to a remote parking lot. From there a van takes you and other guests up to the end of the Temple Lodge service road, saving you the walk. Skoki Lodge doesn't guide its guests to the lodge on the hike in, so you'll be on your own, just like the other backpackers on the 9-mile (15-km) hike in to Skoki Valley.

Whether you choose to camp in the valley, at one of the designated campgrounds, or stay at the lodge, a backcountry visit here will be memorable. Arguments for the lodge include its uniqueness. There are lots of wilderness lodges in mountain ranges all over North America, but few come with the civility and quality of food found here. Accommodations are rustic, but boast the comforts of home. At Skoki Lodge one lives well, sleeping in comfortable if primitive lodge rooms (or adjacent individual cabins), dining well on tasty, healthy food prepared by a dedicated staff, even enjoying a glass of wine with dinner or a cold brew after a hike. Life here is frontier style—there's no running water or showers, no indoor plumbing, etc.— but it's positively luxurious compared with a typical backpackers' camp.

Perhaps the best feature of the lodge is its central location in the Skoki Valley: a guest is well positioned for day hikes to some of the most stunning landscapes

A hiker on a day outing from camp climbs toward the tarn known as Dragon's Drink past the formation called Merlin's Castle. PHOTO BY PETER POTTERFIELD.

The hike into Skoki Valley crosses both Boulder Pass and Deception Pass, with pretty Ptarmigan Lake lying in between. **PHOTO BY PETER POTTERFIELD**

in Banff National Park. The downside is the extra expense, and the fact that the venerable lodge often requires reservations a year in advance. And remember, the backcountry camp is no more than a mile from the lodge, so in terms of geography, there's not much difference when considering location for day hikes.

However you go, you'll start out on the service road by Temple Lodge and soon gain the well-used trail in to the Slate Range. The route works up through the trees into a sprawling open meadow, and from there up to Boulder Pass (7,500 feet, 2,286 m) and the first expansive views of the peaks beyond. From here, Mount Richardson, Pika Peak, and Ptarmigan Peak form the impressive climax of the Slate Range. Pretty Ptarmigan Lake lies below. The trail skirts the lake along its north side, then climbs steeply up to Deception Pass, at 8,200 feet (2,490 m) the high point on the approach, and more spectacular views. The trail descends from the pass and drops into the Skoki Valley with the first tantalizing glimpses of the turquoise Skoki Lakes.

If you're staying at the lodge, continue past a trail intersection to Red Deer Lakes Camp on the main trail, and arrive at Skoki Lodge just a few minutes beyond. The staff greets you with cool drinks and a snack, and shows you to your accommodations. If you are camping, stay on the trail approximately 1 mile (2 km) past the lodge to the Skoki Valley backcountry camp. (Note that there is another legal backcountry

camp that can be a little quieter, at Red Deer Lakes, reached by a 3-mile (4.5-km) hike that leaves the Skoki Valley Trail just before Skoki Lodge.)

Both the lodge and the campground are well positioned for day two of this backcountry journey, the day hike in to the Merlin Valley, and the real payoff to this Slate Range excursion. The route leaves from the lodge, sidehills steeply under a dramatic feature called the Wall of Jericho, ascends a formidable-looking rock bench, then climbs up to Merlin Lake under the craggy peak known as Merlin's Castle. If you've got the juice, continue up another two hours to Merlin Ridge for spectacular views to the west. This world-class day is made into a big loop by returning to camp, or the lodge, via a horse-packers' trail on the north side of the Merlin Valley.

On the third day, you can hike out, or choose to spend more time exploring the enchanting allure of this corner of the Canadian Rockies. Skoki Mountain, Little Pipestone Creek, and Douglas Lake (and the upper Red Deer River) are all appealing day hike destinations from Skoki Valley.

When you do hike out, be sure to take the alternative route called Packer's Pass. It is slightly steeper, perhaps a half hour longer, but more interesting, and so more suited to the descent than the hike in. This route has the advantage of skirting the Skoki Lakes, some of the most scenic mountain lakes in the area, and not something to miss.

HAZARDS

Both grizzly bears and black bears can be found here in the Rockies of Banff National Park, so it's essential that hikers take precautions and follow proper camping practices. Many of the camps near the Skoki Valley are equipped with bear poles and cables that allow you to store your food safely out of the reach of wildlife. Ask the park wardens about bear activity when you pick up your hiking permit.

The route into the Skoki Valley crosses two high passes, where weather can turn violent quickly and visibility can drop unexpectedly. Be prepared for inclement conditions. And while camping, be careful to treat or filter your water to avoid water-borne parasites.

SEASON

Because the route into Skoki Valley is decidedly alpine, the hiking season is somewhat dependent on the previous winter's snowfall. Usually, access is possible from late June to late September, and can be done earlier and later in good weather. A late September hike here, with the larches a burning gold and crisp fall weather, will enhance an already outstanding backcountry journey.

ROUTE

From the Lake Louise townsite, make the five-minute drive up to the Lake Louise ski area off Trans-Canada Route 1. An unpaved access road leads in approximately 1 mile (2 km) to the Temple Lodge Road, and in .5 mile (1 km) to the Fish Creek parking area and the trailhead at 5,600 feet (1,700 m). Park here and hike past the locked gate and up the Temple Lodge Road for approximately 2 miles (4 km) to Temple Lodge. (Note that Skoki Lodge guests are driven up this stretch of road, shaving a few miles off the hike.) The hike ascends a steep but short slope above maintenance buildings for about a hundred yards to the top of the hill.

From there the Skoki Valley Trail is marked by a prominent sign as it enters a wooded area and passes a trail intersection on the left. Don't turn here, but continue straight ahead for 1.2 miles (2 km) to an open area where the trail begins to climb uphill. You leaves the trees behind as you enter open meadows and the first big views of the Slate Range, reaching the Hidden Lake Trail intersection and Ptarmigan Hut (sometimes called Halfway Hut) in 4.5 miles (7.5 km). The old cabin, on the far side of the creek, can offer welcome shelter in nasty weather.

The trail ascends open, rocky ground to the broad summit of 7,700-foot (2,350-m) Boulder Pass in 6 miles (8.5 km), where big overhanging rocks offer shelter if necessary. The view from the summit to the peaks of the Slate Range is

The Packer's Pass descent route goes improbably up through the rock band just left of the waterfall. PHOTO BY PETER POTTERFIELD.

Hiking under the imposing feature known as the Wall of Jericho on the way to Merlin Lake. **PHOTO BY PETER POTTERFIELD.**

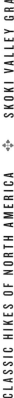
spectacular. The trail descends from the pass to follow the north shore of Ptarmigan Lake before climbing steeply up to Deception Pass, 8,200 feet (2,500 m), the steepest part of the route. From the top of Deception, 7 miles (11 km) from the trailhead, you can actually see down into the Skoki Valley, including the picturesque Skoki Lakes, and back toward the peaks above Lake Louise.

The hard work is over by now as the route gently meanders down from the pass through open meadows and stands of larch trees and into some serious timber. Watch for peekaboo views of the turquoise waters of the Skoki Lakes. The route finishes by winding down through the forest to the valley floor, passing the intersection for Red Deer Lakes Camp at 8.7 miles (14 km) before arriving at Skoki Lodge, 9 miles (14.5 km) from the trailhead. The backcountry campground is another .8 mile (1.2 km) down the trail.

For day two, the route to Merlin Lake leaves from the footbridge near the front porch of Skoki Lodge. This frankly amazing route follows an exquisite trail as it sidehills below the big ridge known as the Wall of Jericho for almost a mile (1.6 km) before reaching a seeming dead end at a steep rocky bench. Some hikers drop down to Castilleja Lake and work up into the cirque holding Merlin Lake from there. My party found a scrambling route that turned the rocky bench on its left side, shaving a bit of time (and elevation loss) off the route.

It's approximately 2 miles (3.5 km) up to Merlin Lake from the valley floor, and it's a pretty spot. Merlin's Castle looms

above, to the northwest, and Mount Richardson and the high peaks of the Slate Range rise dramatically to the south. But don't stop there. Continue higher to a small tarn called Dragon's Drink, about a mile farther, for lunch and a breather, and wonderful alpine ambience. And for a spectacular finish to the day, make the two-hour hike up to the crest of Merlin Ridge, another 1.5 miles (2.2 km) to the west, with almost 1,000 feet of elevation gain. It's a tough, rocky, cross-country route, but the views from the top are not to be missed.

On the descent, make a loop trip of an amazing day by finding the horse-packers' trail that starts from the northeast end of Merlin Lake and drops down the north side of Merlin Valley to the broad, wet expanse of Skoki Valley. This is particularly wise for those camping in the campground, as is makes for a more direct route. The trail descends steeply down from Merlin Lake, hard to follow in places, before reaching the broad, marshy floor of Skoki Valley below the imposing summit of Skoki Mountain.

"Skoki" is said to be an Indian word meaning swamp, or marsh, which aptly describes this section of the valley. Expect to get your boots wet here in the network of shallow creeks and soggy bottoms. Cross the valley floor back to the campground, and climb back up to the lodge on the pretty good trail if you're staying there. Expect this day-long loop trip to Merlin Ridge to take seven to eight hours and cover approximately 10 miles (16 km).

If you have another day in the valley, consider an ascent

of Skoki Mountain, a non-technical but strenuous climb up its western slopes. Other appealing side trips include day hikes along Little Pipestone Creek, or a long day hike up to Douglas Lake (and the upper Red Deer River).

But when it's time to hike out, instead of leaving the way you arrived, follow the route known as Packer's Pass on the upper section of trail back to the ski area. From the lodge, take the way trail directly toward Skoki Lakes. When it appears to dead-end at the waterfall draining the lakes, find the improbable hikers' route up beside the falls, just left, and enjoy the hike along the shore of both lakes before rejoining the normal Skoki Valley Trail before Ptarmigan Lake.

Once back in Lake Louise, if you have an extra day, consider taking the three-hour drive up the Icefields Parkway to Jasper for a look at the Canadian Rockies' other major park.

INFORMATION

Backcountry permits and backcountry camping permits are required. They can be reserved in advance and picked up at the Parks Canada Lake Louise Visitor Centre or at the visitor center in Banff.

LAKE LOUISE VISITOR CENTRE
Box 213
Lake Louise, AB TOL 1E0
403-522-3833 or 403-522-1264
E-mail: ll.info@pc.gc.ca
www.pc.gc.ca/pn-np/ab/banff/visit/visit5.aspx

BANFF INFORMATION CENTRE
224 Banff Avenue
Banff, AB T1L 1K2
403-762-1550
E-mail: banff.vre@pc.gc.ca

BANFF NATIONAL PARK
Box 900
Banff, AB T1L 1K2

Planning a Trip

Alberta's provincial Web site can assist when planning a trip to Banff National Park:
www.TravelAlberta.com

For hikers interested in staying at historic Skoki Lodge, see the Skoki Lodge Web site for rates and details:
www.skoki.com

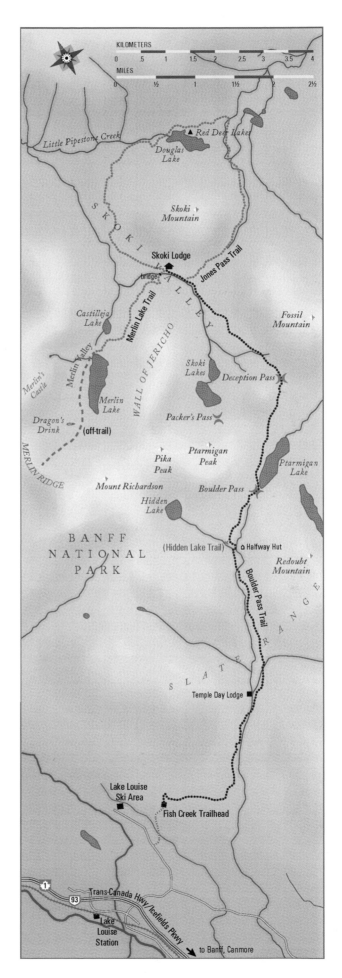

GREY OWL TRAIL
Kingsmere Lake and
Grey Owl Wilderness
Boreal Forest
Prince Albert National Park

Saskatchewan, Canada

DISTANCE: **25 miles (40 km) round-trip**
TIME: **2–3 days**
PHYSICAL CHALLENGE: **1 2 3 4 5**
PSYCHOLOGICAL CHALLENGE: **1 2 3 4 5**
STAGING: **Waskesiu Lake, Saskatchewan**

The great boreal forest of Canada is an over-looked venue for backpacking adventures, but once you venture into it the experience can be addictive. My first foray into the heart of it, the wilds of northern Saskatchewan, was undertaken lightly, with complete ignorance, an adjunct to another story. I had not carried my pack a mile before I came around the bend to find a lynx regarding me implacably, at the edge of the trail. The long, feathery tufts on its ears were clearly visible at 20 feet, the distance between us. The eyes of the astonishingly large cat showed only curiosity before it grew bored and trotted off. I had hoped for a close-up look at a lynx for much of my life, to no avail, and here it was, delivered up to the unworthy, where I least expected it. Luck or karma, I couldn't say, but I had to come back.

There's no better way to experience the great northern forest of Saskatchewan than to make the 25-mile (40-km) hike through the wilderness of Prince Albert National Park to pay homage to one of Canada's earliest conservationists. The story of Grey Owl could hardly be more improbable. Born an Englishman, Archie Belaney immigrated to Canada in 1906 to pursue a frontier fantasy. But a funny thing happened along the way: he honestly embraced the ways of the First Nations people. He married into the Ojibway tribe and became an accomplished woodsman and trapper, no small feat in the unforgiving regions of northern Canada.

On his evolution from pretend frontiersman to authentic conservationist, Belaney later married (one of five marriages for him) a Mohawk woman he christened Anahareo, took the name Grey Owl, gave up his ways as a trapper, and went to work as a naturalist for the Canadian park system. He and Anahareo built a cabin on the shores of Ajawaan Lake in a remote corner of Prince Albert Park, and lived there with a pair of beavers, Jelly Roll and Rawhide. It was a hard life—the winters don't bear thinking about—but idyllic in its way. The complicated, oft-married, and wily Grey Owl wrote books that became bestsellers in Canada, making a celebrity out of him and the rustic cabin he

OPPOSITE: *Not for nothing is Saskatchewan known as the Land of Living Skies, as prairie weather kicks up dramatic atmospheric conditions.* PHOTO BY PETER POTTERFIELD.

The cabin, home to iconic Canadian conservationist Grey Owl—born Archie Belaney—is today much as it was 75 years ago.
PHOTO COURTESY OF PARKS CANADA/PRINCE ALBERT NATIONAL PARK.

called Beaver Lodge. Today, the two- or three-day journey to visit his home, the birthplace of an iconic movement, is a fascinating backcountry outing.

Prince Albert National Park, a big one at almost 4,000 square miles (10,400 sq km), holds greater allure. The landscape here is an ecotone, an overlapping of prairie and boreal forest that creates a unique "edge effect" with unreal botanical diversity. This rare environmental juncture makes good habitat for the mixed forest of birch, spruce, tamarack, aspen, and jack pine of the southern boreal forest, as well as some of the few remaining remnants of native prairie. Peat bogs, wetlands, taiga, and tundra are components in the complex, interconnected habitat. This is something special, a place where rare fescue and mixed-grass native prairie bumps up right against the billion-acre boreal forest. The edges of such distinctly different ecozones come with wildlife in abundance and variety, not just my Canada lynx, but wolves (Prince Albert is world headquarters for gray wolf research in the forest), woodland caribou, plains bison, elk, and black bear.

The latter don't present much of a problem here but I think that's because there just aren't enough people to create the kinds of encounters that result in conflict. I met some park wardens who agree, and who think that might change as more people are drawn to these authentic wilds. But for now solitude is the theme when hiking in Prince Albert: you look around and suddenly realize you are alone, the only two-legged creature for miles and miles. I did the hike up to Grey Owl's cabin by myself, and never saw a soul. It's a little scary, especially when you think about all those wolves and bears wandering around out there in the pristine ancient forest.

There's a decidedly primeval vibe here. I remember making a water run from my base camp at the head of Kingsmere Lake, a big body of water. At more than 7 miles (11 km) long and 5 miles (8 km) wide, it's far enough across that you can barely see the opposite shore. I had to walk all of 10 feet from the tent to fetch a pot full of water from the clear lake. The sky was still dramatically pink in the west, but a full, fat, yellow moon sat just above the trees on the opposite horizon. Merganser families swam arrogantly by just offshore. Loons flapped noisily on the surface of the lake trying to get airborne. They are clumsy takeoff artists, but there's nothing like drifting off to sleep in the far north to the haunting calls of a pair of loons.

The hike itself is unlike any other, but quite manageable: the trailhead is just 20 miles (33 km) from the small, comfortable town of Waskesiu Lake. The drive out to the trailhead is a veritable wildlife park, so take your time and pay attention. From the trail-head, it's about 11 miles (17 km) out to the most appealing camp, right at the head of Kingsmere Lake. From there, it's a pleasant half day hike up and over the ridge to Ajawaan Lake and Grey Owl's modest cabin. You can do it in two days easily, but three is better. The extra time lets you absorb the majesty of the great forest, enjoy the quiet and the solitude, and maybe get a little freaked out at night by all those unfamiliar noises floating into camp on the breeze.

LOGISTICS & STRATEGY

Saskatchewan's biggest city, Saskatoon, is the gateway to Prince Albert Park, but the hamlet of Waskesiu Lake, about three hours away, is the place from which to stage the hike. Saskatoon's airport has good connections from all over North America, and an easy rental car counter. You'll likely have to take multiple flights to get here, so a workable strategy is to arrive when you can, and plan to stay in an airport or other local hotel if it's late. Begin your journey to the park the following day after picking up necessary supplies and equipment in town.

Take Highway 11 up through the wheat and canola fields to the town of Prince Albert, two hours north of Saskatoon. This bustling town has big grocery stores and an outdoor shop for last-minute shopping. From the town of Prince Albert, drive up Highway 2 another hour, turning off at Highway 245 for the short drive into Prince Albert National Park and the hamlet of Waskesiu Lake.

The village sits right on the eastern shore of Lake Waskesiu. It can get pretty busy in high summer, but even then remains relaxed and informal, and it is small enough that you can walk from one end to the other. Campgrounds, inns, and lodges offer accommodations, and the local restaurants provide a range of dining choices. Pick up your hiking permit at the Parks Canada visitor center right in town, on the lakeshore by the public beach. You'll pay a fee for both the hiking permit and the camping permit. It's wise to choose "active deregistration," especially if you are hiking alone. That way, if you don't return on time to deregister, the wardens will know you are missing and come looking for you.

A primitive but effective bear-proof food storage structure is found at Northend Camp: just store your food up top and remove the ladder. In a pinch, the added bit of elevation is just enough to make it possible to use a cell phone from the platform. PHOTO BY PETER POTTERFIELD.

Prince Albert National Park is dominated by lakes, and so is as much about canoeing and fishing as it is about hiking. If you have time on the day you arrive, think about doing the hike through the amazing Boundary Bog. It's a fascinating outing through one of the classic peat bogs in the area, so well-interpreted in signage that you could easily spend half a day, making a good warm-up to the Grey Owl hike. I also rented a canoe for a paddle through Hanging Heart Lakes, and cruised the park's unpaved roads looking for wildlife.

When it's time to leave for Grey Owl's cabin, follow the Kingsmere Road north past the Waskesiu Marina and Birch Bay for 20 miles (33 km) to the trailhead at the Kingsmere River, the end of the road. The 13-mile (20-km) hike to Grey Owl's cabin starts here.

You'll notice at the trailhead a boat launch ramp, which reveals another option for reaching Grey Owl's cabin. Instead of hiking both ways, it is possible to hire a guide and freight canoe (a large canoe with a squared-off stern to accommodate a small outboard motor) to run you up to the top of Kingsmere Lake. If you choose that option, it's wise to take the boat up, and walk back. Kingsmere Lake is a serious body of water, and while it might be smooth as glass one minute, it can be churned by big wind into dangerous whitecaps the

next. You can hike back to the trailhead in pretty much any conditions, but sometimes canoes and kayaks can't navigate the storm-tossed water.

If you choose the guided run up the lake, you'll experience a classic boreal forest portage, which can be quite a clambake. You launch your canoe at the trailhead, paddle about 500 yards (457 m) downstream, then haul out again at a purpose-built dock. The portage here has been used for a hundred years, so a rail system has been constructed. A wheeled cart rides on rails from the near end of the portage on the river to Kingsmere Lake. You load the canoe on the cart, strap it down, and push it a little less than a mile (1 km) down the rails until you reach Kingsmere Lake proper. The canoe option adds interest for some people, but also expense and planning time. Just remember that hiking the route both ways is rewarding as well, and preserves solitude, so the decision comes down to personal preference.

From the trailhead by the boat launch, the route to Grey Owl's cabin follows the eastern shore of Kingsmere Lake, often within sight of the water, for 11 miles (17 km) to the north end of the lake and the Northend Campground. The trail crosses a large marshy area to start, but soon enters the forest. Elevation is not an issue here. The terrain sits at about 5,800 feet (1,780 m) with only a few hundred feet variance. The hiking topography is mostly flat, with moderate ups and downs as the trail takes you on a

rare forest excursion with few distractions. The trail drops down to beaches twice in the hike out to the north end of the lake, and passes two intermediate campgrounds along the way: Westwind Camp and Sandy Beach Camp.

I recommend camping at the Northend Campground, which sits appropriately at the top of sprawling Kingsmere Lake, offering expansive views to the south. The location makes it sunny in good weather. The tent sites are run out in the trees just yards from the lake. Sunrise happens on your left, sunset on your right. Mosquitoes and flies can be annoying up here in the forest, but I found the breeze at the north end of the lake kept them to a minimum. From the Northend Campground, the hike over to Ajawaan Lake and Grey Owl's cabin takes about an hour each way. Camping is not permitted near the cabin, or even on Ajawaan Lake, so you have to use one of the Kingsmere Lake campsites.

Some people prefer Sandy Beach Camp, about 8 miles (13 km) from the trailhead, and about 3 miles (5 km) short of Northend Camp. The appeal of Sandy Beach is this: the campsites are situated on a pretty little beach, and it can be a little quieter here if there's a big party at the north end, which apparently can happen as Northend Camp is sometimes used by boaters. Camping at Sandy Beach can make sense too if you got a late start on the hike and don't have the time or inclination to go all the way to Northend

Camp. Sandy Beach is still within day-hiking distance of Grey Owl's cabin.

I spent two nights at Northend Camp, where I had the place to myself the whole time. A tall tower made of steel-clad timber poles offers food storage safely out of the reach of bears and other wildlife. You climb up, drop your food bag, and simply take the ladder down after you've stored your food. The upper platform, incidentally, offers just enough elevation above the terrain to get a cell phone signal, which could prove quite useful. The park maintains a huge pile of firewood here, chopped and split, behind the food storage tower, for use in the fire pits at each campsite. Sitting around the campfire watching loons and ducks on the lake during sunset is absolutely the thing to do in the evening at Northend Camp.

From Northend Camp, the route to Ajawaan Lake and Grey Owl's cabin follows the north shore of the lake for a few hundred yards before turning north off the beach and into the forest. The route climbs up and over a small ridge before reaching the south end of Ajawaan Lake, which offers the classic, picturesque view of the cabin. From there it's just 20 minutes along the west shore of Ajawaan Lake to the cabin site itself, where you'll find two cabins, not one.

The main cabin is down on the lakeshore, and has an opening on the water side that permitted access for the beavers to actually enter the cabin from the lake, where Grey Owl and Anahareo built a sort of pen inside for the animals. It's frankly hard to believe they could live there, with beavers, which are nocturnal, but they did. The other cabin is up the hill a few hundred feet, near the gravesites for Grey Owl, Anahareo, and their daughter Shirley Dawn. The little graveyard is surprisingly moving.

The hike from Northend Camp to Grey Owl's cabin can easily be done in two or three hours round-trip, but think of taking most of the day to absorb the ambience of this wilderness abode. When it's time to hike back to the car, a fit hiker can easily complete the 11 miles (17 km) from Northend Camp back to the trailhead in four hours. But a reason to come here is to savor the experience of hiking in this great forest, so take time to stop at Sandy Beach and Westwind camps for a different perspective on impressive Kingsmere Lake.

When driving back to Saskatoon for the flight home, detour slightly to drive the scenic parks road at the south end of Prince Albert National Park, and its greater potential for wildlife. Route 263 runs south from the village of Waskesiu Lake for 12 miles (20 km) through the park before joining Highway 2 north of Prince Albert. I saw a number of bears on that drive.

Sunset from Northend Camp on Kingsmere Lake, Prince Albert National Park. PHOTO BY PETER POTTERFIELD.

TOP: *Vast Kingsmere Lake offers genuine opportunity for solitude deep within the boreal forest of Canada—and makes for a short water run from camp.* PHOTO BY PETER POTTERFIELD.

BOTTOM LEFT: *The Grey Owl Trail is generally very well maintained, but spring flood can make the bridge crossings interesting.* PHOTO BY PETER POTTERFIELD.

BOTTOM RIGHT: *The long walk to and from Grey Owl's cabin reveals the solitude and primeval vibe of the boreal forest.* PHOTO BY PETER POTTERFIELD.

HAZARDS

Black bears and wolves are among the diverse wildlife found in Prince Albert National Park. Problem encounters with either animals are rare, the wardens report, but that's partly due to the fact there aren't many visitors to the backcountry here. It's imperative to practice proper bear-country camping, including cooking at some distance from your tent and storing food out of the reach of animals. Make noise so you don't surprise bears on the trail.

TOP: *The relatively low elevation of the Grey Owl Trail makes it navigable in early season, when the wildflowers put on striking displays.* PHOTO BY PETER POTTERFIELD.

BOTTOM: *The subtleties of the deep forest walk make the 25-mile (40-km) round trip a surprisingly interesting and engaging hike.* PHOTO BY PETER POTTERFIELD.

Biting flies and mosquitoes are actually more of a problem, and can reach levels that rival places such as Alaska. Bring plenty of bug repellent and other appropriate equipment, such as head nets. And prepare for violent weather, which can come up unexpectedly. Even in summer, storms can roil up quickly enough to put you in danger.

SEASON

The climate here is "continental," with long, cold winters and warm summers, and marked differences between day and night temperatures. (Even in summer, take my word for it, nights can be quite cold.) But because Prince Albert National Park is at a relatively low elevation, below 6,000 feet (1,830 m), the hiking season here is a long one. The trip to Grey Owl's cabin can be done in most years as early as mid-May and as late as mid-October. Early and late season trips have the advantage (sometimes) of fewer bugs. But weather can present problems at any time of year, so know the forecast before you go.

ROUTE

From the village of Waskesiu Lake, take the Kingsmere Road north out of town past the Waskesiu Marina. Drive along the northeast shore of Lake Waskesiu, where the pavement ends, and complete the 20-mile (33-km) drive to the Kingsmere River parking lot and trailhead. A nearby campground, the Southend Camp, is a short walk away for those who wish to spend the night at the trailhead.

The Grey Owl Trailhead is just up the hill, above the boat ramp, on the edge of the forest. Follow the trail down through an expansive marshy area for approximately half a mile (.8 km) until the trail emerges near the southeast shore of Kingsmere Lake south of Westwind Camp. Follow the trail north until you reach the camp at 2.5 miles (4 km) from the trailhead. There are two tent sites here. North of the camp, the route drops down to the beach for a good 100 yards, one of the longest stretches of beach on the route, before rejoining the trail and heading back up into the woods.

For the next 3 miles (4 km), the route follows the gently undulating trail through a dense climax forest with occasional glimpses of the lake from high points. The trail is largely in good condition, but some of the bridges have been knocked off their foundations by heavy spring flows and require care to negotiate. Navigating is no problem, as the trail is obvious and easy to follow, allowing one to get into a relaxed, Zen state while enjoying the rhythm of this extraordinary forest walk. In season, wildflowers line the trail. This is a super hike, if a quiet one.

Some maps show a third interim camp, called Chipewyan Portage Camp, at about 4.5 miles (7 km) from the trailhead, but I never saw it and am not sure it is still in use. The well-marked trail continues through the trees until it reaches Sandy Beach Camp at 8 miles (13 km) from the trailhead. Three tent sites are here near the lakeshore, two double sites and one single.

From Sandy Beach, the trail cuts east, farther from the lake and deeper into the forest, until it nears the Northend Camp at 11 miles (17 km) from the trailhead. Expect to spend five hours or so hiking from the trailhead to Northend Camp. A comfortable picnic area, with tables, is adjacent to the campground, which has a half dozen tent sites.

From Northend Camp, the 2-mile (3-km) route to Ajawaan Lake and Grey Owl's cabin starts out on the beach, then cuts inland after several hundred yards. The route goes up and over a low, wooded ridge to reach the south end of Ajawaan Lake, and the first glimpse of Grey Owl's cabin. A well-used trail parallels the west shore of the lake to reach the waterside cabin. The second cabin, and graveyard, are up the hill, accessed by an obvious trail with steps. Expect to take just an hour to reach the cabins from Northend Camp.

The return trip to camp, and back to the trailhead, simply retraces your steps.

INFORMATION

All overnight visitors must register at the Information Centre in Waskesiu prior to their trip. A park use permit will be issued and both hiking permit fees and backcountry camping fees apply.

PRINCE ALBERT NATIONAL PARK
Northern Prairies Field Unit
Box 100
Waskesiu Lake, SK S0J 2Y0
306-663-4522
E-mail: panp.info@pc.gc.ca
www.pc.gc.ca/pn-np/sk/princealbert/index.aspx

Boat Shuttles and Guided Freight-Canoe Trips

WASKESIU MARINA ADVENTURE CENTRE
Summer: 306-663-1999
Winter: 306-763-1278
E-mail: waskesiumarina@sasktel.net
www.waskesiumarina.com/tours.htm

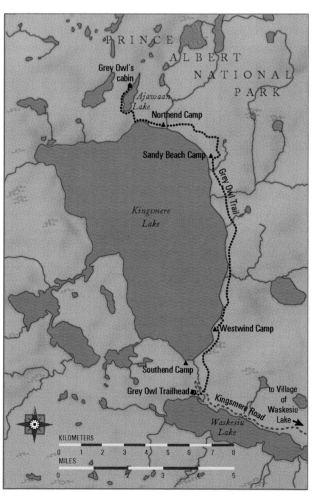

PRESIDENTIAL RANGE TRAVERSE
Appalachian Trail
White Mountains
New Hampshire, United States

DISTANCE: 26 miles (42 km) one-way
TIME: 3–4 days
PHYSICAL CHALLENGE: 1 2 3 4 5
PSYCHOLOGICAL CHALLENGE: 1 2 3 4 5
STAGING: Manchester, New Hampshire; Portland, Maine;
or Boston, Massachusetts

The vaunted Presidential Range Traverse, perhaps the most demanding section of the 2,000-mile (3,220-km) Appalachian Trail, may well be the best hike in the East. The route climbs over a succession of peaks more than 5,000 feet (1,500 m) high, and one over 6,000 feet (1,829 m). Deep, in-cut valleys combine with the highest peaks in the East to make for daunting elevation gains and heartbreaking losses. Add to that the potential for some of the worst weather on the continent and you've got a wilderness outing of both serious challenge and epic appeal.

Mount Washington, at 6,288 feet (almost 2,000 m), the undisputed monarch of the Presidentials, has been branded the stormiest place in the world, a reference to its record for the highest wind speed ever recorded, 231 mph. Conditions are seldom that bad, but the potential for sudden, severe weather means this hike calls for prudence over valor. The Presidentials can be wet and windy and cold, even in summer. Because a lot of people are drawn here, these treacherous conditions frequently result in injuries to hikers, even deaths.

But don't make the mistake of viewing this stunning route as some sort of grim ordeal. Summers can be mild, and while you have to be wary of potential storms, this wilderness walk—much of it above tree line—can be a glorious, if strenuous, jaunt. Adding to

A hiker travels the "Monroe flats" on the Crawford Path near Mount Monroe, on a classic section of the Presidential Traverse.

High in the Presidentials, above tree line, cairns like these show the way. They are spaced closely together because whiteout conditions are common. In the White Mountains, many hikers who have become lost in bad weather have perished. PHOTO BY CAMERON MARTINDALE.

the allure here is the fact that the Appalachian Mountain Club has developed along this route a system of refuges that is unusual for American backcountry. Three European-style huts, offering meals, bunks, and provisions, are spaced along the route at roughly a day's hike from each other. The comfortable lodges can be reserved in advance, meaning you can do this physically demanding hike in relative comfort, and with a lighter pack. But this is an area just as well suited to camping. Using your tent and stove, where permitted, is a good way to experience the terrain in a style in keeping with its wilderness heritage.

For all but the final few miles, the route follows the Appalachian Trail. This oldest and best-known of America's long-distance continental routes runs for 2,167 miles (3,488 km) along the ridge crests and across the major valleys of the Appalachian Mountains from Katahdin, Maine, to Springer Mountain in north Georgia. The AT, as the route is universally known, began as a vision of forester Benton Mac-Kaye. It was opened as a continuous trail in 1937 and designated as the first National Scenic Trail by the National Trails System Act of 1968.

There's yet more history here: part of the traverse, from Crawford Notch to Mount Washington, follows the Crawford Path, the oldest continuously maintained foot trail in America, dating from 1819.

In fact, the extensive trail system in the White Mountains predates the AT by a century, and most of the trail signs here carry both the local trail name as well as the AT moniker.

LOGISTICS & STRATEGY

The route recommended here covers 26 miles (42 km) from Crawford Notch to the Appalachia Trailhead on US Highway 2. While the hike can be done in either direction, it is described from south to north, the better strategy. Going that way gives the hiker a few days to warm up before tackling Mount Washington and the other high peaks of the traverse.

This is New England, where nothing is too far from anywhere else, and so Bostonians and New Yorkers will drive to the trailheads. For those coming from farther afield, Boston is a good choice of airport, from there it's a straight shot up Interstate 93. Airports at Manchester, New Hampshire, and Portland, Maine, also are within three hours' drive of the White Mountains. The route begins at Crawford Notch State Park, about 30 miles (48 km) north of North Conway, at the AT/Webster Cliff Trailhead off Highway 302, and ends at the Appalachia Trailhead, on US Highway 2, about 5 miles (8 km) west of Gorham.

At present, no permit is required to hike the route from Franconia Notch to Appalachia, but you will need to follow the rules on backcountry fires and camps. These regulations, which change yearly, are posted at the White Mountain National Forest Web site under "rules for campers." Keep in mind that much of the Presidential Range is in designated wilderness, or other restricted-use areas, where camping is controlled or even prohibited. The route also passes through three state parks, which have different regulations. You will need to buy a Forest Pass, a parking permit that can be purchased on an annual or weekly basis, if you intend to park at Crawford Notch or Appalachia.

Three of the eight huts operated by the Appalachian Mountain Club (AMC) are spaced along this route, all of which offer meals, beds, and basic provisions: Mizpah Spring, Lakes of the Clouds, and Madison Spring. The huts offer bunkroom accommodations, running water, and full-service lodging with breakfasts and dinners prepared by the hut crew. From Crawford Notch to Appalachia, the huts make it unnecessary to bring a tent or brave nighttime temperatures outside, a fact that opens up the possibility of doing this route a bit earlier or later in the season.

You'll need to know that you have a bunk, so if you intend to use the huts while on the hike be sure to reserve space in advance through the club's telephone reservation system. It is possible to purchase space on arrival, but that depends on vacancies, a rare thing at the popular huts during summer. At about $90 per night, the huts may seem expensive, but you get a lot in return, including a kitchen staff. Meals are included in the cost of accommodation. The AMC also operates a shuttle service between popular trailheads in the White Mountains, making it easy to get back to your car—or to get to the trailhead from which you want to start. Shuttle rides can be reserved in advance.

Be aware that this is a rugged route despite the proximity of huts and other surprising amenities, such as the cafeteria near the summit of Mount Washington. From the start at Crawford Notch to the finish at Appalachia, the Presidential Traverse is one of the most difficult sections of the AT. Much of this 26 miles (42 km) is above tree line, where camping is strictly prohibited. The weather can be horrible, even dangerous. Elevation gain and loss on this section is extreme, so allow a few days to traverse this route over peaks such as Mount Eisenhower, 4,780 feet (1,457 m); Mount Franklin, 5,004 feet (1,525 m); Mount Washington, 6,288 feet (1,917 m); and Mount Madison, 5,363 feet (1,635 m).

HAZARDS

Weather in the Presidentials can be deadly, and for that reason this hike isn't recommended for novices. Mount Washington weather is indicative of what you'll face in the Presidentials. The summit lies in the path of historic storm tracks and, because of its elevation, the peak is biologically and ecologically similar to the subarctic zone. Washington has received measurable snowfall during every month of the year, and average snowfall is more than 250 inches a year. As of

One of the many outcrops of white quartz encountered along the way in the White Mountains, with Mount Adams in the background.
PHOTO BY CAMERON MARTINDALE.

2003, the highest temperature ever recorded on the summit was 72 degrees Fahrenheit (22°C), but the annual average temperature on the mountain is only 27 degrees (–28°C). The summit is in cloud 70 percent of the time, and hurricane-force winds—75 mph (120 kph) or higher—occur on average an unbelievable 104 days per year. Hikers contemplating this route must come prepared to deal with extreme conditions. In the 150 years that records have been kept, more than 100 hikers have perished due to falls, weather, exposure or other factors.

One often overlooked hazard is the nuisance of mosquitoes and blackflies. These insects can be unbearable without appropriate measures, such as effective repellent and head nets.

SEASON

The hiking season in the White Mountains is June (maybe late May in some years) through September (early October if you're lucky on weather), with July usually seeing the warmest temperatures. September, and even October, can have some of the best hiking conditions, with stable weather patterns, clear skies, and fall color. April and May often produce difficult conditions, with deep, wet snow. Winter months are surprisingly busy in these mountains, as hikers, skiers, and snowshoers with appropriate skills venture into the Whites as weather patterns permit. At any time of year, however, severe storms can produce dangerous conditions in the White Mountains.

ROUTE

The start to the hike is found within New Hampshire's Crawford Notch State Park on New Hampshire Route 302, about 30 miles (48 km) north of North Conway (45 minutes' drive) and 60 miles (96 km) south of Littleton (1 hour 15 minutes' drive). Crawford Notch is a major pass through the White Mountains, one that has been used by wagons for hundreds of years. The trailhead is in a parking lot on the east side of Highway 302. Look for the sign with the Appalachian Mountain Club's shuttle schedule posted, and the trailhead for the AT/Webster Cliff Trail.

The AT/Webster Cliff Trail starts out fairly level as it crosses the Saco River, but steepens as it ascends up to good views of Crawford Notch itself. Above, the route turns northward and continues climbing over several steep knobs on the way to Mount Webster. What follows is a very tough five hours, as more than 3,000 feet (900 m) of elevation gain leads up and over a number of false summits to the top of Mount Webster at 3,910 feet (1,200 m). From the top, the trail descends slightly along the ridge only to climb up again toward the summit of Mount Jackson, a mile and a half (about 2 km) distant. Jackson is only 200 feet higher than Webster, but it's a strenuous climb from the col over boulders to reach the top. From the summit, at 4,310 feet (1,314 m), there are good views of the entire Presidential range, notably Mount Washington, and even the Mizpah Spring Hut on the side of Mount Pierce. From the summit, the trail descends slightly to reach the Mizpah Spring Hut, 6.5 miles (10.5 km) from the parking lot at Crawford Notch State Park. The Nauman Campsite is next to the hut. Built in 1965, the Mizpah Spring Hut is one of the most modern on this section of trail.

Working up the slopes of Mount Washington with Mount Adams in the middle and Mount Madison on the right.
PHOTO BY CAMERON MARTINDALE.

A moss-covered rock on the Randolph Path.
PHOTO BY CAMERON MARTINDALE.

The 5-mile hike from Mizpah Spring Hut to Lakes of the Clouds Hut is a highlight of the Presidential Range Traverse, traveling the entire way above tree line and offering the summits of mounts Pierce, Eisenhower, Franklin, and Monroe. But beware, this bald ridge can be extremely exposed in bad weather, so be prepared for temperatures on the ridge to be 20 or even 30 degrees colder than at the hut. From Mizpah Spring Hut, the AT/Webster Cliff Trail climbs steeply to the bare rock summit of Mount Pierce at 4,310 feet (1,314 m), and good views of Eisenhower, Franklin, and Washington. Just past the summit, the trail drops and at a junction on a shoulder connecting Pierce and Eishenhower the route turns right and becomes the AT/Crawford Path, which leads all the way to Mount Washington.

The AT goes not to the top of Eisenhower but around the peak, so take the short Mount Eisenhower Loop trail if you want to go to the 4,780-foot (1,457-m) summit with its great views. The AT/Crawford Path traverses the east flank of Eisenhower and continues over Mount Franklin, 5,004 feet (1,525 m). Beyond, the AT traverses the east flank of Mount Monroe, so take the Mount Monroe Loop trail if you want to enjoy the view of Mount Washington from the 5,385-foot (1,642-m) summit of Monroe. The AT/Crawford Path reaches the Lakes of the Clouds Hut, on the broad flank of Mount Washington, 5 miles (8 km) from Mizpah Spring Hut.

This hut, being close to the popular summit of Mount Washington, is one of the largest and most popular of all the huts along the trail, hence its nickname, Lakes of the Crowds. Though it has a capacity of almost 100 people, it is frequently at capacity. If you arrive here without a reservation be prepared to be turned away, except in emergencies, when the hut crew may let you pay for a sleeping space on the dining room floor.

From the Lakes of the Clouds Hut the AT/Crawford Path winds between the two Lakes of the Clouds and starts the ascent of Mount Washington's summit cone. The upper part of the mountain is basically a big boulder field up which the trail climbs with only a few switchbacks. The way through the rocks is marked by white-painted blazes that identify the AT route.

The summit of Washington, which is also a New Hampshire state park, is a busy place. There's a road as well as the venerable Cog Railway; the railway, built in the 1860s, is said to have the steepest grade of any railroad in the world—14 percent. There is also a visitor center, cafeteria, a weather observatory and various structures including radio antennas. Wilderness it is not. The summit is visited by up to 250,000 people per year; about a quarter of those

are hikers. Though the area is famous for having the worst weather in the world, literally, Mount Washington's most notorious conditions occur during winter storms. Summer storms can be severe as well, as conditions are legendary for turning very bad, very quickly. The entire route from Pierce to Madison is exposed to weather, so be prepared.

From the summit of Washington, continue on the AT/Trinity Heights Connector for a few hundred yards to where it ends at the AT/Gulfside Trail. Turn right here. The AT will follow the Gulfside for the rest of the Presidential Range Traverse to Madison Spring Hut.

The rocky trail drops steadily from the summit of Washington, crosses under the cog railroad tracks, and skirts the Great Gulf on the way to Washington-Reagan Col. The Great Gulf is the largest ravine in the White Mountains. Washington and the peaks of the northern Presidentials (Jefferson, Adams, and Madison) arc around to form the headwall of the Great Gulf. The AT winds around the west side of the recently renamed Mount Reagan and down to Sphinx Col, then along the ridge to the junction with the Mount Jefferson Loop trail. The loop trail leads over the summit with its great views, while the AT/Gulfside passes to the east of the summit and drops steadily to Edmands Col, the low point between Jefferson and Adams. Several trails meet at Edmands Col, including the north end of the Mount Jefferson Loop. The AT continues, ascending from the col past Storm Lake (a seasonal pond) and on to a place famous for bad weather, Thunderstorm Junction, a major trail intersection marked by a gigantic cairn.

ABOVE: *One of two Lakes of the Clouds in the col between Mount Washington and Mount Monroe.* PHOTO BY JERRY MONKMAN.

From here Lowe's Path goes up Mount Adams, to the south. (Lowe's Path and the Airline Trail can be used as a loop over the summit of Adams for more great views.) The AT/Gulfside descends to Madison Spring Hut in the col between Adams and Madison. The historic hut, built in 1888, was rebuilt in the 1940s after fire destroyed the original.

If you don't want to go to the summit of Madison, take the popular Valley Way Trail 3.5 miles (6 km) from the hut to the parking lot at Appalachia. Take care to stay on the Valley Way as there are many trail junctions on the way down. The summit of Madison, 5,367 feet (1,636 m), is .5 mile (1 km) above the hut via the AT/Osgood Trail. If you go to the top, the easiest and most protected—if slightly longer—route down is to take the AT/Osgood Trail back to the Madison Spring Hut and pick up the Valley Way for the descent to Appalachia. Appalachia is on the south side of US 2, approximately 5 miles (8 km) west of Gorham and a mile east of Lowe's Country Store.

ABOVE: *The Madison Spring Hut as seen from the trail.* PHOTO BY CAMERON MARTINDALE.

OPPOSITE: *Rime ice forms in the autumn cold near the summit of Mount Adams, the summit marker behind.* PHOTO BY CAMERON MARTINDALE.

INFORMATION

WHITE MOUNTAIN NATIONAL FOREST HEADQUARTERS

71 White Mountain Drive
Campton, NH 03223
603-536-6100
www.fs.fed.us/r9/forests/white_mountain

CRAWFORD NOTCH STATE PARK

2057 US Route 302
Harts Location, NH 03812
603-374-2272
www.nhstateparks.org/explore/state-parks/
crawford-notch-state-park.aspx

Hut and Shuttle Information

APPALACHIAN MOUNTAIN CLUB HUT RESERVATIONS AND TRAILHEAD SHUTTLE SERVICE

603-466-2727
E-mail: AMClodging@outdoors.org
www.outdoors.org

Maps and Guidebooks

AMC WHITE MOUNTAIN GUIDE WITH MAPS

800-262-4455
www.outdoors.org/publications/index.cfm

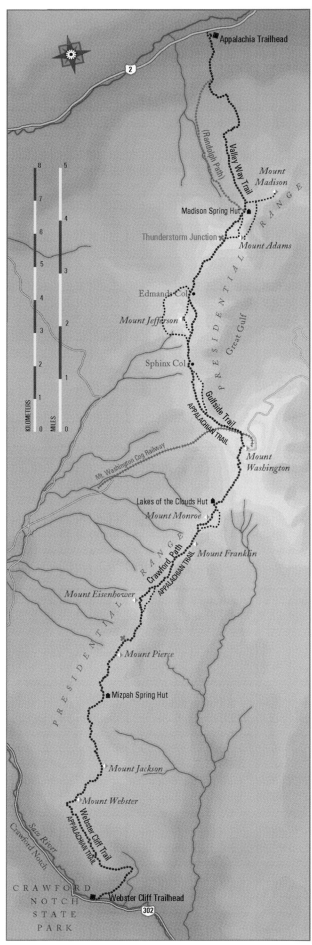

SAWTOOTH TRAVERSE
Sawtooth Wilderness
Idaho, United States

DISTANCE: 28 miles (45 km) one-way
TIME: 3–4 days
PHYSICAL CHALLENGE: 1 **2** 3 4 5
PSYCHOLOGICAL CHALLENGE: 1 **2** 3 4 5
STAGING: Stanley, Idaho

Just driving into the hamlet of Stanley, Idaho, when you get that first glimpse of the Sawtooths, can get your heart rate up. The rocky peaks rise abruptly from the edge of town, impossibly steep and impressively jagged. This is the Sawtooth Wilderness, a place so wild it was first preserved in 1937 as a primitive area, then designated official wilderness in 1972. That means these great mountains have remained absolutely untouched for most of the last century. Here's a place with more than 400 alpine lakes and 300 miles of rivers, and yet it is so off the beaten track that almost no one comes here. In the space of its 217,000-acre domain, the Sawtooth Wilderness harbors more than 50 peaks above 10,000 feet (3,050 m), an unreal concentration of big mountains by any standard.

But the way to appreciate these peaks is to get up in them, and get to know them, by doing this legendary traverse that completely crosses the range from east to west in four spectacular days. I admit it was day two on this route that made a true believer out of me. Working up 2,000 feet (610 m) of switchbacks took me from the Redfish Lake Creek valley floor to Alpine Lake, nestled in its cirque below Packrat Peak. But it was not until I climbed the final mile up to the crest of the ridge itself—well above 9,000 feet (2,743 m)—and peered over into the Baron Lakes basin that the scope of the rugged Sawtooth Range

Monte Verita Peak as seen from Baron Lakes.
PHOTO BY PETER POTTERFIELD.

Pristine campsites beneath 10,000-foot (3,050 m) peaks make backpacking in the Sawtooths something special. PHOTO BY PETER POTTERFIELD.

hit home. The imposing summits of Monte Verita, Warbonnet, and Tohobit dominated the massif rising above Baron Lakes, while Decker Peak loomed across the valley to the south, and Braxon and Horstman filled the horizon to the east.

From this ridgetop vantage, the wild beauty of the landscape offered mute if irrefutable evidence of why those mountain lovers lucky enough to know the Sawtooths speak of them with frank awe. The cluster of 10,000-foot (3,050-m) peaks in my immediate field of vision was as dramatic as any I've seen, and reason enough to do this four-day traverse. But when you realize that the Sawtooths harbor so many of these imposing peaks in such a compact area, the distinctive character of these mountains becomes apparent: this is genuine North American wilderness, rugged beyond belief, and one in which the motivated backcountry traveler can still find solitude.

Everyone who spends time hiking in the Sawtooths goes home talking about these mountains in clichéd superlatives, and having been there, I now understand why. The 35-mile-long by 20-mile-wide (57-km-long by 32-km-wide) Sawtooth Range is uniquely made geologically and visually striking. Classic uplift mountains, they were then carved by glaciers into jagged

pinnacles of mostly pink granite. The result is not only uncommon beauty but interesting topography (not to mention great rock climbing and hiking).

I had long wanted to explore the Sawtooths but quickly discovered that getting reliable information on the best places to go here was easier said than done. I wouldn't go so far as to say a veil of secrecy protects these mountains, but it's clear that those who know the range best tend to keep their secrets close. This remote, compact range of steep mountains, twisting valleys, and hidden alpine basins lends itself to exploration and discovery. The fact is, finding the most interesting corners of the Sawtooths can take persistence and time—and really good advice.

I eventually discovered perhaps the signature route through this stunning American wilderness. The Sawtooth Traverse starts at scenic Redfish Lake, more than 6,500 feet (1,981 m) high, on the eastern side of the Sawtooth Wilderness. The hike follows the Redfish Lake Creek drainage up to a high divide above Alpine Lake before dropping into the magical Baron Lakes basin below a veritable wall of jagged, rocky peaks. Several side trips, like the one to Saddleback Lakes, makes this hike the Sawtooth classic it has become. The route eventually follows Baron Creek out to the South Fork of the Payette River and to the place called Grandjean Trailhead.

Airline pilots say central Idaho is one of the darkest places in the nation to fly over at night, because so few people call it home, and that's part of the allure. This is not Yellowstone or the Grand Canyon; you won't find busloads of people here. Three hours from the small but modern airport in Boise, Stanley protects itself by being remote. This is no gentrified mountain town, certainly no Aspen. But Stanley is as friendly as it is unpretentious, funky but comfortable, small but well suited to its role as gateway to the Sawtooths.

The Sawtooths are clearly worth the trouble it takes to get here, but beware, they can be addictive. The steep valleys between the rugged peaks make for fascinating backcountry travel on more than 350 miles (563 km) of trail. The fact that the Sawtooth Wilderness has been protected so well for so long means that mind-boggling stands of old-growth timber greet you around many twists in the trail. And the peaks here form the headwaters of the great rivers that run through central Idaho: the North Fork and

OPPOSITE: *Cresting the divide between Redfish Lake Creek and the Baron Lakes basin, with the dramatic spires of Warbonnet Peak beyond.* PHOTO BY PETER POTTERFIELD.

Middle Fork of the Boise River, the South Fork of the Payette River as well as that of the legendary Salmon River. The mountains and rivers within the wilderness area itself represent the climax of the Sawtooth National Recreation Area, which in turn is just part of the huge Sawtooth National Forest.

LOGISTICS & STRATEGY

Staging for this hike is done from the hamlet of Stanley, Idaho, approximately three hours by car from the capital city of Boise and its convenient airport. From the airport, head east on Interstate 84 four miles to Highway 21, and drive north on this extremely twisting, turning expanse of highway. In winter, Highway 21 may be closed, which means you have to reach Stanley via Sun Valley over Galena Summit, a longer drive, but that's not an issue for a summer hike.

Stanley is a far cry from the well-heeled tourist cities of the Rocky Mountains. It is definitely not Jackson Hole, or Park City, or even Sun Valley, just an hour to the south over Galena Pass. Stanley is unpretentious and small but well equipped and well situated to offer hikers everything they need to venture into the Sawtooths. With overnight accommodations, restaurants, and outdoor shops, funky Stanley has it all, and scenery to boot. The rocky peaks of the range rise right from the edge of town, making a dramatic backdrop to this rustic cluster of buildings. One of the popular places to stay and dine is a few miles outside of town, the Redfish Lake Lodge, at Redfish Lake, which is also the trailhead used to start this hike.

For small hiking groups, there's no need to visit the Stanley ranger station on Highway 75 just south of town, as hiking permits can be self-issued at the trailhead. But, if you plan to leave a car at Grandjean Trailhead or Redfish Lake Trailhead, you will need to purchase a Trailhead Parking Pass in Stanley, or in any Sawtooth National Forest ranger station. That still leaves you plenty of time to explore the hamlet and its surroundings, and check out the local restaurants and services. I picked up some fuel canisters at the local outdoor store as well as a can of bear spray, since you can't fly with either of those. Most Sawtooth hikers don't bother with bear spray, but I think it's prudent when one hikes in bear country.

This classic hiking traverse begins at Redfish Lake and ends at Grandjean Trailhead, a basic route of only about 21 miles (34 km). But the whole point of this hike is that it gets you into the heart of the Sawtooth Range, and at high elevation, where world-class high-country exploration is at your doorstep. On the Sawtooth Traverse, at least one extra day should be considered the minimum, and two is better, to savor the alpine realm reached via this route.

Trailhead transportation for the hike requires two vehicles, or taking advantage of informal shuttle services in Stanley. Before the first day of your hike, spot one car at Grandjean Trailhead, located off Highway 121 (you passed the turnoff to Grandjean on your way to Stanley from Boise). From town, it's 40 miles (64 km) back west and south to the Grandjean turnoff on Highway 21, and another 7 miles (11 km) to the trailhead via the access road. Retrace your route in the other car back to Stanley. The local bakery is where everybody meets up, and that's a good place for a coffee to go and a trail lunch sandwich.

From Stanley, it's about 7 miles (11 km) by car to Redfish Lake, south of town on Highway 75. Find the backpackers' parking lot near the large Redfish Lodge, where a water taxi makes what would be a 5-mile (8-km) hike to the end of the lake into a 10-minute sightseeing run. The water taxi is the way to go, well worth the expense. The small boat drops you off at a dock at the south end of the lake, and from there it's a moderate, ascending hike up the Redfish Lake Creek drainage to good campsites about 3 miles (5 km) and few hundred feet up from the lake. I don't recommend going farther. Instead, make camp here (or at Flat Rock Junction, a few miles farther on). From your camp, head off on an excursion to Saddleback Lakes, a three-hour day trip from the valley. This area near the famous Elephant's Perch climbing area is one of the highlights of the Sawtooth Traverse. Three lakes nestle in the scenic alpine cirque, surrounded by a half dozen towering peaks, including Elephant's Perch, Decker Peak, and Redfish Point. You can easily spend an entire afternoon exploring the basin.

The next day the route ascends up the valley from your camp, past Alpine Lake, then over a 9,000-foot (2,745-m) divide into the Baron Lakes drainage, and down to the lakes where good campsites abound. Use this as your base for exploration into Braxon Lakes, Stephen Lakes, and other alpine basins nearby. Be open-minded, consider moving your camp for one night if the mood strikes, or just take long day hikes from your Baron Lakes camp. Being up here in the magical realm of the high Sawtooths is the reason to come.

On the final day, when it's time to hike out, you make a long (12-mile, 19-km) but easy hike downhill

TOP LEFT: *The trail passes massive ponderosa pines as it approaches the South Fork of the Payette River near the terminus of the traverse at Grandjean Trailhead.* PHOTO BY PETER POTTERFIELD.

BOTTOM LEFT: *The Sawtooth Wilderness lies deeply protected within the Sawtooth National Forest.* PHOTO BY PETER POTTERFIELD.

BELOW: *Mosses grow on a log at Saddleback Lakes.* PHOTO BY PETER POTTERFIELD.

OPPOSITE: *Exploring the hidden corners of the Sawtooth Range midway on the traverse brings you to places such as Braxon Lakes.* PHOTO BY PETER POTTERFIELD.

out the Baron Creek drainage to the South Fork of the Payette and then on to Grandjean Trailhead. There's not much at the place called Grandjean besides a campground and informal lodge, but the little general store here carries cold beer that tastes mighty good after four days in the backcountry. From Grandjean, it's about an hour's drive back to Stanley, where the rest of your gear is, or a two-hour drive back to Boise if you've got your stuff in the car.

This is a hike that can be easily done on one's own by any fit group of hikers, but there are good reasons to go with the venerable hiking outfitter in Stanley, Sawtooth Mountain Guides. These guys are old hands in these mountains, and they guide everything from yurt-based ski trips to high-standard rock climbs to backpacking trips. Founder Kirk Bachman accompanied me on this hike, and his presence made all the difference. I might have found this route on my own, but I never would have found all the secret, beautiful places Kirk showed me on our four days in the Sawtooths. Nor would I have had the history and background on the area that only years of experience can bring. Sawtooth Mountain Guides can also make your trip easier and quicker by simplifying trailhead transportation and food.

HAZARDS

For such a glorious route, there are relatively few dangers to this hike other than the usual Rocky Mountain considerations of wildlife (bear, snakes, etc., even wolverine on this hike), and the usual dangers of high-altitude weather prone to sudden changes, with the ensuing potential for lethal hypothermia. Local hikers tell me the bears here in the Sawtooths are not habituated to people and tend to keep their distance, but you never know, so take precautions. You can get snowed on any month of the year here, especially up high, but Sawtooth weather actually tends to be better than most mountain environments of similar elevation. Even here in the pristine Sawtooths, it's necessary to treat or filter your water.

SEASON

The Sawtooths are high and alpine, so the hiking season is dependent on the previous winter's snowfall. Most years this route can be done from June 15 to the end of September. Hikers who go early in the season should be adept at using an ice ax for the high divide above Alpine Lake. In mid-season, beware of sudden thunderstorms.

ROUTE

Most hikers stay in town, as I did. I met my partner at the local bakery so we could caravan in both cars over Banner Pass to Grandjean Trailhead, leaving one there on the west side of the Sawtooths near the South Fork of the Payette River off Highway 21, approximately one hour (47 miles, 76 km) west and south of Stanley. Return to town, then drive south on Highway 75 for approximately 7 miles (11 km) to the turnoff for Redfish Lake; continue 2 miles (3 km) to the backpackers' parking lot at the north end of the big lake, one of several large lakes in the Sawtooths created by big blocking moraines. The Redfish Lake Lodge operates a water taxi that speeds you up the 5-mile-long (8-km-long) lake, saving a two-hour hike and giving you a scenic perspective from the lake surface up the big valley ahead.

The fast boat ride up the lake makes short work of the first 5 miles (8 km) of trail, and it's fun to boot, so it's definitely the way to go. The boat drops you at the upper (south) end of the lake at a small dock. From the dock, hike southeast on the Redfish Lake Creek Trail #101. Approximately 3 miles (4.8 km) from the dock, look for appealing campsites near the creek, or continue on to Flat Rock Junction at 4 miles (6.4 km). Make camp somewhere in this vicinity, or just drop your packs and look for the cross-country route up to Saddleback Lakes (sometimes called Shangri La or, by climbers, the Elephant's Perch).

The route up to Saddleback Lakes is well used by now and easier to find than it used to be, but it's still steep and rough and slightly occult. Find it this way: about 2.5 miles (4 km) from Redfish Lake, the Redfish Lake Creek Trail crosses a stream coming down from Braxon Peak. Look for a trail leading south, cross the creek and look for the way trail leading uphill toward the spectacular cirque.

The 1.5-hour hike up to Saddleback Lakes is well worth the time. A visit to this stunning series of high-country tarns and lakes nestled below the imposing walls of the Elephant's Perch, one of the premier backcountry climbing walls in the Sawtooths, is a reason to come here. This side trip reflects the classic Sawtooth style of hiking: traveling through the range, but taking time to explore the extraordinary features off the beaten track.

The next morning, continue to Flat Rock Junction at 4 miles (6.4 km) from Redfish Lake, and turn uphill where Trail 101 leaves Redfish Lake Creek and works steeply upward toward Alpine Lake, approximately 2.5 miles (4 km) and 1,800 feet (550 m) above the junction, about two hours' hiking. Another mile (2 km) and another 800 feet (245 m) takes you up and over Baron Divide, where you descend the steep switchbacks down to Baron Lakes in approximately 4 miles (7 km) from Alpine Lake. Good campsites abound in this area, including some on rock slabs and some in open meadows below the dramatic bulk of 10,000-foot-high (3,050-m-high) Monte Verita Ridge.

From base camp at Baron Lakes, use the next day (or two) to explore the surrounding high country. One nearby alpine basin not to miss is Braxon Lakes. This pair of alpine lakes is reached by hiking the Baron Creek Trail downhill for about a mile, then cutting right, eastward, cross-country, across a shoulder on a moderate bushwhack and down into the Braxon Basin, approximately 1.5 hours from camp. The lakes here have outstanding fly fishing, and make a perfect daylong outing from Baron Lakes. If you have another day, consider hiking due north over a pass and drop into Stephens Lake and the Fishhook Creek drainage. Other alpine

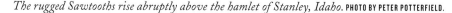

The rugged Sawtooths rise abruptly above the hamlet of Stanley, Idaho. PHOTO BY PETER POTTERFIELD.

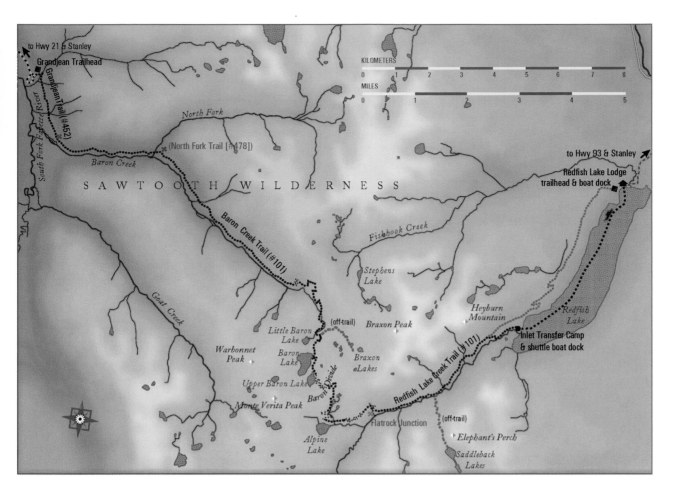

basins and ridge walks lie within reasonable reach of your Baron Lakes camp.

When it's time to hike out to Grandjean, follow the Baron Creek Trail (still #101) down beside roaring Baron Creek Falls and then an honest 12 miles (19 km) all the way down the valley toward the South Fork of the Payette River and on to Grandjean. You'll reach the intersection of the North Fork Trail (#478) leading off to the right, north, in about 8 miles (13 km) from Baron Lakes. Stay on the Baron Creek Trail and continue west. Just before the river, approximately 10 miles (16 km) from the lake, Baron Creek Trail intersects with Trail #452. Turn right here for the final 2 miles (3 km) to Grandjean on some hot stretches of trail and unwelcome elevation gain. It's a long walk for the final day, but easy, as the route is mostly downhill, losing more than 3,000 feet (915 m) before it reaches Grandjean Trailhead at 5,200 feet (1,585 m) in about five hours.

From the trailhead, drive 7 miles (11 km) back out to Highway 21, and turn right for the 40 miles (64 km) back to Stanley.

INFORMATION

All wilderness users must have a permit for wilderness use. Self-issued wilderness permits are available at trailheads for groups under eight members total.

SAWTOOTH NATIONAL FOREST
2647 Kimberly Road East
Twin Falls, ID 83301
208-737-3200 or 800-877-8339
www.fs.usda.gov/sawtooth

For current trail conditions and other local information:
STANLEY RANGER STATION
HC 64, Box 9900
Stanley, ID 83278
208-774-3000

Guide Services

SAWTOOTH MOUNTAIN GUIDES
P.O. Box 18
Stanley, ID 83278
208-774-3324
http://sawtoothguides.com

Planning a Trip

The state of Idaho's travel Web site provides information to help plan a trip to Idaho:
www.visitidaho.org

CHILKOOT TRAIL
Klondike Gold Rush National Historic Park, Chilkoot Trail National Historic Site

Alaska, United States; British Columbia and Yukon Territory, Canada

DISTANCE: 33 miles (53 km) one-way
TIME: 4–6 days
PHYSICAL CHALLENGE: 1 2 3 4 5
PSYCHOLOGICAL CHALLENGE: 1 2 3 4 5
STAGING: Whitehorse, Yukon

The very place names on this storied route—the Golden Stairs, the Scales, Happy Camp, the Stone Crib—are redolent of the suffering and hard effort on the part of 1898 gold miners. These hardy souls trudged up into the wild Coast Range with their ungodly loads and visions of wealth to be scraped from the Yukon gold fields. There's no mistaking the history here: both sides of the trail are littered with rusting relics, equipment the miners jettisoned out of exhaustion. Even today, the sad jetsam of their backbreaking burdens remains, strewn along the way, giving the trail an authentic aroma of human struggle.

Who would have thought that more than a century later the backcountry journey those miners blazed, driven by lust for riches, would become one of the iconic wilderness routes in North America? Interesting terrain and big scenery come in equal measures here on the Chilkoot. Temperate old-growth coastal rain forest, steep, rocky passes, and an exhilarating 20-mile (32-km) ramble through alpine basins, high plateaus, and the boreal forest set the trail apart from other backcountry routes. But in the same way the Anasazi ruins of southern Utah add a unique element to Southwest hikes, the detritus left behind by those tough miners adds an irresistible Gold Rush component to the Chilkoot Pass hiking experience.

It's a reason to come, but there are many others. This 33-mile (53-km) adventure is unique, traversing a corner of North America where the Yukon, British Columbia, and Southeast Alaska come together in an odd, complicated convergence of borders. The geography makes doing the Chilkoot not just a hike, but a multifaceted travel experience with frankly unreal variety, featuring the wild west coast of Southeast Alaska, the remote interior of British Columbia, and lively Whitehorse, Yukon, as the starting point. Exotica such as antique railway lines and travel by floatplane further colors the experience.

All the moving parts can complicate logistics. A hike that covers two countries, one province, one state, one territory and two national parks can present some serious trailhead transportation issues. The Chilkoot Trail demands some advance planning and attention to detail, but the hike is worth the trouble.

And while the route is closely linked to the miners who followed it for a few years at the turn of the previous century, those treasure-seekers were not the first to use this great trail. One of the few glacier-free corridors through the intimidating Coast Range of British Columbia, the Yukon, and Alaska, the Chilkoot Pass had for centuries been a crucial trade route for the Native peoples of the coast, notably the Tlingit, on their way to the interior.

This irrefutable fact of geography is why the Chilkoot remains one of the most compelling recreational backcountry routes in North America: it's a natural. The route rises quickly from tidewater to crest Chilkoot Pass at 3,300 feet (1,006 m), but instead of dropping back down, it meanders more than 20 miles (32 km) through an alpine wonderland while losing only a thousand feet to its terminus at Bennett Lake. Those final three days reveal an unforgettable stretch of trail. An abundance of North American wildlife, including moose, wolf, coyote, and grizzly bear, make this a quintessential wilderness walk.

The American frontier is exotic to visitors from abroad, and the international border here adds yet another twist to hiking the Chilkoot. There's no official mid-route border station, but you will need your passport. Travel documents are checked in Skagway, as the trail is managed jointly by the US Park Service and Parks Canada. Coupled with the large contingent

OPPOSITE: *Hikers climbing toward Sheep Camp get their first view of the Coast Range glaciers.* PHOTO BY PETER POTTERFIELD.

of international hikers who are drawn to this North American classic—Japanese, Australians, Kiwis, Scandinavians, and Germans, to name a few nationalities represented during my own journey here—the border gives the route a polyglot atmosphere, not unlike the Inca Trail or even the Everest Trek.

LOGISTICS & STRATEGY

Because the Chilkoot Trail starts in Skagway, Alaska, and ends at Bennett (on Lake Bennett), British Columbia, getting to the start and the finish can be a puzzle. While the trail can be hiked in either direction, almost everyone chooses the west-to-east option, from Skagway to Bennett, and for good reason. Leaving from Skagway is the route the miners followed, and it puts the steepest part of the trail, the Golden Stairs, on the uphill side. That may require better aerobic fitness for grinding up the slope, but for most that's preferable to torturing your knees coming down this extraordinarily steep section. And since the weather on the Chilkoot can be seriously bad, by starting at the coast and working inland, most of the wind and rain rolling in off the Pacific will be at your back.

Ironically, this hike is best staged at neither the beginning nor the end, but elsewhere: Whitehorse, Yukon. Even though it's in a different province from the terminus of the trail, and in a different country from the start of the trail, Yukon's biggest city is stra-

The detritus left more than a century ago by miners headed to the Yukon gold fields still remains even here, east of the Chilkoot Pass on the Canadian side. PHOTO BY STEFAN WACKERHAGEN.

tegically situated between both, and holds plenty of transportation and trailhead options. Whitehorse is so conveniently located for all sorts of adventure up here in the far north, there are even direct flights from Europe. But most travelers will arrive here from Vancouver, British Columbia.

Whitehorse is the de facto capital of this unique part of North America, the only sizable town where the Yukon, British Columbia, and Southeast Alaska are joined. Vast expanses of wild country, and a sparse human population, give this region an authentic out-there feel. Situated astride the Alaska-Canada Highway, Whitehorse offers an oasis of civilization, and the best staging area not just for the Chilkoot Pass hike but for other adventures in the Yukon, such as a canoe trip down the Yukon River, a trek into the Tombstone Range, or a climbing trip into the Cirque of the Unclimbables.

The hiker has multiple options for reaching the start of the Chilkoot Trail in Skagway, Alaska, from Whitehorse: you can drive, fly, or take the historic White Pass & Yukon Railway. The latter option is recommended, as it gives one an opportunity to sample even more of the Gold Rush history. The miners who trudged so gamely over Chilkoot Pass to reach the gold fields did so for only two years. When the White Pass & Yukon Railway was completed in 1901 (over a pass just south of the Chilkoot) it made the arduous hike over the Chilkoot a moot point: miners could now simply take the train to the gold fields. These days, the historic railway is an excursion for tourists: the tracks climb up to the 3,300-foot (1,000-m) summit of White Pass before dropping down to sea level on the Inside Passage at Skagway in just 20 miles (32 km).

The cruise industry has changed this remote corner of North America into a busy summer tourist area. When I boarded the restored rail cars of the White Pass Railway in Fraser, British Columbia, outside of Whitehorse, I did so with busloads of tourists returning to their cruise ships in Skagway. The one-way trip requires just three hours to go up and over the pass and down to Skagway on the Inside Passage. Glimpses of the water from Inspiration Point announce one's imminent arrival in town, where Chilkoot hikers disembark at the railway station near the harbor.

Skagway is a favorite stop with cruise ships doing the standard summer run between Seattle and Alaska. With its restored Gold Rush façade (replete with saloon can-can girls bawdily calling from the

balconies), the place has the feel of theater or an amusement park, but it's all about having fun. For a few hours, the streets are jammed with cruise-ship passengers enjoying the brief time they have in town. The presence of five or six huge vessels idling at the piers is a slightly jarring juxtaposition—the hulking ships loom above, dwarfing the town. But the mighty whistles soon sound, calling the passengers back, the big ships leave, and the place reverts to the funky Southeast Alaska town it has always been.

Once in Skagway, you've got time to head over to the National Park Service Trail Center, near Broadway and Second Avenue. This ranger station represents Klondike Gold Rush National Historic Park on the US side, and Chilkoot Trail National Historic Site on the Canadian side. This is where you'll show your passport and pick up your previously arranged hiking permit. Hiking permits and camping permits are required during the summer season, and it is strongly advised that you reserve your hiking permits by phone or fax before arrival. Otherwise, you are taking a chance on getting one of the handful of hiking permits handed out daily on a first come, first served basis. Expect to pay a hefty fee for hiking permits and camping permits for this multinational route.

The Trail Center in Skagway is where you get the latest information on current Chilkoot conditions. When I last did the Chilkoot in 2007, the rangers informed my party that a dangerous bear had been harassing hikers on the British Columbia side of the hike, and advised us to hook up with other hikers to make a larger group size. The ranger also noted that high water from recent heavy rain and snowmelt had submerged several bridges on the Alaska side of the pass, so we should be prepared to wade. Thus, reality was underscored: despite the fact we'd be hiking in national parks the whole way, the usual wilderness hazards of wild animals and dangerous weather remain a big part of the equation.

Numerous hotels and restaurants in Skagway make the standard approach the wise one: overnight in Skagway, live well, then make an alpine start for the trailhead early the next morning. The other option is to pick up your permits the afternoon you arrive and immediately head for the Chilkoot Trailhead, 15 miles (24 km) from town, and spend the night near the trailhead (there are lodges here, as well as Dyea Campground), or hike a few miles down the trail to Finnegan's Point Camp (4.3 miles, 7 km). Several trailhead shuttle services operate regularly from downtown Skagway to the Chilkoot Trailhead.

Hikers cross the Taiya River on a suspension bridge on day one of the Chilkoot Pass Trail. PHOTO BY PETER POTTERFIELD.

Most hikers will take five days to complete the route, but it can easily be done in four days by a fit party, and is arguably more enjoyable in six days. The longer itinerary gives you a day or two to loiter on the British Columbia side of Chilkoot Pass, which is extraordinarily beautiful country and not a place to hurry through.

The standard trip is to leave Skagway in the morning via the 20-minute shuttle drive to the trailhead in Dyea, and hike for four hours and camp at Canyon City the first night. Then, hike to Sheep Camp (the last camp before Chilkoot Pass) in another four hours on the second day. Then, hike up and over the pass to Happy Camp (the first camp north of the pass) in a tough six hours the third day. And, finally, hike to Lindeman City Camp or Bare Loon Lake Camp the fourth and final night. I was pressed for time and shaved a day off the usual route by hiking the first day all the way to Sheep Camp, easily reached by mid-afternoon.

The end of the trail is Bennett, on the shore of Lake Bennett, which has no services, only a train station (with a dining room for rail passengers only), and the remnants of an old miners' village, highlighted by an extraordinary hundred-year-old wooden church. The question from Bennett is, how to get back to White-horse? Most hikers opt to take the train back to Fraser, BC, and on by bus to Whitehorse. For those hikers who staged in Skagway, simply take the train in the opposite direction back to Skagway.

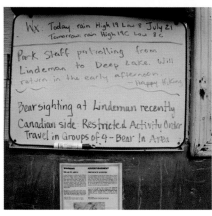

TOP: *A float plane from Alpine Aviation in Whitehorse, Yukon, lands in Bennett Lake to pick up hikers completing the Chilkoot Pass Trail between Skagway and Bennett.* PHOTO BY PETER POTTERFIELD.

BOTTOM LEFT: *Some camps along the Chilkoot Trail require that backpackers camp on platforms, such as this one at Sheep Camp, to avoid impacts on the alpine environment.* PHOTO BY PETER POTTERFIELD.

BOTTOM RIGHT: *The message board at the Lindeman City warden's cabin warns hikers to be aware of an aggressive grizzly bear roaming the area.* PHOTO BY PETER POTTERFIELD.

My party opted to return to Whitehorse in a float plane from a Whitehorse charter operator, Alpine Aviation. The bright red aircraft appeared right on time and landed on the lakeshore in Bennett, right by the train station, to fetch us, which made us the envy of all the other hikers, who were stuck there waiting for the train. Not only were we back in Whitehorse in time for a beer on the deck that afternoon, we got an astounding 25-minute sightseeing flight into the bargain.

Any competent hiking party can do the Chilkoot route entirely on its own, as most do. Many hikers, however, will choose to work with one of the approved guide services in Whitehorse or Skagway to simplify logistics. The better guide services can arrange permits, rail tickets, and trailhead transportation, a float plane for the return trip from Lake Bennett, and even provide a guide/cook to accompany you on your Chilkoot adventure. Working with a guide service

can add to the expense, but can make your hike easier and more enjoyable, especially for those arriving from some distance. I chose to use Nature Tours of the Yukon, which handled everything from permits to food to trailhead transport, a strategy that saved me time and hassle.

HAZARDS

Grizzly bears and black bears are found in abundance along this route. My party saw both, so it is imperative to be educated on how to travel safely in bear country, check with rangers about bear activity, and carry bear spray for protection. Abundant wildlife of other species presents more of an added allure than a danger, but hikers should keep a respectful distance from any of the wilderness denizens. Weather is the second serious threat to hiker safety on this route, which is extremely exposed to storm systems coming off the Gulf of Alaska. Hypothermia is a real danger on this route. Snow and persistent rain make the use of quality outerwear and camping gear essential, as there is no way to bail out off this route—you either have to go back, or finish it. Finally, the growing popularity of the Chilkoot means that it is necessary to treat or filter all your water.

SEASON

Because it rises to more than 3,000 feet (914 m), the Chilkoot is most definitely an alpine route, and that limits its season to summer months. June through mid-September is optimal most seasons, but a heavy snow year can cut that short at either end. May through October may be possible some seasons, weather permitting. Off-season travelers should be adept at using an ice ax to travel safely over Chilkoot Pass.

ROUTE

The 33-mile (53-km) Chilkoot Trail begins near the Taiya River in Alaska and ends at Bennett, British Columbia. There is no midway bailout point or significant trail variation available.

From Skagway, Alaska, the trailhead shuttle vans follow the shore of Taiya Inlet toward Dyea townsite, what's left of a bustling Gold Rush village that once rivaled Skagway for supremacy. The Chilkoot Trailhead itself, virtually at sea level, is marked by a simple wooden sign, almost ramshackle, but there's a certain gravity to it, even for modern hikers, given the epic struggle of those who plied this route so long ago. The good trail starts out along the Taiya River through a classic Alaskan old-growth temperate rain forest.

Less than 2 miles (3 km) down the trail hikers reach a low, often swampy area, where the river sometimes comes up over a low, boardwalked section of trail built to keep hikers out of the mud. But the way soon climbs higher on the bank on a dry trail before reaching Finnegan's Point Camp a little over 4 miles (6.4 km) from the trailhead. This is a camp frequently used by hikers who get a late start on the trail. Most hikers camp farther along the river trail at Canyon City Camp (7.8 miles, 13 km from the trailhead) for the first night. As the camp names suggest, this was a busy place at the turn of the last century, and artifacts of all descriptions can be seen rusting away along the river trail. A couple of hundred yards beyond Canyon City Camp is a spur trail to the old townsite.

From Canyon City the trail continues along the river with minor ups and downs until it reaches Pleasant Camp at 10.4 miles (17 km) and begins a steep, 2-mile (3-km), 1,000-foot (300-m) ascent that offers the first open views of the snow-capped Coast Range. The way levels out before reaching Sheep Camp at 12 miles (20 km) from the trailhead. This is a busy camp, as everyone stays here because it's as close as you can legally camp to Chilkoot Pass. Park rangers hold evening programs here that include safety discussions, bear activity reports, and even sing-alongs. A small cabin provides a cooking shelter in bad weather.

The following day, up to Chilkoot Pass, is definitely the crux of the route. Get an alpine start, if only to be ahead of other hikers, and follow the trail as it leaves the river and heads up toward the steepest part of the hike. When I was here in 2007, a bridge across a tributary of the Taiya had a torrent of water running *over* it. From camp, a series of switchbacks starts up the slope, the beginning of a 3,000-foot (900-m) elevation day. The trail crosses a number of small streams. At 4 miles (7 km) from Sheep Camp, the rocky ledge known as the Scales is reached. This was the place where nineteenth-century miners had to demonstrate to the Royal Canadian Mounted Police that they carried sufficient provisions and gear to enter the Klondike. Soon the trail fades as the route climbs onto rock and scree slopes

and crosses the occasional snowfield to the beginning of the infamous Golden Stairs. Here the route is marked by 6-foot-high orange pylons, which seem like overkill on a sunny day, but in the whiteout I climbed up in were welcome trail markers. In early season, the Golden Stairs section of trail is a long, undulating snow slope, icy in places, right up to the top of the pass.

After several false passes, the pylons lead up a final slope up to the crest of 3,300-foot (1,000-m) Chilkoot Pass, 5.5 miles (9 km) from Sheep Camp. A Canadian warden station lies just across the pass, where the trail markers change from the US pylons to the Canadian circles on metal poles. This is a glorious place in good weather, but I had the bad luck to climb it in a whiteout with freezing rain. The small warden's station, empty when I was there, is always open for use as a warming hut. Welcome to Canada.

The next 4 miles (7 km) to Happy Camp is really the scenic highlight of the trip, aggressively alpine at more than 3,000 feet (900 m) of elevation. The route traverses complicated basins and contours around lakes where actual icebergs bob about. We saw a large grizzly bear working up the hillsides across a creek, but it ignored our presence. The trail here meanders through authentic wilderness. Even the low cloud and murk I hiked through didn't detract from this hard beauty. The trail on this side remains high, with only minor ups and downs, and we arrived at the

TOP: *A pair of backpackers ascends the Golden Stairs in extreme conditions: a full-on whiteout with light snow and freezing rain.*
PHOTO BY STEFAN WACKERHAGEN.

BOTTOM: *The author negotiates high water above Sheep Camp.*
PHOTO BY STEFAN WACKERHAGEN.

Camp, and meanders mostly level through astounding back-country. Keep your eyes peeled here, as always there are reminders of its Gold Rush past in the form of artifacts and puzzling pieces of old equipment strewn about.

There are three possible camps east of Happy Camp: Deep Lake, Lindeman City, and Bare Loon Lake Camp, 3 miles (5 km), 6 miles (10 km), and 9 miles (15 km) respectively from Happy Camp. Lindeman City makes the most sense, as it is almost exactly halfway to Lake Bennett, the end of the trail, and marks the site of a once sizable settlement of miners. Here hikers will find a quiet camp stretched along the shore of expansive Lindeman Lake, by far the biggest on the route so far. The "city" of course is long gone; only a warden's station and small historical exhibit remain.

The final day on the Chilkoot drops down from the alpine zone and into the boreal forest once again, following sandy trails past Bare Loon Lake, the final camp, and definitely one to consider if you have an extra night. Bare Loon Lake is only 3 miles (5 km) from Lindeman City Camp, but makes a good base for exploration. The way follows ever wider sandy trails, with views opening up to expansive Bennett Lake, before reaching the terminus of the Chilkoot Trail at Bennett itself, 7 miles (11 km) from Lindeman City and 33 miles (53 km) from the trailhead.

What was once the significant community of Bennett has dwindled to one amazing hundred-year-old church and a recently restored train station used by the White Pass & Yukon line.

INFORMATION

A hike on the Chilkoot Trail requires advance planning. For current information on permits and trail condition, contact either Parks Canada or the US Park Service, which manage the trail jointly.

PARKS CANADA—YUKON
Suite 205
300 Main Street
Whitehorse, YT Y1A 2B5
867-667-3910 or 800-661-0486
E-mail: whitehorse.info@pc.gc.ca
www.pc.gc.ca/lhn-nhs/yt/chilkoot/index.aspx

KLONDIKE GOLD RUSH NATIONAL HISTORIC PARK
P.O. Box 517
Skagway, AK 99840
907-983-2921
www.nps.gov/klgo/planyourvisit/chilkoottrail.htm

TOP: *Backpackers on the long alpine section of trail east of Chilkoot Pass in typical Coast Range conditions.* PHOTO BY PETER POTTERFIELD.

BOTTOM: *Filling water bottles from a side stream along the Taiya River on the Chilkoot Pass Trail.* PHOTO BY PETER POTTERFIELD.

appropriately named Happy Camp, 8 miles (13 km) from Sheep Camp and still above 3,000 feet (900 m), by two o'clock. Your early start pays off here: Happy Camp is usually empty, allowing the best choice of campsites, until other hikers trickle in later in the afternoon. The tent sites here are on wooden platforms, so bring short lengths of cord to use in place of tent stakes. A large, comfortable hut makes cooking pleasant even in bad weather. By evening, the hut is a scene, full of hikers from all over the world.

The character of the Chilkoot route changes abruptly: it climbs steeply from sea level at Skagway to the pass, but from there descends only slightly over three days to 2,000 feet (600 m) at Lake Bennett. That makes the next day on the trail, between Happy Camp and Lindeman City, yet another long meander through fascinating alpine highlands, dotted with lakes and cut through by deep gorges. The way is easy, on pretty good trails, if muddy in places, as the route passes above Long Lake, drops down to Deep Lake

Shuttle Services

Currently, the park service lists these shuttle operators in Skagway:

DYEA DAVE
907-209-5031 or 907-983-2731

FRONTIER EXCURSIONS
907-983-2512 or 877-983-2512

KLONDIKE TOURS & TAXIS
907-983-2400

Guide Services

NATURE TOURS OF YUKON
P.O. Box 31187
Whitehorse, YT, Y1A 5P7
867-667-4868
E-mail: joost@naturetoursyukon.com
www.naturetoursyukon.com

PACKER EXPEDITIONS, LTD
P.O. Box 601
Skagway, AK 99840
907-983-3005
E-mail: guide.manager@packerexpeditions.com
www.packerexpeditions.com/alaska-tours

Check the Klondike Gold Rush National Historic Park Web site for an up-to-date list of approved shuttle providers and guide services.

Floatplane Transport Between Lake Bennett and Whitehorse

ALPINE AVIATION
P.O. Box 6
Whitehorse, YT Y1A 2B0
867-668-7725 or 867-393-1482
Email: alpineaviation@gmail.com
www.alpineaviationyukon.com

Planning a Trip

Travel Yukon can help hikers plan their visit:
www.travelyukon.com

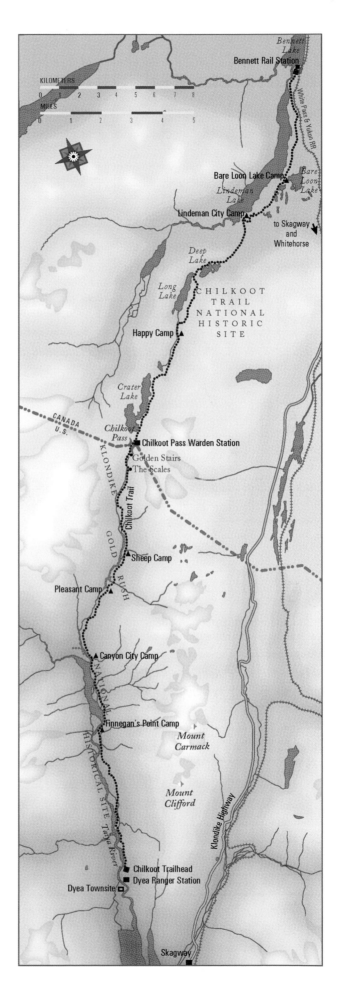

MOUNT RUSHMORE– HARNEY PEAK LOOP
Black Hills
Black Elk Wilderness
South Dakota, United States

DISTANCE: **25 miles (40 km) loop**
TIME: **3–4 days**
PHYSICAL CHALLENGE: **1 2 3 4 5**
PSYCHOLOGICAL CHALLENGE: **1 2 3 4 5**
STAGING: **Rapid City, South Dakota**

In decades of hiking I can't remember a more surreal experience than that first day in the Black Elk Wilderness. Trudging up the Centennial Trail through the craggy rock outcrops and ponderosa pines in blissful tranquility, I suddenly caught sight of the unmistakable visage of George Washington gazing imperturbably down at me over the treetops. Abe Lincoln peered quietly over his shoulder. The pair of gigantic heads, rendered in white granite with remarkable detail, loomed above me plain as day, no binoculars needed. Perched right on the boundary of the wilderness area, the Mount Rushmore National Memorial and its sculpted façades adds a unique element to this backcountry journey through the much wilder Black Elk.

"We *will* see faces," my local partners had promised, despite my skepticism, and they proved themselves correct. But the contrast was striking nonetheless: here we were on a three-day wilderness journey during which we would encounter maybe three backpackers in 25 miles (40 km) of trail. But just over there, maybe 2 trail miles away, we knew 10,000 tourists milled around the monument's viewpoints, their cars and idling tour buses filling the parking lots.

A spur trail here offers convenient access and better views, if you're so inclined, of the famous patriotic

Mount Rushmore and its famous faces lie just 2 miles outside the Black Elk Wilderness, and can be clearly seen from the Centennial Trail without venturing onto the grounds of the busy national memorial. PHOTO BY PETER POTTERFIELD.

Custer State Park adjoins the Black Elk Wilderness and harbors one of the largest herds of free-roaming bison in the Lower 48.
PHOTO BY PETER POTTERFIELD.

monolith and its four presidents (Thomas Jefferson and Teddy Roosevelt were hidden, far back in their niche, from our perspective). Or you can do as I did, and remain in the bosom of the wilderness area to preserve a wilder experience. This amazing route takes in not only Mount Rushmore, close up or at some remove, just as you wish, but Harney Peak as well, at 7,242 feet (2,200 m) one of the highest peaks in the United States east of the Rocky Mountains. From its summit tower you can see parts of four states: South Dakota, Montana, Wyoming, and Nebraska.

But more than their geographic high points, these Black Hills carry a certain mystical vibe. "Hills" is in fact a bit of a misnomer for a sprawling mountain range that stretches more than a hundred miles, from Wyoming deep into South Dakota. Its signature, otherworldly rock spires give it aptly named provinces, such as the Needles or Cathedral Spires. And this, don't forget, is the Paha Sapa, the sacred ground of the Sioux or Lakota people. This was the center of the universe, the place where renowned Sioux leaders Red Cloud and Sitting Bull sought vision and direction. The wilderness itself is named after Black Elk, the famous Oglala Sioux holy man and chief. For him, the summit of Harney Peak was very big medicine indeed, the very place of his life-changing spiritual visions.

It wasn't until 1980 that the Black Elk Wilderness finally was set aside. Now this 13,600-acre wilderness area nestled in the embrace of the surrounding 35,000-acre Norbeck Wildlife Preserve, both flanked by sprawling Custer State Park, makes a fabulous place for backpacking. More than 50 miles (80 km) of trails snake through the area, with so many options that you can touch all the highlights here without passing through the high-traffic areas of Mount Rushmore and Sylvan Lake—although you should take the time to see both. My suggestion is to come quickly. A devastating pine beetle infestation is eroding the famed blackness of the Black Hills with patches of brown, threatening this delicate ecosystem.

After exploring the Black Hills over the course of decades, I eventually settled on a favorite route. This elaborate loop connects multiple trails to create a custom journey that ends where it starts, at Iron Creek Trailhead. From there, the Centennial Trail travels north to Horsethief Lake Trail, and south to the Grizzly Bear Creek Trail, eventually returning to the car on the Norbeck Trail in a truly amazing 25-mile (40-km) circuit that includes views of Rushmore and the top of Harney Peak. One could link any of a dozen trails here to create a custom trip for the time and mileage you wish. But none can rival this unique route for hitting all the highlights in just three easy days.

LOGISTICS & STRATEGY

Rapid City is the logical staging point for any hike in the Black Hills. Good connections through an easy airport make getting into the city convenient, where food, lodging, good coffee shops, and big outdoor stores make backcountry trip preparations quick and civilized. Beware that while South Dakota is a huge outdoor adventure state, we're not talking about hiking and backpacking. You'll be in a small minority when compared to the pheasant hunters, big game hunters, and fishermen who drive the outdoor industry in the state.

"Rapid," as the locals call it (Pierre, South Dakota's capital, is called "Peer"), is close enough to the Black Hills that you can do the hike directly from town. But my advice is to spend at least a day or two exploring the Black Hills at close range to get your bearings, and take in the scope and scenery of the remarkable landscape. Custer State Park is ground zero for both wildlife and scenic beauty in the vicinity of the Black Elk Wilderness, encompassing both the ineffably beautiful Sylvan Lake and some of the largest bison herds in the United States.

I chose to base for one night at the Custer State Game Lodge, one of several state-owned lodges in the park that cater to tourists, with an emphasis on hunters. For bison aficionados, the fall roundup is the time to be here, but you can see the bison at any time of year. The lodge is just minutes from most of the highlights in the park, and has a big restaurant that makes it an excellent overnight base before beginning the Black Elk Wilderness excursion described here. But note, too, that dozens of accommodations and restaurants can be found just a little farther away in the towns of Custer, Hill City, and Keystone, located around the perimeter of the wilderness.

The loop recommended here covers its 25 miles (40 km) in three pretty equal days of 7 or 8 miles (11–13 km) each, including the summit run up Harney Peak, but a bit more with exploration and side trips from each camp. Begin off Highway 87 about 7 miles (11 km) east of Sylvan Lake at the Iron Creek Horse Camp and Trailhead. Follow the Centennial Trail, with stunning, open views of the surrounding mountains, as it meanders north right up to the boundary with the Mount Rushmore National Memorial. Take the 2-mile (3-km) spur trail in and out of the memorial if you want an up-close view of the presidents. The main loop route continues on the Centennial Trail farther north to the Horsethief Lake Trail, and turns hard left there to the first camp in the high-country pine forest a mile or two (2–3 km) from the intersection.

Day two follows the Horsethief Lake Trail to the Grizzly Bear Creek Trail and up to its intersection with Harney Peak Trail. The latter is a major backcountry highway, carrying significant day hiker traffic from beautiful Sylvan Lake up to the tower at Harney Peak, where everyone wants to go. You'll be on that trail for a few miles when you make your side trip to the summit, but site your camp beyond (west), where the Grizzly Bear Creek Trail intersects with the Harney Peak Trail to preserve your solitude. My party encountered no one at either of our camps on a 2010 trip in the Black Elk.

After pitching camp, follow the Harney Peak Trail for an hour to the summit, standing way above everything else at more than 7,200 feet (2,000 m). The stone watchtower was built in 1940 as a fire lookout, and today offers an outstanding panorama of the Black Hills. Take some time on the outcrops nearby to seek out some solitude, to savor the power of the place, to gain some insight into why this mountaintop held such power for Native Americans who lived here. This moment is a reason to come here.

Day three surprises with some of the most scenic trails on the entire loop, and some of the most meaningful venues to Native peoples. From camp, follow the Norbeck Trail as it descends steeply into

---

The complicated trail intersection where the Grizzly Bear Creek Trail joins up with the Norbeck, Cathedral Spires, Sylvan Lake, and Harney Peak trails in the space of a few hundred yards.
PHOTO BY PETER POTTERFIELD.

A backpackers' camp above Horsethief Lake Trail in the dense lodgepole and ponderosa pine forest of the Black Elk Wilderness.
PHOTO BY PETER POTTERFIELD.

Dawn light illuminates Harney Peak (right), standing aloof from the other rocky spires and pinnacles that characterize the Black Hills of the Black Elk Wilderness. **PHOTO BY PETER POTTERFIELD.**

a pretty valley bottom, where it is purported the Sioux held vision quest ceremonies in the meadows. The route follows the creek past the Upper Iron Creek Trailhead (a bail-out point to the highway if that is desired) before finishing up the loop back to your car. If you have an extra day, spend it at the high camp and use the time for exploration, or a side trip to Sylvan Lake.

Note that the Black Hills are often described by hikers as wet, but my party found hot and dry conditions, even in the spring season. We actually had trouble finding water on some sections of the trip, although we often walked by good flows at midday. It was an exceptionally dry year, and we ended up pumping water out of shallow pools near our camps. One critical pool was near the intersection of the Centennial Trail and Horsethief Lake Trail, and another near the intersection of the Grizzly Bear Creek Trail and the Harney Peak Trail.

If conditions are dry when you go, take note and tank up on water where you find it. There will be plenty. You may end up carrying more water than you want to, but that's preferable to pumping from marginal sources. Our party found the best flows in Grizzly Bear Creek and the big creek along the Norbeck Trail. A small spring had pumpable pools near the intersection of Grizzly Bear Creek Trail and the Cathedral Spires Trail, the site of our second camp.

If you have two vehicles and wish to incorporate Sylvan Lake into your hiking itinerary, leave one car there. After your ascent of Harney Peak, spend a final night at your high camp and hike out to Sylvan Lake the following day. Whatever you do, don't miss striking Sylvan Lake and its rock spires; just don't expect to have it to yourself. The same goes for Mount Rushmore. If you haven't seen it, you have to go—just be prepared for the polyglot crowds drawn to such a unique monument of such national import.

The Black Hills harbor much more in the way of interest, including the historic townsite of Deadwood, Wind Cave National Park, and the improbable but thought-provoking Crazy Horse Memorial. Visiting some of these places is time well spent on your way back to Rapid.

HAZARDS

For such a high payoff hike, there are relatively few dangers when hiking in the Black Elk Wilderness. Weather can present problems in the Black Hills as in any mountain environment, but conditions are milder here than in the Rockies nearby. Still, it's wise to come prepared for inclement conditions, and to pay attention to weather, as thunderstorms can bring violent conditions.

Harney Peak, the highest point in South Dakota, is now adorned with a fire lookout tower built in the 1930s. In its wild state, the peak was where Sioux medicine man Black Elk had his famous vision: "I was standing on the highest mountain of them all, and round about beneath me was the whole hoop of the world. And while I stood there I saw more than I can tell and I understood more than I saw; for I was seeing in a sacred manner the shapes of all things in the spirit, and the shape of all shapes as they must live together like one being." PHOTO BY PETER POTTERFIELD.

Backpackers pump water from the ample flow of Grizzly Bear Creek, but water sources can become an issue by late summer. PHOTO BY PETER POTTERFIELD.

There are no bears to worry about in the Black Elk Wilderness, so you can leave your bear spray at home. However, a surprising increase in the number of mountain lion sightings emphasizes the fact that the population of deer and antelope in the wilderness attracts these predators and makes the threat from cougar attack real. The best strategy is to pay attention and to try to avoid close contact.

Treat, or filter, all water, and take precautions against disease-bearing ticks, which are a scourge of the region.

SEASON

Despite their altitude, among the highest points east of the Rockies, the Black Hills have a much longer hiking season than their Rocky Mountain brothers farther west. While May through late September is considered the traditional season for long hikes in the Black Elk, lucky weather can extend that season by almost a full month on either end. Early May was a

scorcher the year I explored this area, and mid-April would have been fine for hiking. Check with rangers on snow conditions and creek levels to ascertain whether the route is open.

ROUTE

Whether you're coming from the State Game Lodge in Custer State Park, Rapid, or one of the surrounding Black Hills communities, the best landmark is Sylvan Lake. Follow Highway 87 (the Needles Highway, named for the rocky pinnacles that line parts of the road) east from Sylvan Lake for approximately 7 miles (11 km) to where it crosses the Centennial Trail. Watch for signs to the Iron Creek Trailhead. Turn north here onto an unpaved road and drive toward the Iron Creek Horse trailhead and campground. Park here at approximately 4,900 feet (1,500 m) elevation.

Follow the Centennial Trail, #89, north as it runs past open views, including distant views of Harney Peak, for 3.5 miles (5.6 km), right up to the boundary with the Mount Rushmore National Memorial. The best views of the presidential faces from the Centennial Trail can be found here; scramble up on the rocky hills to the right of trail for the best vantage points. The views of Rushmore from here are amazing, but if you want more take the spur trail (just short of

A backpacker admires the faces of George Washington and Abe Lincoln from the quiet of the Black Elk Wilderness, a stark contrast to the busy scene at the Mount Rushmore National Memorial a few miles away. PHOTO BY PETER POTTERFIELD.

Hikers travel east on the Norbeck Trail, the final leg of the big loop, through an area where members of the Sioux tribe formerly held their famous vision quest ceremonies. PHOTO BY PETER POTTERFIELD.

2 miles, 3.2 km, each way) and venture into the memorial itself for a close-up look at the faces.

From the intersection with the spur trail to Mount Rushmore, continue north on the Centennial Trail with lots of minor ups and downs to its intersection with the Horsethief Lake Trail, #14, and take a sharp left (south) here. Hike almost due south for an hour, where good camping can be found a mile or two (2–3 km) from the intersection as the trail climbs higher, to approximately 5,700 feet (1,740 m). Here at 7.2 miles (11 km) from the trailhead, look for appealing campsites in the open forest. Some have views (or are close to views) of the expanse of the nearby peaks and rocky spires of the Black Hills. The water source, however, is lower on the trail, just beyond its intersection with the Centennial Trail, so you'll have to carry it on your way up or make a water run later, after pitching camp. Be sure to explore the ridgetops near camp to find the best vantage point for scenery and the sunset.

On day two, continue up the Horsethief Lake Trail for 1.5 miles (2.5 km) until it intersects with the Grizzly Bear Creek Trail, #7. Turn right here and begin the rather steep climb up the hill toward the intersection with the Harney Peak Trail and the second night's camp. A good creek with deep pools runs along Grizzly Bear Creek Trail for most of the way, until it steepens significantly near the top on a series of switchbacks. Reach the intersection of the trail leading to Harney Peak at 4.5 miles (7.2 km) from camp. Continue past the intersection on the Cathedral Spires Trail, #4, a few hundred yards to good campsites near the highpoint of the trail, approximately 6,700 feet (2,040 m), quite high considering we're in South Dakota. A small but reliable spring can be found nearby.

Note that multiple trail intersections where the Grizzly Bear Creek Trail, the Harney Peak Trail, the Cathedral Spires Trail, and the Norbeck Trail come together can cre-

ate confusion. Even the trail names on the map are ambiguous, so don't worry too much about the trail names but look instead at where they go. The Grizzly Bear Creek Trail intersects a trail that goes north to Harney Peak. The trail you've arrived on now turns south toward Sylvan Lake, and becomes the Cathedral Spires Trail. A few hundred yards down that trail the Norbeck Trail makes a left turn back toward the trailhead.

Set up camp and prepare for your summit hike to Harney Peak, approximately an hour and 1 mile (2 km) away, and 600 feet (185 m) higher. When the spur trail intersects with the main Sylvan Lake–Harney Peak Trail, #9, expect to see day hikers making the popular trip between those two landmarks. The hike is steep but short, ending at the unlikely stone tower with its spectacular 360-degree views of the Black Hills. The old fire lookout can offer welcome shelter in bad weather, but better viewing, with less company, can be found on the outlying rock outcrops nearby. Take a moment for contemplation, and you might get an inkling of what Black Elk felt here.

On the final day, descend from camp a few hundred yards down the Cathedral Spires Trail, #4, to where it intersects with the Norbeck Trail, #3, and turn left, southeast. The trail descends quickly and steeply from 6,600 feet (2,100 m) to the valley bottom at 5,400 feet (1,680 m). This Black Hills loop finishes strong, and the final section of trail turns out to be a highlight of the trip.

The route drops down through the ponderosa pine forests with several sections of steep switchbacks. In just 3 miles (5 km) from camp, the Norbeck Trail takes you out of the Black Elk Wilderness and into Custer State Park for a bit before reentering the wilderness on its southern boundary. The trail meanders through pretty creek-side meadows where the Sioux once held their vision quest ceremonies.

You'll hike past the Upper Iron Creek Trailhead in 4 miles (6.4 km) from camp (Highway 87 is just south of the trail at this point). The trail continues east, but cuts well north of the road to return to your car at the Iron Creek Horse trailhead and campground, 7 miles (11 km) from camp.

INFORMATION

All wilderness visitors to the Black Elk Wilderness must obtain the required Wilderness Use Visitor Permit before entering the area. Only one permit per group is necessary, and there is no fee for the permits. Self-issue registration boxes are located at each trailhead, so there's no need to stop at a ranger station.

For more information and current trail conditions, contact the Custer ranger station or the US Forest Service headquarters in Custer.

HELL CANYON RANGER DISTRICT
330 Mt. Rushmore Road
Custer, SD 57730
605-673-4853

US FOREST SERVICE
Black Hills National Forest
1019 N. 5th Street
Custer, SD 57730
605-673-9200
fs.usda.gov/blackhills

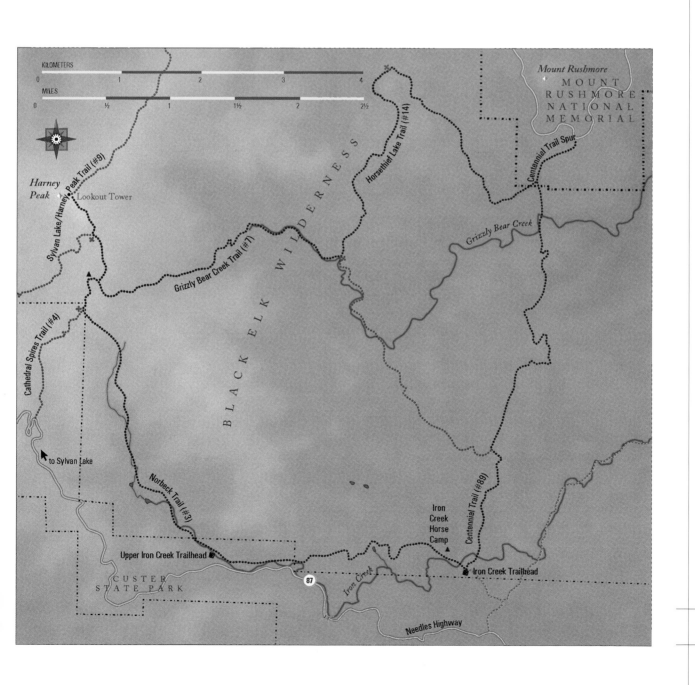

HIGH UINTAS BASINS
High Uintas Wilderness
Utah, United States

DISTANCE: **30–40 miles (50–66 km) round-trip**
TIME: **4–5 days**
PHYSICAL CHALLENGE: **1 2 3 4 5**
PSYCHOLOGICAL CHALLENGE: **1 2 3 4 5**
STAGING: **Salt Lake City, Utah**

Any backcountry journey through the High Uintas Wilderness will demonstrate how aptly it is named. I've been in here a half dozen times, and the lowest camp I ever had was at 10,200 feet (3,100 m). Even the trailheads here are above 10,000 feet. The whole place is so high I suffered from altitude sickness when I flew out from sea-level Seattle and hiked in to Naturalist Basin on the same day. But the Uintas quickly become addictive for those who treasure big wilderness and solitude. Remember that majestic mountain country you saw in the film *Jeremiah Johnson*? That was the Uintas.

The 450,000-acre wilderness area protects almost 70 miles (113 km) of the east–west-oriented range, which includes Kings Peak, the highest mountain in Utah. In fact, *all* of Utah's peaks over 13,000 feet (3,962 m) are here in the High Uintas. Huge, glacial carved cirques and expansive high basins, sometimes miles across, characterize the range, making for fascinating backcountry travel often right at the edge of tree line. A long hike in the Uintas takes you in and out of the forest, then up on the ridges for hundred-mile views, and down into the verdant basins for big exploratory loops on the benches.

The Highline Trail, a trunk line that runs the length of the range, offers a direct way into the heart of the High Uintas. One 65-mile (100-km) length of

Cresting the somewhat intimidating Rocky Sea Pass, the 11,266-foot (3,433-m) barrier that keeps visitation to Rock Creek Basin low. PHOTO BY PETER POTTERFIELD.

the Highline Trail, from Hayden Pass to Chepeta Lake, has become a classic. But for me the Highline is a means to an end, a good trail offering access to fantastic alpine exploration, which here in the High Uintas is in a couple of classic basins: Naturalist Basin and Rock Creek Basin.

You could call this wilderness trip a tale of two basins, for one is famously beautiful and often visited, the other just big and bad and remote enough to put a nice edge on the whole experience. Visiting them both in one backcountry journey makes for a delightfully diverse excursion through one of America's greatest remaining wild places. This four- or five-day trip shows you a high-altitude Garden of Eden, with more contiguous terrain above timberline than anywhere in the country. The 30-mile (48-km) route (that's the minimum distance and does not include exploratory walks) takes you on a varied journey at the ecotone between forest and alpine, in and out of stands of Engelmann spruce and lodgepole pine, into expansive meadows, and across ridges of tundra that stretch for miles.

Naturalist Basin may be the prettiest spot in Utah, and its proximity to the trailhead makes it perhaps the most visited area in the High Uintas Wilderness. But I've camped here for three nights at a time and never seen a soul, not one human, as the geography allows those who wish for solitude a way to find it. The topography here is like a giant bowl with concentric circles of emerald green benches working up

the sides, each a few hundred feet higher than the last. Mount Agassiz reigns over the basin from the west side, finishing off a mountain tableau of exceptional beauty.

And the perfect foil to pretty Naturalist Basin is rugged Rock Creek Basin, another half day down the trail but well guarded by imposing Rocky Sea Pass. You see the pass rising ahead as you approach, gnarly and intimidating. Like the boundary to a kind of twilight zone, there's something about this pass that keeps people away. Truly, that thousand feet of hiking, that hour on the trail, creates a psychological barrier that preserves the lonely quality of Rock Creek Basin on the other side. Here, you find the real deal, a basin so big and wild you could explore for days and not see it all, or anyone else. I've never seen anyone but a ranger in Rock Creek Basin.

Touring the High Unitas demands some time, as meandering around in the basins is the raison d'être of the hike. Wander the benches in Naturalist Basin and sooner or later you'll end up at Faxon Lake, regally situated at the head of the basin with a glorious view of the terrain laid out below. And it might take days of looking, but you'll eventually come upon Rosalie and Gladys lakes tucked up against the big ridge way over there in Rock Creek Basin, perhaps with a moose standing knee-deep in the water. This is impressive American wilderness, and taken as a package, it's tough to beat the combination of these two basins.

LOGISTICS & STRATEGY

Salt Lake City is both the gateway to the Uintas and the most practical place from which to stage the hike. With the trailhead just two hours from town, an alpine start from Salt Lake has you on the trail by 7 or 8 A.M. The trailhead is located off Utah Highway 150, about 35 miles (57 km) from Kamas. For those who wish to be a bit nearer, tony Park City is about 45 minutes closer than Salt Lake, and the town of Kamas, less than an hour from the trailhead, has some lodging available.

LEFT: *A backpackers' camp in upper Naturalist Basin under the imposing bulk of 10,247-foot (3,070-m) Mount Agassiz.* PHOTO BY PETER POTTERFIELD.

OPPOSITE: *Naturalist Basin is filled with lakes, both large and small, located on benches that rise from the basin floor to the flanks of the surrounding ridges.* PHOTO BY PETER POTTERFIELD.

Four nights should be considered the minimum for this (at least) 30-mile (48-km) route, and five is better. The mileage noted does not include day hikes and basin exploration, which can easily double it. Hiking both these basins is all about getting into the High Uintas on the Highline, then exploring the enchanting mountain landscapes you've entered.

From the Highline Trailhead near Hayden Pass, hike two hours to the trail junction for Naturalist Basin. Turn left, north, here and hike into the basin. Within 2 more miles (3.2 km) you are at the threshold of Naturalist Basin proper, after only four hours total on the trail. Find a camp, a really good one (more on that later) and spend two nights in Naturalist Basin. That itinerary allows one full day to explore this, perhaps the prettiest high mountain basin I have ever seen.

On day three, hike out of Naturalist Basin back to the Highline Trail, turn left, east, and hike toward Rocky Sea Pass. Within two hours you come to a trail crossroads near Pigeon Spring, and the beginning of the thousand-foot climb up to Rocky Sea Pass. For some reason the pass seems to separate the men from the boys, the wheat from the chaff—those who want to go from those who don't. Hardly anybody takes on the challenge, yet it is just not that difficult. An hour and you're up, way up at 11,350 feet (3,460 m), with incredible views in all directions.

If you leave Naturalist Basin late in the day and don't have time to make the hike up and over Rocky Sea Pass into Rock Creek Basin, no worries. There are good campsites right at the base of the climb up to the pass, at Olga Lake, just off the trail to Four Lakes Basin, and in the meadows just north of Pigeon Spring. Camping here allows an early start on Rocky Sea Pass the following day.

Whereas Naturalist Basin is really pretty, Rock Creek Basin is wild, imposing, and impossibly big. This is impressive country. From Rocky Sea Pass, drop down into Rock Creek Basin and camp another two nights here in splendid isolation. People have to be in there somewhere, but I haven't seen them. The basin is big, or maybe I've just been lucky. Once you are off the Highline Trail, it's easy to follow the trail system within the basin to various lakes, benches, meadows, and hidden corners of Rock Creek Basin, and explore further by traveling cross-country. As scenic as Naturalist Basin is, the impact and scale of Rock Creek Basin emerges as the highlight of this route.

Two nights in Rock Creek Basin is the minimum, especially considering the time and effort invested to get here. Make sure you take at least one full day to explore this wild basin; two is better. Use the last day for the hike up and over the pass to head back to the car. If you have time on the hike out, you could detour in to Four Lakes Basin, or hike down to see Grand-daddy Lakes Basin. Even if they don't rival Naturalist or Rock Creek for beauty, they show you more of the unique High Uintas country. The fact is, a multitude of variations can be applied to this route, but the best one may be simply to spend more time in either Naturalist Basin or Rock Creek Basin.

Know going in that you will see people in Naturalist Basin. The trailhead is close to Salt Lake, and the buzz has garnered a growing fan base of devotees. But for all the talk one hears about the traffic here, I camped for three nights and saw not a soul until I hiked down by Jordan Lake. Jordan Lake is the big one in Naturalist Basin, right on the trail, and the southwest corner makes a very pretty camp. Want solitude in Naturalist Basin? Don't camp at Jordan Lake. Go up on the higher benches, take some time to scout a good camp among the many lakes and tarns, and you can find privacy.

Altitude is definitely a factor in Naturalist Basin, so you might have to take it easy for a day or two. The basin is so high it defies belief. On my first visit, I hiked up a bench or two to gain some privacy for my camp, and when I looked at my altimeter saw I was above 11,000 feet. It was open, with awesome views, but not unduly exposed. Hiking a bit farther is worth the extra trouble to find a great camping spot. Then spend a day, that's plenty, to explore the benches and lakes scattered all around the basin.

Conversely, there is no way to see all or even most of Rock Creek Basin in a day. Two is way better. And privacy is no big deal: a hundred yards off the trail and you are truly by yourself. I like to camp at the unnamed lakes north of the Highline Trail near the entrance to the basin (as you roll in off the pass) the first night. The altitude there is 10,800 feet (3,300 m), even on the floor of the basin. If I have time, another hour on the trail leads farther north to the vicinity of Rosalie Lake, another good choice for a couple of nights. Moose sometimes hang out here. This is awesome American backcountry, rugged and wild and empty.

I navigate around Rock Creek Basin using a combination of cross-country travel and an informal network of trails that are in reality like way trails. We're not talking big maintenance here. To find your way around, carry the Trails Illustrated map, it's got the basin routes right, whereas the quads for some reason don't. After you've contoured in the shadow of a ridge all day, navigating by topography, it's nice to know that if you walk around that lake you can, with certainty, pick up that trail you see on the map and follow it back to the Highline.

If you've got the time on the way out of Rock Creek

RIGHT: *The geography of Naturalist Basin features a ring of basins, each one higher than the last, harboring quiet nooks and crannies, alpine meadows and crystalline mountain lakes.* PHOTO BY PETER POTTERFIELD.

OPPOSITE: *Part of the pleasure of visiting Naturalist Basin in the High Uintas is the opportunity it affords for off-trail roaming in more remote regions.* PHOTO BY PETER POTTERFIELD.

Basin, explore the open ridges that lead north from Rocky Sea Pass itself before dropping back down toward Pigeon Spring. The high, open terrain makes for easy cross-country travel, and the views back down into the northern part of Rock Creek Basin are spectacular. From the top of Rocky Sea Pass, it's about a five-hour hike back to the trailhead.

The Uintas make a supremely satisfying back-country excursion, combining interesting travel, five-star scenery and a surprising lack of people. Naturalist Basin is exquisite, and Rock Creek Basin impressive, and that towering ridge separating you from the rest of the world is as much a psychological barrier as a geologic one. But the two places, when visited together, create a wilderness journey to rival any.

HAZARDS

Altitude, weather, and wildlife are all a part of the Uintas experience. Avoid the headaches and lassitude of altitude sickness by acclimating before the hike; even a night or two in Salt Lake helps. Black bear are known to be in these mountains, so practice proper camping techniques for bear country, including preparing meals at some distance from your tent and storing food properly.

Sudden storms can happen any time of year in the Uintas, and at 10,000 feet (3,050 m) and above the potential for hypothermia is real. Make sure your clothing and camping gear can adequately protect you in severe weather.

SEASON

The High Uintas are so high that the season is predictably short. When the trailhead is above 10,000 feet (3,050 m), and a lot of camps near 11,000 feet (3,350 m), don't expect to be able to get in here much before late June, or much after late September. You can luck out on weather and pull off an early October trip, which would be cold but pretty, but don't count on it. Predictably, with all the lakes and marshy areas, bugs are pretty bad in midsummer.

ROUTE

From Salt Lake City, drive Interstate 80 eastbound 30 miles (48 km) to US Highway 40, turn south and drive 5 miles (8 km) to Highway 248, turn southeast and follow it 20 miles (32 km) to the town of Kamas. From there, drive 35 miles (57 km) on Highway 150 to the Highline trailhead near Butterfly Campground, a few minutes beyond Mirror Lake and just short of Hayden Pass. The parking lot is well signed and is about 500 yards off the highway, right about 10,000 feet (3,050 m) elevation.

On the drive in, stop at the kiosk on Highway 150 to fill out your use permit and pay the recreation fee (bring cash for that purpose, an envelope drop allows an after-hours purchase). Keep the permit on your dashboard while in the parking lot at the trailhead. The hiking permit is self-issued at the trailhead; just fill out the register as you start the hike.

From the Highline trailhead, the route actually drops a few hundred feet in the first mile or so, which is a nice way

A backcountry camp just west of Rocky Sea Pass, a good option for hikers arriving too late in the day to make it over the pass. PHOTO BY PETER POTTERFIELD.

A backcountry cook finds shelter from the Rock Creek Basin winds to construct an elaborate meal. PHOTO BY PETER POTTERFIELD.

to start, but five days from now that final uphill stretch of trail to the car will test your resolve, possibly your spirit. Hike past the junction to Mirror Lake, then in about 1 mile (2 km) enter the High Uintas Wilderness Area. Follow the trail as it gently undulates up and down past Scudder Lake to the next intersection, the turnoff for Wilder, Wyman, and Packard lakes. Continue eastbound on the Highline Trail just over 4 miles (6.4 km) from the trailhead to the well-signed intersection with the Naturalist Basin Trail.

Turn left, north, here and hike up toward the basin. The route ascends gradually, reaching the first basin trail intersection in just over a mile (1.6 km) from the Highline. There are two good options here: take a left at this first intersection to look for camps on the higher benches to the west, or continue into the basin, turning off to the east before reaching Jordan Lake to camp at, or near, Evermann Lake. A third

option is to go a bit farther, past Jordan Lake, to camp at or near Shaler Lake. If it's midweek and off-season, take a chance with the southeast corner of Jordan Lake.

Find a place you like and settle in for a couple of nights. I found a fabulous spot, just a half hour from the entrance to the basin. The secret is to look on the benches above the basin floor at the fringes of the basin. Spend the next day exploring; a full day is enough time to see every major lake by making a big loop on the higher benches before returning to camp. If you have the time, a third night in Naturalist Basin gives you more time for exploration, including roaming the high country above the meadows.

When it's time to leave Naturalist Basin, retrace your steps back to the Highline Trail. Turn left, east, and head toward Rocky Sea Pass. The trail is mostly level as you travel eastward. In two hours and 4 miles (6.4 km), reach

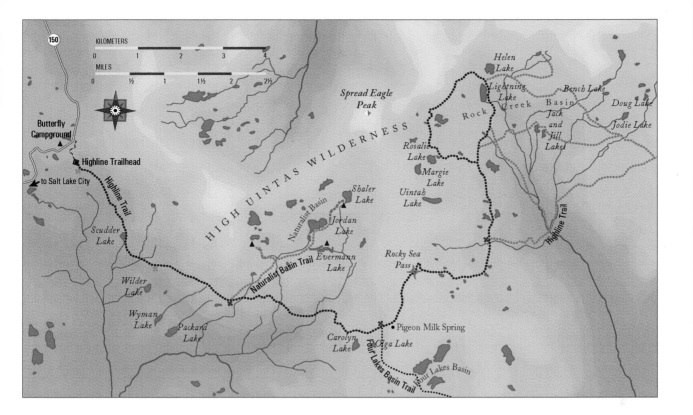

the intersection with the trail to Four Lakes Basin, which leads to the south. Stay on the Highline Trail here, heading east, and start up the lower slopes of the big ridge toward Rocky Sea Pass. It took my reasonably fit party an hour to hike from the Four Lakes Basin Trail intersection to the top of the pass, another hour to hike down into Rock Creek Basin. The hike down provides a perfect vantage from which you can pick out an appealing camp from the many lakes and meadows on the basin floor. It's hard to go wrong in Rock Creek Basin.

From your base camp, spend the next day or two exploring Rock Creek Basin. There's a lot to see here. Make sure to visit the lakes in the northwest corner of the basin, including Uintah, Margie, and Rosalie, and the country over by Lightning Lake and lovely Helen Lake above that. It will probably take you another day to visit the lakes in the northeast part of the basin, beyond Jack and Jill Lake, to Bench, Doug, and Jodie lakes. Meadows, patches of dense forest, and hidden benches make wandering around Rock Creek Basin with a day pack a lot of fun.

When it's time to leave the basin, plan on an hour to work back up to the top of the pass via the Highline Trail. Take time at Rocky Sea Pass to explore the high-country ridges extending nearby. Cell phones work from the exposed

ridges above the pass, but almost nowhere else on the entire journey.

From the pass, it's a half hour down to Pigeon Spring and the intersection with Four Lakes Basin Trail, and from there four to five hours for the 8 miles (13 km) back to the parking lot.

INFORMATION

Permits are required to hike in the Uinta Wilderness, but they can be self-issued at the trailhead near Butterfly campground.

KAMAS RANGER DISTRICT
Wasatch–Cache National Forest
50 East Center Street
Kamas, UT 84036
435-783-4338

DUCHESNE RANGER DISTRICT
Ashley National Forest
85 West Main Street
Duchesne, UT 84021
435-738-2482

OPPOSITE: *The Highline Trail ascends the dramatic eastern escarpment of Rocky Sea Pass on the way back to the car.* PHOTO BY PETER POTTERFIELD.

NORTHERN LOOP TRAIL
Mount Rainier National Park
Washington, United States

DISTANCE: **35 miles (56 km) loop**
TIME: **4–6 days**
PHYSICAL CHALLENGE: **1 2 3 4 5**
PSYCHOLOGICAL CHALLENGE: **1 2 3 4 5**
STAGING: **Seattle, Washington**

Crescent Mountain reigns over Crescent Lake opposite the Yellowstone Cliffs just west of Windy Gap on the Northern Loop Trail.
PHOTO BY PETER POTTERFIELD.

If Mount Rainier is the undisputed monarch of the Cascades, the Northern Loop Trail is its treasured road less taken. The loop has long taken the cognoscenti, that handful of hikers who knew about it, into the most pristine backcountry in all of Mount Rainier National Park. It was a simple fact of geography: located in the remote and hard-to-get-to northern reaches of the park, it was far from the busy attractions that bring most visitors, such as the Paradise visitor center high on the south slope with its access to glaciers, or the Grove of the Patriarchs and its revered giant red cedars.

On the Northern Loop, the appeal is different: lonely stretches of trail, changing perspectives on the 14,410-foot (4,400-m) mountain, one of the highest passes in the park, natural bridges, meadows afire with wildflowers, and raging rivers flowing out of the glaciers. The Northern Loop traverses a landscape very little changed in centuries. And a fluke of nature has not just preserved these qualities, but in a violent act of weather and geography, served to isolate this epic backcountry route even more completely. An almost biblical storm in the early autumn of 2006 washed out the Carbon River Road in the northwest corner of the park, permanently cutting off automobile access used for decades to reach the route. The Northern Loop now is longer, harder, and some would say better.

More than anything but rain, Mount Rainier symbolizes the Cascade Mountains and the Pacific Northwest. Rising from its lowland valleys like a vision, Rainier shows as much relief as Everest. Draped in a mantle of ice, 35 cubic miles (146 cubic km) of it, Rainier is a veritable showstopper rising almost 10,000 feet (3,050 m) above its surrounding terrain. Even from Seattle, 50 miles (81 km) away, it's a view that moves people. Captain George Vancouver saw the peak from his ship in Puget Sound in 1792 and felt obliged to name it after his naval crony, Rear Admiral Peter Rainier. But to the native Salish people of the Northwest, it was spiritual Tahoma. To modern-day residents, it is simply The Mountain.

As striking as it is from a distance, Rainier is best experienced at close range. The hiker within its

embrace is on more intimate, more rewarding terms with the mountain and its surrounding wilderness than even the climbers on its slopes. Here's a place where humbling ancient forests of Douglas fir and western hemlock, expanses of lovely alpine meadows (locally called "parks"), the roaring, glacier-fed rivers, add irresistible appeal to this verdant landscape.

It's all about topography. Climb up past the giant trunks of old-growth trees so high they disappear in the canopy far above and suddenly the moody gloom of the forest gives way to brilliant sunlight at Berkeley Park, or the breathtaking expanse of Grand Park. These surprise stretches of open meadows reveal a carpet of mountain lupine, or avalanche lilies, or Indian paintbrush swaying in the breeze in a chorus of colors. Cross 6,735-foot (2,050-m) Skyscraper Pass and you'll be digging for your Gore-Tex, stopping to watch, mesmerized, ragged streamers of clouds blowing across the glaciers of Rainier's summit dome, seemingly very close from such a high, alpine vantage point. Hiking alongside the Carbon Glacier, and skirting just below the Winthrop Glacier, you'll see before your eyes the birth of a river as both streams emerge from the snouts of the glaciers. Where else in the Lower 48 can you experience something like that?

a wonder to behold. The largest, the Emmons, is 5 miles (8 km) long and a mile (2 km) wide, a remarkable river of ice for the Lower 48. Perhaps more than any other attribute, it is the presence of so much ice that makes a hike around Rainier unique.

LOGISTICS & STRATEGY

The gateway to Rainier is through Seattle. The airport is just an hour and a half from Mount Rainier National Park, or you can spend a couple of days in the city buying gear and provisions before heading for the mountain. Most hikers rent a car for the journey to the national park and the trailhead at Sunrise Visitor Center.

Every hiker will need to obtain the necessary backcountry permits. This process is a bit easier for the Northern Loop Trail than it is for more popular routes, such as the Wonderland Trail. Seventy percent of all wilderness campsites and zones are reservable, the remaining 30 percent are issued on a first come, first served basis on the day a trip begins. The first come, first served slots go quickly, even mysteriously, and cannot be counted on to be available when you want to start your trip. Off-season hikers will have an easier time getting permits for the camps they want for the Northern Loop, whether they reserve in advance or take a chance on the daily allotment.

Each year, reservation requests are accepted on March 15 for the entire season through September, so the best strategy for obtaining permits is this: go to the Web site (see below), download and complete the reservation form, and fax it to the Longmire Wilderness Information Center on March 15 or soon after, with a credit card number to cover the fees. It might be well into May before you find out if your permit has been approved. And when your backcountry permit request is approved, you still must show up at the ranger station by 10 a.m. the day of your hike or you will lose the permit. If you cannot make it to the park by that time, call ahead so the rangers don't give away your permit.

What permits do you ask for? Hikers on most Mount Rainier trails are restricted to camping in designated sites. There are nine legal camps on the

Distinctive radial ridges called "cleavers," a result of the mountain's violent volcanic past, emanate down from high on Rainier into the backcountry surrounding it. These ridges are what create a successive series of obstructing passes set above valleys deeply dug out by raging glacial torrents. Features including Skyscraper Pass require the hiker to climb high above the lowland river valleys of the West Fork of the White River, and the Carbon River during the course of the Northern Loop. You'll earn your rewards on this hike, as there's very little consistently level trail. This route is usually climbing to high ground such as Windy Gap, or descending steeply into big river valleys. Expect to lose and gain more than 9,000 feet (2,745 m) during the 35 miles (56 km) on this trail.

The upside is unrivaled views of Rainier from constantly changing directions. In fact, a highlight of the Northern Loop is the differing perspectives it offers on Rainier as you complete the route. Granite Creek, Lower Curtis Ridge and the high passes on the route offer vantage points that show the ever-changing profile of Rainier and its glaciers. And even in this age of climate change, the glaciers of Rainier remain complete Northern Loop Trail, but they are not necessarily evenly spaced. That means you'll walk right by some camps as you head to the next, depending on your desired destination that day, and your starting point. Planning is complicated by the fact some camps are separated by relatively short mileage but by substantial elevation gain, so don't forget to factor that in. Camps are listed in the route section below.

For experienced backcountry enthusiasts who don't mind going a few miles off the trail on some days, or climbing a few thousand feet higher, or camping away from water sources, there is another option: take advantage of a limited number of "cross-country zones" that can add flexibility, and a degree of solitude, to camping on the Northern Loop. Regulations are strict for these zones, group size is limited to five people, and the terrain is often difficult to negotiate. Rangers emphasize that cross-country camping is suitable *only* for those adept with map and compass, and for those in excellent physical condition for enduring the additional challenge of cross-country travel. But if you qualify, call the Wilderness Information Center to inquire about what cross-country zones are available.

In the summer, the first come, first served permits can be obtained at any ranger station in the park during their hours of operation. Obtain permits at: the Longmire Wilderness Information Center at Longmire, the Jackson Visitor Center at Paradise, the Ohanapecosh Visitor Center at Ohanapecosh, the White River Wilderness Information Center at the White River entrance, the Sunrise Visitor Center at Sunrise, and the Carbon River ranger station at the Carbon River entrance. For the Northern Loop, the White River, Sunrise, and Carbon River locations make the most sense.

The Northern Loop's off-the-beaten-path feel derives from its remote location, far from the usual attractions of the park, such as the Paradise visitor center. But the major storm and subsequent flooding event of 2006 made the trail even harder to visit by washing out the Carbon River Road that previously reached Ipsut Creek Campground. Now you have to walk or ride a bike from the Carbon River entrance the 5 miles (8 km) to Ipsut Creek, which adds significant length to the route. Though an inconvenience for many, this is a positive development for serious backpackers as it protects the pristine qualities of the Northern Loop. Use the situation to your advantage when strategizing your hike.

Basically, you have two options. The recommended route described here is to do a big 35-mile (57-km) loop starting at the Sunrise Visitor Center by combining the full length of the Northern Loop Trail with a section of the Wonderland Trail. The second option is to bail out at the northern terminus of the route, making a one-way 25-mile (40-km) hike of the Northern Loop Trail by incorporating the washed-out Carbon River Road to finish, and using two cars. Both options will show you the wild side of Mount Rainier Park, and give you days hiking under the magical presence of the mountain.

Sunrise Visitor Center is the place to begin, its ranger station and other services (including food service in season) prove helpful, and the 6,400-foot (1,950-m) elevation there starts you out with an altitude advantage. The primary strategic decisions to make are where you want to camp, and therefore what to put on your permit request. The nine legal campsites on the loop provide enough flexibility to accommodate your itinerary. For instance, Berkeley Park Camp is only 3.5 miles (5.5 km) from the start, but if you arrived at Sunrise late in the day, that could well be your best option. Likewise, Redstone Camp is only 5 miles (8 km) from Fire Creek Camp. That sounds like a too-short day until you realize that the route loses 2,000 feet (600 m) down to the White River, then gains it all back climbing up to Redstone.

LEFT: *Avalanche lilies in springtime.* PHOTO BY SETH POLLACK.

CENTER: *Bear grass in bloom.* PHOTO BY PETER POTTERFIELD.

RIGHT: *The meadows of the Northern Loop, locally called "parks," are famous for outrageous wildflower gardens in mid-summer.* PHOTO BY PETER POTTERFIELD.

The "Lower Crossing" is in—but just barely. This lower ford of the Carbon River at the northern end of the Northern Loop Trail routinely washes out in spring, forcing hikers to go 2 miles out of their way to a bigger suspension bridge. Here, a party of hikers is fortunate to cross the Carbon in bad weather before the log is swept away.
PHOTO BY PETER POTTERFIELD.

The number of camps is sufficient to accommodate individual fitness levels and the number of days planned for doing the hike. Three nights will be enough for some parties, six will be preferable for others. Fit parties will want to investigate camping options in cross-country zones, which adds mileage and time to the hike.

HAZARDS

The eruption of Mount St. Helens in 1980 proved without a doubt that the Cascade volcanoes remain active. For that reason, any trail in the park comes with a set of hazards unique to hiking in North America: mud flows, glacier outbursts, floods, lahars, pyroclastic flows, and other events relating to Rainier's volcanic origins. While it is unlikely that an eruption will happen without warning, mud flows and other glacier-generated floods can and do happen suddenly, so every hiker must come to grips with this weird reality. If you do go, rangers recommend that should you hear rumbling or see rivers rise rapidly, do *not* run downstream, but move to higher ground as fast as possible.

As for more common threats: winter lasts nine months a year on Rainier, and summer only a few weeks, so climate can potentially be hazardous any time of year. Catching all the wind and rain that rolls in from the Pacific, Mount Rainier generates its own weather, often bad. Conditions change without warning. Newcomers are aghast at how quickly a hot, sunny day can turn into a cold whiteout, particularly at higher elevations, such as Windy Gap. Snow can fall in such places any time of year, clouds can hide landmarks, and chilly, damp weather can cause hypo-

thermia in the unprepared. Proper clothing and good equipment can protect you from the elements, and a map and compass, or GPS receiver—as well as the experience to use them—can help you find the way in a cloud. Snow-covered stream crossing can be hazardous, and snow-covered trails and passes may require the skills necessary to negotiate hard snow.

While black bears live in the park, these animals seldom cause problems; still, be sure to take the precaution of hanging your food bags out of reach when in camp, on the bear poles provided. Cougars are present and leave tracks, but are rarely seen, and few incidents have been reported.

SEASON

The best weather in the Pacific Northwest almost always comes in July and August, so that would seem to be the time to do the route. But those months are also the busiest, by far, in terms of visitation to Mount Rainier National Park. If you want to hike the Northern Loop in the prime of the summer, you'll need to get an early start on your hiking permit, and be prepared to have company along the trail. An alternative plan might be to go early in the season, if you've got the backcountry skills, including proficiency on snow-covered trails and route-finding. Another option is to go later in the season, when fall color, cool temperatures, and stable weather patterns can make for ideal hiking conditions and snow-free travel. In general, the Northern Loop is in hiking condition most years from July to October, but beware that heavy snow years can delay its opening, and early snow can close it prematurely.

ROUTE

The Northern Loop of Mount Rainier as described here can be broken down into four useful sections. There are nine backcountry camps (counting Ipsut Creek) along the route, shown below in italics. Allowing for both trail mileage and elevation gain, the following route description can be used for trip planning: determine the features that are most attractive to you, how many overnight stays you're contemplating for the hike, and then decide which camps best serve your purposes. With that information, you can apply for your permit reservation.

The route begins at the Sunrise Visitor Center, a 14-mile (22-km) drive up the hill from the White River entrance station off Washington Highway 410. Find the Sourdough Ridge Trailhead at the north end of the parking lot.

Sunrise (road access) to Fire Creek Camp, 7.5 miles (12 km)

From the trailhead, at 6,400 feet (1,950 m), hike west on the Sourdough Ridge Trail with good views of Rainier to the five-trail intersection in just over 1 mile (2 km) from Sunrise. Find the Wonderland Trail and follow it west for less than a mile (2 km) to the intersection with the Northern Loop Trail. Turn right here and hike north into the open meadow below. This is Berkeley Park: enjoy the views, and in season, the riot of wildflowers. There's no camping here; the legal *Berkeley Park Camp* is another 1.5 miles (2.5 km) north on the trail. From the trailside camp the route climbs up to good views of Mount Rainier, then descends to stunning Grand Park, one of the most impressive meadows in the park. Take time to explore the meadow before dropping down into the forest to the turnoff for *Fire Creek Camp* at 4,800 feet (1,375 m).

LEFT: *Rainier is infamous for making its own weather. A party of hikers is forced to make camp near Windy Gap when the fog becomes so thick that merely staying on the trail is problematic.* PHOTO BY PETER POTTERFIELD.

BELOW: *A backpackers' camp under the storied and seldom-visited Yellowstone Cliffs just below Windy Gap.* PHOTO BY PETER POTTERFIELD.

Mount Rainier and the resident elk herd as seen from Grand Park, a popular side trip on the Northern Loop Trail.
PHOTO BY PETER POTTERFIELD.

*Mount Rainier as seen
from Grand Park.*
PHOTO BY SETH POLLACK.

Fire Creek Camp to Yellowstone Camp, 8.5 miles (14 km)

From *Fire Creek Camp*, return to the Northern Loop Trail and turn right, west, to gradually descend almost 2,000 feet (610 m) to the West Fork of the White River. There's no bridge at the trail crossing, so be prepared to wade during periods of high water. Take care, as this crossing can prove problematic. Once across the river, catch a glimpse of Van Horn Falls before ascending steep forest slopes on dozens of switchbacks for 2 miles (3 km) and 1,500 feet (460 m) to the trail junction for pretty Lake James, which is worth a look down the short spur trail. From the intersection, continue west, still climbing via switchbacks, to the turnoff for *Redstone Camp*. Turn left here if you plan to camp, or continue west on the trail into the real heart of the wilderness accessed by the Northern Loop Trail. In 1.5 miles (2.5 km), reach aptly named Windy Gap, where a side trip of just under 2 miles (3 km) can be made out to see Natural Bridge. In 1.4 miles (2.5 km) from the Windy Gap trail intersection, the route drops into a narrow valley, with Tyee Peak and the Yellowstone Cliffs dominating the view on the right, and gnarly Crescent Mountain on the left. Turn left at the intersection for the spur trail to reach *Yellowstone Camp* at 5,200 feet (1,590 m).

Yellowstone Camp to Mystic Camp, 9 miles (15 km)

From *Yellowstone Camp* descend gradually at first, then steeply via switchbacks, down forested slopes for almost 3 miles (5 km) and 2,500 feet (762 m) of elevation loss to the Carbon River. If you plan to exit via *Ipsut Creek Campground*

and the Carbon River entrance station, cross the Carbon River here, at the so-called Lower Crossing. If the river is too high, and it often is, you'll have to continue 1 mile (2 km) farther south (upstream) to cross the river on the suspension bridge. Once on the western side of the river, hike north on the Wonderland Trail to *Ipsut Creek Campground*, then hike the final 5 miles (8 km) down the washed-out Carbon River Road (now regraded into a trail) to the entrance station and the parking lot.

If you are not exiting via Ipsut Creek but doing the full loop route: upon descending to the Carbon River, don't cross the river, but continue south along the east bank of the Carbon River 1 mile (2 km) to the suspension bridge. The *Carbon River Camp*, tucked under Mother Mountain and the Echo Cliffs, is just across the bridge on the west side of the Carbon River. If you don't intend to camp there, continue south on the east side of the river on what is now the Wonderland Trail. The route rises alongside the Carbon Glacier (the snout is virtually at trailside as you hike up) a steep 1.5 miles (2.5 km), hot and dry in summer, ascending 1,800 feet (550 m) to *Dick Creek Camp*. From Dick Creek, the route ascends more gradually another 3.5 miles (6 km) into gentler terrain, meandering through small meadows with peekaboo views of Rainier. The route finally enters Moraine Park before cresting a ridge, with its sublime views of the Willis Wall, the north face of Rainier, and dropping down to Mystic Lake, at 4,500 feet (1,372 m). Less than half a mile (1 km) farther along the trail, you reach *Mystic Camp*, 9 miles (15 km) from *Yellowstone Camp*.

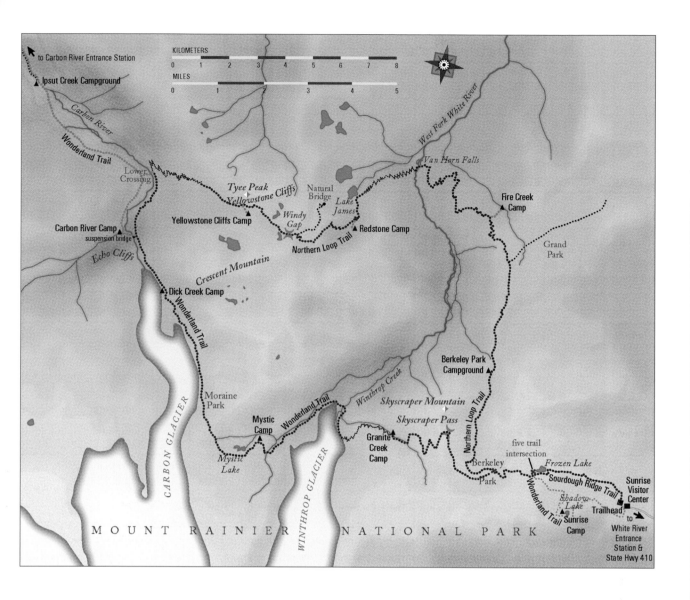

Mystic Camp to Sunrise Visitor Center (road access), 9 miles (15 km)

From *Mystic Camp*, the route descends to cross Winthrop Creek (check before setting out that the creek has not washed out the crossing) before climbing a steep 1,000 feet (305 m) to *Granite Creek Camp* at 4 miles (7 km). The Wonderland Trail climbs out of Granite Creek an additional 500 feet (150 m) to Skyscraper Pass (one of the highest points on any trail at Mount Rainier at 6,740 feet, 2,050 m), passes through the meadows of Berkeley Park, and returns to the five-trail intersection near Frozen Lake. If you are camping one final night, follow the Wonderland Trail 1 mile (2 km) to *Sunrise Camp* at Shadow Lake, 8.5 miles (14 km) from *Mystic Camp*. If you're going to exit via the Sunrise Visitor Center, from the five-trail intersection at Frozen Lake follow the Sourdough Ridge Trail 1.4 miles (2.5 km) back to the Sunrise Visitor Center and your vehicle, 9 miles from *Mystic Camp*.

INFORMATION

MOUNT RAINIER NATIONAL PARK
Tahoma Woods, Star Route
Ashford, WA 98104
360-569-2211
E-mail: MORAInfo@nps.gov
www.nps.gov/mora

SUNRISE VISITOR CENTER
360-663-2425

Hiking Permits

LONGMIRE WILDERNESS INFORMATION CENTER
Mount Rainier National Park
Tahoma Woods, Star Route
Ashford, WA 98104
360-569-6650
www.nps.gov/mora

SOUTH RIM TRAIL
High Chisos Mountains
Big Bend National Park
Texas, United States

DISTANCE: **16 miles (26 km) round-trip**
TIME: **2–3 days**
PHYSICAL CHALLENGE: **1 2** 3 **4 5**
PSYCHOLOGICAL CHALLENGE: **1 2** 3 **4 5**
STAGING: **Chisos Basin, Big Bend National Park, Texas**

Like the Black Hills of South Dakota, the Chisos Mountains of Texas come as a surprise. Rising steeply out of the Chihuahuan Desert to altitudes of almost 8,000 feet (2,440 m), these peaks are some of the highest mountains east of the Rockies. Rising from the banks of the Rio Grande, the High Chisos incorporate an impressive number of ecozones in the span of a few dozen miles, and a diversity of wildlife and birdlife that reflects their position on the cusp of both east and west, and north and south. But the biggest allure of Big Bend is the outstanding hiking that can be found here in these unexpectedly high mountains.

Named for the actual Big Bend, that sudden, magnificent, unlikely course change the Rio Grande makes in a graceful loop to the northeast before resuming its usual course as it flows to the southeast, Big Bend National Park encompasses the Chisos mountain range in its entirety, and a tableau of big desert and big river ecosystems as well. Big Bend is a big park, more than 800,000 acres, and its stretch of the Rio Grande covers almost a quarter of Texas's thousand-mile border between the United States and Mexico. This Texas-sized domain—preserved rather late, in 1944—protects not just the High Chisos and their extensive trail network and unique high-country landscape but 1,200 square miles (3,108 sq km) of the Chihuahuan Desert ecosystem. Big Bend is a big deal, really three parks in one: desert, river, and mountain.

You can find more than 150 miles (241 km) of trail in Big Bend National Park, some so remote and deep within an arid wilderness environment they are positively dangerous. But the reason to come here is the South Rim Trail through the High Chisos Mountains. Mount Emory is the highest peak in the Chisos, at 7,825 feet (2,385 m), but others reach over 7,000 feet (2,135 m), including neighboring Toll Mountain at 7,415 feet (2,260 m). You'll walk right by both these peaks on the way to the Chisos's south-

Emory Peak, the highest of the High Chisos, as seen from the Laguna Meadow Trail. PHOTO BY PETER POTTERFIELD.

ern rim, a stunning vantage point more than 2,500 feet (762 m) above the desert floor. Stretching for 4 miles (7 km) like a giant balcony, the rim from some points offers a glimpse down to the Rio Grande, protected here as a Wild and Scenic River, and beyond that to the mountains of Mexico.

The landscape of Big Bend remains wild. While the amazing South Rim Trail offers a way to experience perhaps the most appealing part of it, it's not tame. There's a chance you might see a Mexican black bear on this hike, and a way better chance of seeing a mountain lion. Dozens of lion sightings happen each month, and one cougar was recently found drowned in a large *tinaja*, or tank, a natural depression in the rocky terrain that forms a pool after rain. Those big tarantulas walking around on the trail can get your attention, too. The natural world thrives here, including endangered peregrine falcons who live in eyries along the inaccessible cliffs of the rim, flourishing on the rich hunting

Highway 385 approaches Persimmon Gap, the gateway to Big Bend National Park. One of the most remote in the national park system, Big Bend requires a four-hour drive at the 85 mph speed limit from even the closest airport. **PHOTO BY PETER POTTERFIELD.**

grounds along the river. So successfully do the falcons breed here, trails are often closed to protect nesting pairs.

As rugged as the environment may be, the hike itself is not arduous. The route recommended here is a moderate two- or three-day overnight backcountry journey of about 16 miles (26 km), if you walk the entire rim loop. But there's no reliable water source on the hike and that means you've got to carry all the water you'll need. Packing water adds weight, but it's not a significant problem for a short backpack such as this one, and is a small price to pay for this unusual backcountry experience.

Life in this place has never been easy, and humans have long struggled to exist here. Archeologists know people have lived in these mountains, the ancestral home of the Chisos Indians, for ten thousand years. Europeans are relative newcomers to the High Chisos. As explorers arrived, Mescalero Apaches established a base in the remote and rugged peaks as late as the 1700s while raiding nearby Spanish settlements in what is now Mexico. While the Apache Indians were ultimately driven out, Comanches later used the Chisos during the storied "Comanche Moon" phase, a period of feared nighttime raids in the mid-nineteenth century, as a base for attacking settlers, by then arriving in bigger numbers. Today you can actually drive parts of the famous Comanche Trail on

your visit to Big Bend. Ranchers and miners soon followed the settlers, and this unique landscape astride the Rio Grande became the home of Americans and Mexicans, not Native Americans.

Big Bend is not just close to the border, it *is* the border, and so predictably it has long been a quirky place that defies the realities of an international frontier. The Mexican hamlet of Boquillas del Carmen was for decades a favorite of visitors to the park, who often waded across the Rio Grande to enjoy the south-of-the-border ambience in the bucolic town, perhaps a beer in the cantina or an overnight stay at the local inn, no border formalities required. There was even talk of creating an international peace park, mirroring the model of Waterton-Glacier. Alas, such casual transborder socializing came to an end after 9/11, along with Boquillas's traditional way of life. The village is now a virtual ghost town. Recently, Mexico's tragic drug war violence has touched the fringes of the park, but not the High Chisos.

Rich in culture, wildlife, and scenery, rugged Big Bend nonetheless remains one of the least visited of all the US national parks, with only 300,000 visitors a year. The Grand Canyon sees twice that many people in a single month. But long distances from population centers, and the scarcity of water, have protected this landscape well enough to preserve the wilderness experience here. The five-hour drive from

The park notifies hikers on their way into Chisos Basin that the wildlife considerations of hiking in the High Chisos Mountains are not to be taken lightly. PHOTO BY PETER POTTERFIELD.

LOGISTICS & STRATEGY

Big Bend National Park is so far from anywhere that the South Rim hike suggested here is best staged from within the park itself, or a handful of nearby communities. People in Texas will probably drive to the park, upwards of 500 miles (Texans seem immune to the mind-numbing realities of 12-hour drives), but most of us have to fly. The closest major airport to Big Bend is Odessa/Midland, about four hours by car from the park, closer to five hours by car to the trailhead.

From the airport, the standard route to Big Bend is to follow Interstate 10 33 miles (53 km) west to the town of Monahans. Take a left (south) on Highway 18, and go 50 miles (80 km) to Fort Stockton. This is your last chance for big grocery stores. Take a left on US Highway 385, and drive 55 miles (88 km). Here, US 385 intersects US Highway 90 near the city of Marathon, your last chance for supplies (limited) and gas. Continue south on US Highway 385 to Big Bend National Park. From Marathon you'll reach the park boundary in about 30 miles (48 km), the park headquarters at Panther Junction is another 30 miles (48 km), and the Chisos Basin area in about 6 more miles (10 km).

Note that some people take minor highways through Alpine, Texas, and end up entering the park farther west, near the communities of Terlingua and Story

the nearest airport down two-lane blacktop highways at legal 85 mph speed limits is unique these days in North America. And the backcountry journey out to the ragged edge of the country's southernmost mountain range can bring unexpected surprises. It could inadvertently make you the envy of every birder in the Lower 48: that Colima warbler you see chirping from the piñon branch on the Laguna Meadow Trail may be just one of 450 bird species in the park, but you're not going to see it anywhere else in the United States.

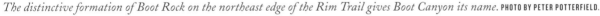

The distinctive formation of Boot Rock on the northeast edge of the Rim Trail gives Boot Canyon its name. PHOTO BY PETER POTTERFIELD.

A bold Mexican jay approaches a hikers' lunch stop hoping for a handout. PHOTO BY PETER POTTERFIELD.

Butte. These towns are closer than Marathon and present yet another option for staging the hike, with motels and small groceries, despite being an hour from the trailhead. From Story Butte, it's about 5 miles (8 km) to the park entrance, but almost 30 (48 km) to Panther Junction and 6 more (10 km) to Chisos Basin.

The park headquarters and post office are at Panther Junction, but all of the action is in Chisos Basin, at 5,400 feet (1,646 m). That's where the lodge, shops, restaurants, store, campground, visitor center and other amenities are located. Chisos Basin is the center of the universe for Big Bend. Truly, the basin is the place to stay. The trailhead for the hike recommended here is right in the basin, next to the lodge and the small market by the parking lot for the visitor center. Be sure to reserve your accommodations at the lodge in the basin (the term is a bit of a misnomer, as the lodge is really a motel-style lodging in one of three buildings). Any extra expense is made up for in terms of proximity: you can walk to the trailhead, restaurant, and ranger station.

Hiking and camping permits must be picked up in person within 24 hours of your hike. You can't reserve one in advance or do it by phone, and that puts an element of uncertainty into the whole affair. For overnight trips the permit will include a specific campsite in the backcountry. There are 42 such legal backcountry camps in the High Chisos Mountains, but only about a dozen are well situated for the South Trail Rim. It used to be that you could camp wherever you wanted to in the park, but that changed in the late 1980s, when open backcountry camping was replaced by designated backcountry camps.

So that's the game when backpacking in Big Bend: get to the visitor center as soon as you arrive and see which camps are available for tomorrow's hike. Actually, for most of the year, one can usually get a camp pretty close to the one you want. Exceptions include spring break, when lots of Texas college kids come here, and holidays such as Thanksgiving and Christmas. I timed my visit for the week after spring break,

stopped at the park entrance ranger station on arrival, and got the very best campsite on the rim: SW4. A week earlier and I could not have obtained a campsite anywhere in the High Chisos. Don't worry too much about the annual trail closures from February through May most years. The park closes the eastern part of the Rim Trail to protect nesting peregrine falcons, but that still leaves the central and western parts for hiking and camping.

The hike itself is quite straightforward: you take one of two trails out to the start of the South Rim loop, do the rim hike, spend a night or two, and return by either of those same two trails. A middle route can come in handy to make a shorter trip, bail out, or deal with trail closures on the eastern rim. That's all there is to it. But the names of the trails in the High Chisos change like you wouldn't believe. It looks confusing, but it's not, so don't be put off. For instance, instead of being called the Rim Trail, this 5-mile (8-km) section, the sweet part of the route, is labeled on maps as three different trails: the Northeast Rim Trail, the Southeast Rim Trail, and the Southwest Rim Trail. But it's really all the same trail.

Here's how it works: from the big Chisos Basin Trailhead near the visitor center parking lot, hike to the South Rim via the Laguna Meadow Trail, which takes you to the western part of the rim, or hike out via the Pinnacles and Boot Canyon trails, which take you to the eastern part of the rim. If you hike out via Laguna Meadow, you start the rim walk at the west end, hike 5 miles (8 km) to the east, and then return to Chisos Basin via the Boot Canyon and Pinnacles Trail. Conversely, if you hike out via the Pinnacles, Boot Canyon, and Northeast Rim trails, you'll hit the rim on the eastern extremity, so just hike the 5 miles

A hiker approaching the intersection of the Boot Canyon Trail and the Northeast Rim Trail. PHOTO BY PETER POTTERFIELD.

(8 km) around the rim to the west and return via the Laguna Meadow Trail. A spur of the Boot Canyon Trail hits the Rim Trail a little west of midway, and that can prove useful to shorten the hike, or get around trail closures.

Whichever route you decide to take, it's going to be a 15 or 16 mile (24–26 km) loop hike total, start to finish, from Chisos Basin, with a camp somewhere near the rim. At the southern end of the loop, positioned all around the Rim Trail (which on park maps is called the Northeast Rim Trail, the Southeast Rim Trail, and the Southwest Rim Trail) are 12 legal backcountry camps. They are designated by codes that reflect the section of trail they are located on. For instance, the camps on the Northeast Trail are named NE1, NE2, etc., and the Southwest Trail camps are designated SW2, SW3, etc.

When doing the route as a one- or two-night backpack, which is recommended, you'll want to camp near the rim, so try to reserve campsites with the prefix NE, SE, or SW. The entire Rim Trail is only 5 miles (8 km), so no matter where you end up camping, you'll be able to do some sightseeing along the length of the Rim Trail from your camp. Most of the camps are situated under at least some tree cover; each camp has at least one tent site and animal-proof storage cans. My preferred camp is SW4, right on the apogee of the Rim Trail, near great views down to the Rio Grande and into Mexico.

Remember, there is no reliable water on the hike out to the South Rim. You might find some, but you can't count on it. The only solution is to carry the water you need. About one gallon per person per day is what you should have with you. For an overnight trip, you'll need to carry about two gallons. You might be able to get away with less, but this is not the sort of place to take chances with water.

HAZARDS

A growing population of mountain lions (sometimes called panthers in Texas) and Mexican black bears are known to live in the park. Attacks on humans are rare, but at least two have occurred in the past decade, and encounters with lions are on the increase. Store your food in animal-proof containers provided in each camp, be vigilant, and report any sightings of predators to a park ranger.

Water is the big problem when hiking in the High Chisos. The rangers have many stories of people who died a half mile from their car because they got lost on a day hike. Tales like that underscore the importance of ensuring your access to water even if things go wrong or your plan falls apart. There is almost no reliable water on any of the backcountry routes, so that means you have to carry *all* you need. Make prudence the better part of valor, and take more than you

The ultimate destination for hikers is the Southwest Rim Trail, where the views to the south are unrivaled. PHOTO BY PETER POTTERFIELD.

The Big Bend of the Rio Grande winds through Big Bend National Park. PHOTO BY PETER POTTERFIELD.

think you require. Look at it this way: the necessity of carrying water keeps the crowds down.

SEASON

Fall and spring are the best seasons for hiking in the Chisos Mountains, but winter can often be just as enjoyable if weather allows. Snow is rare in these peaks, but it does happen. The summers can be hot, but cool spells make high mountain hikes tolerable during some weather patterns. Thunderstorms make summer the wettest season in the park.

Peak season for visitation to Big Bend is March, largely due to its popularity during spring break. Note that parts of the Rim Trail are closed between February and early spring to protect nesting peregrine falcons, so if you plan to do the entire Rim Trail, the best time to hike is October through January.

ROUTE

The 16-mile (26-km) route described here can be done in either direction; it is described here as a clockwise loop because the route is most frequently done that way: in via the Pinnacles–Boot Canyon Trail and out via the Laguna Meadow Trail. However, the reverse works just as well—a counterclockwise loop in via the Laguna Meadow Trail and out via the Pinnacles–Boot Canyon Trail. This may be best when the eastern part of the rim is closed to protect the falcons. In fact, it doesn't really matter which way you go.

From the Chisos Basin Trailhead at the southwest corner of the visitor center parking lot in the Chisos Basin developed area, take the Basin Loop Trail south to the junction with the Basin Loop/Pinnacles Trail. Bear left here and continue on the Pinnacles Trail as it ascends steeply (gaining 1,800 feet, 525 m) over brushy, undulating ground on the east side of the basin and through the pine and juniper forest toward the plateau between Toll Mountain and Emory Peak. The stretch below the Emory Peak Trail Junction switchbacks steeply uphill past cactus and yucca plants.

At 3.5 miles (5.6 km) the trail reaches the junction with the Emory Peak Trail, which branches off to the west near the rock spires of what's called Pinnacle Pass. If it's early in the day, you might consider the 2-mile (3-km) round-trip side trip to the top of Emory, at 7,832 feet (2,387 m) the highest peak in the Chisos Mountains. Beware that the last few hundred feet require some minor scrambling. If you are not going to the top of Emory, continue south past the trail junction on what is now called the Boot Spring Trail.

Hike south on the Boot Spring Trail as it winds through the canyon, which covers some of the greenest and wettest parts of the park, and may even have water. (Look for the famous "boot" rock formation that gives the canyon its name.) At 1 mile (2 km) reach the junction with the Colima Trail. Continue past the trail junction .3 mile (.5 km) to the junction with the Juniper Canyon Trail, which leads left, and east, down to the desert. Continue straight here on the Boot Canyon Trail another .5 mile (.8 km) to the junction with the Northeast Rim Trail. Turn left here to begin the 5-mile (8-km) South Rim Trail loop. (If the Northeast Rim Trail is closed for the falcons, continue on the Boot Canyon Trail 1 mile, 2 km, out to its intersection with the Southeast Rim Trail.)

Hike eastward on the Northeast Rim Trail until it turns south and west and becomes the Southeast Rim trail. A number of legal campsites are clustered on the eastward corner of the Rim Trail loop, NE 1–5 to SE 1–4, which are near the midway point of the circuit. Stunning views to the south, southeast, and southwest can be found along this stretch of trail, clearly the most scenic in the park, and the reason to come here. In some places this striking vantage, some 2,500 feet (762 m) above the desert floor, permits views to the Rio Grande and into Mexico. Note that this is the section of trail closed in late winter and early spring to protect nesting peregrine falcons.

At 3.3 miles (5.4 km) from the Boot Canyon–Northeast Rim Junction, you arrive at another junction, this one the terminus of the southern spur of the Boot Canyon Trail. Continue past this junction on what is now called the Southwest Rim Trail, and follow it westward until it curves around to the north. At 1.7 miles (2.7 km) from the terminus of the Boot Canyon Trail, the Southwest Rim Trail intersects the Colima Trail. Three legal wilderness campsites, SW2 to SW4 are on this section of trail, and make excellent overnight campsites. This is another stretch with outstanding views, among the best of the rim vantage points.

At this intersection, you can turn right (east) on the Colima Trail and hike 1 mile (2 km) to the Boot Canyon Trail, and retrace your steps from there to the Emory Peak Trail intersection (1 mile, 2 km) and the Chisos Basin Trailhead in 4.3 miles (6.9 km).

The recommended route, however, which makes a loop of the South Rim Trail excursion, bears left (west) at the Colima Trail Junction another .8 mile (1.3 km) to the intersection with the Laguna Meadow Trail and the Blue Creek Trail. The latter turns left, south, and downhill toward the desert. Take a moment to enjoy the view on the bench provided. Turn right (north) here and hike back to the Chisos Basin Trailhead through the piñon and juniper forest on the Laguna Meadow Trail. From the Blue Creek Trail intersection, the route travels past the rocky west slope of Emory Peak, through the namesake meadow as it descends gradually through the hilly terrain for 1,600 feet (490 m) through meadow and open forest, reaching the trailhead in 3.8 miles (6 km) back in Chisos Basin.

INFORMATION

All overnight backcountry use requires a permit. Permits must be obtained in person, within 24 hours of your hike, and can be obtained at all visitor centers during normal operating hours.

BIG BEND NATIONAL PARK
P.O. Box 129
Big Bend National Park, TX 79834
432-477-2251
www.nps.gov/bibe

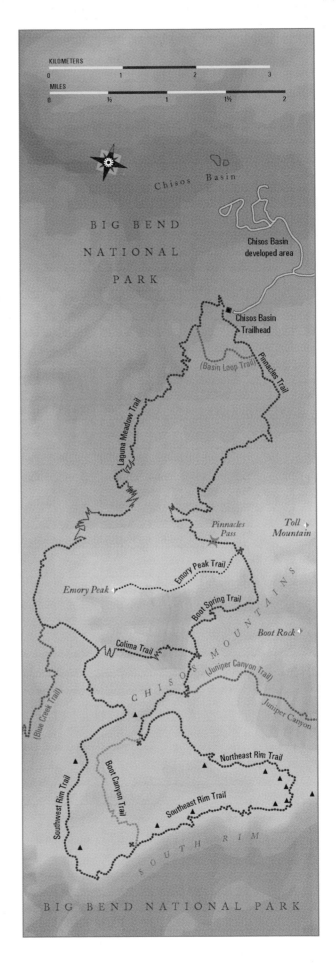

MIRROR LAKE AND EAGLE CAP

Wallowa Mountains
Eagle Cap Wilderness

Oregon, United States

DISTANCE: 25–30 miles (40–50 km) round-trip
TIME: 3–4 days
PHYSICAL CHALLENGE: 1 2 **3** 4 5
PSYCHOLOGICAL CHALLENGE: 1 2 **3** 4 5
STAGING: LeGrande, Oregon

As you approach from a distance, the Wallowas of eastern Oregon rise up out of the plain dramatically enough to evoke memories of the Grand Tetons. Stuck out here where Oregon and Washington come together at the Idaho border, between the Snake River and the Blue Mountains, this compact range, about 50 miles (81 km) long, harbors the biggest concentration of alpine terrain in the state of Oregon. That translates into some of the best hiking in the northwest, traversing long glacier-sculpted valleys, winding up broad meadows, and contouring around distinctive granite peaks. This is appealing, satisfying terrain, best appreciated on foot. The defining feature of Wallowas high country might just be all those alpine lakes, and there are lots of them.

The best of the Wallowa Mountain backcountry is contained within the Eagle Cap Wilderness, at 361,500 acres the largest in the state. Dramatic Eagle Cap peak sits squarely in the middle of the range. When you do this hike, and make the walk-up ascent to the very summit of Eagle Cap, you can look out over the entire range and see what makes it unique. From Eagle Cap, all the major drainages of the

Hikers take in the view of Eagle Cap across Glacier Lake, not as busy as the Mirror Lake side. PHOTO BY KEITH GUNNAR.

Eagle Cap rises regally above its namesake wilderness area, reflected in the waters of Mirror Lake. PHOTO BY COOPER ATKINSON.

Wallowas radiate out below you in every direction. Once thought to be the highest peak in these mountains, Eagle Cap in fact falls a bit short, its 9,595 feet (2,925 m) not quite a match to nearby Sacajawea's 9,843 feet (3,001 m).

No less than thirty peaks in the Wallowas rise to altitudes above 8,000 feet (2,440 m), all separated by meadows, valleys, and lake-filled basins that make the alpine zone here a hiker's paradise. There's a lot of water in the Wallowa Mountains. Oddly, in what is generally a pretty arid place, more than 200 miles (324 km) from the wet Cascades farther west, Eagle Cap gets more than 100 inches (254 cm) of rain per year. That contributes to the thriving forests and lush meadows in the high country. This route, in fact, starts out along the lovely upper reaches of the East Fork of the Lostine River, a stream that boasts a legal designation as Wild and Scenic for more than 15 miles (24 km) of its length. The Wallowas embrace wilderness in spades.

There's nothing fancy about this hike; it's merely a direct route into the most aggressively scenic corner of the Eagle Cap Wilderness, right up to imposing Eagle Cap itself. For the amount of time and effort applied, this hike delivers an unexpectedly high-octane return. A pretty trail up the East Fork of the

Lostine River takes you right to spectacular Mirror Lake. Nestled just beneath Eagle Cap, in certain lights the lake reflects the peak perfectly. A camp here makes an ideal home base for exploring the astounding Lake Basin, just next door, and hiking to the top of Eagle Cap. You can expect to see Rocky Mountain bighorn sheep and mountain goats, and may see bear and cougar.

Locals in the West seem compelled to compare their nearby mountains to European ranges, so it's not really surprising that the Wallowas are known here as "the Alps of Oregon." That might work for the chamber of commerce, but to me they look a lot more like the Sierra than the Alps: all that exposed, clean, white, exfoliated granite in the mountaintops and ridges recalls the famous crags of the Yosemite high country. Wandering in the complicated topography of Lake Basin around Eagle Cap is unbelievably scenic, with two of the highest peaks of the range standing right here: Sacajawea and the 9,845-foot (3,000-m) Matterhorn.

Set aside in 1940, when this part of Oregon remained largely undeveloped, the wilderness here was preserved early enough to protect the landscape effectively. There is history, though, including a mid-nineteenth-century gold rush, and extensive habitation by the Nez Perce and other Indian tribes, notably the Shoshone. A band of the Nez Perce actually hid in these rugged mountains until they were led away in 1877 by their leader, Chief Joseph, who is famous for his remark, "I will fight no more forever." His father is buried a few miles from Eagle Cap.

Perhaps the major issue now is that Eagle Cap's powerful allure will in the future attract lovers of backcountry in unmanageable numbers. The remoteness here has provided a degree of de facto insulation from overuse, and currently all you need is a parking pass and self-issued permit to see this remarkable mountain landscape. The driving distances involved take real commitment to get out here, but that won't dissuade the committed wilderness pilgrim for long. Not many backcountry experiences this direct, dare I say easy, can rival this one.

LOGISTICS & STRATEGY

Eagle Cap is a long way from population centers. The closest major airport is Boise, Idaho, about 230 miles (370 km) from the trailhead, or Portland, Oregon, about 355 miles (570 km) from the trailhead. The most efficient way to get here is in a rental car from either airport, via Interstate 84. Expect to take about three hours to drive the 175 miles (282 km) from Boise to La Grande, Oregon, or five hours for the 300 miles (483 km) from Portland.

A lot of people choose to stage the hike from La Grande. Considered the gateway to the Wallowas, it's right on the interstate, about 60 miles (97 km) from the town of Lostine, and the turnoff to the trailhead, via Highway 82. Another option for staging is Enterprise, Oregon, a tourism center for the Wallowas and home to the Wallowa Mountain Visitor Center, about 10 miles (16 km) beyond Lostine. The trailhead is 17 miles (28 km) from Lostine, located at Two Pan Campground at the end of the Lostine River Road.

The three- to four-day route described here ascends from the trailhead up to Mirror Lake, spectacularly situated under Eagle Cap, in five to six hours of hiking. Establish a base camp somewhere in the vicinity of Mirror Lake, but ensure you are at least 200 feet (60 m) from the lakeshore (on any lake in Eagle Cap) to comply with wilderness rules. The best idea, in fact, is to get some distance from the lake, up on nearby benches, or into the granite outcrops nearby, options that can help you enjoy a little privacy on this increasingly popular route.

From your base camp near Mirror Lake, take at least one day to explore Lake Basin to the north and east of your camp. At least half a dozen alpine lakes can be visited by making a trail loop through the 2-by-4-mile (3-by-7 km) basin chock full of alpine lakes, often reflecting granite peaks. With an early start you may have time for the side trip to Glacier Pass on your hike back to Mirror Lake. If you can take a second day for further exploration, use it for the ascent of Eagle Cap itself. The summit is accessed by good trails and requires no technical climbing skills to reach (snow conditions permitting). The view from the top alone is worth the trip up here. Some fit parties can both explore Lake Basin and climb Eagle Cap in a day, but that's a lot of wild high country to cover in twelve hours of daylight.

When I say put your base camp at Mirror Lake, I mean somewhere in the vicinity. Within a mile of the lake are a number of good camps that can offer a degree of privacy. This is the classic hike in the Eagle Cap Wilderness, the favorite, so you cannot expect solitude. It has become a popular destination precisely because Eagle Cap and Lake Basin are the prettiest places within the extraordinary wilderness. You are likely to see other hikers, particularly on summer weekends and holidays. But this is eastern Oregon, so we're not talking about the kind of pressure you would get in Yosemite or the Grand Canyon.

The powerful allure of the place does make it incumbent on us all to tread lightly. Eagle Cap Wilderness is a favorite of the locals, and as the word gets out, it draws outdoor enthusiasts from farther afield. Simple strategies like doing the route midweek, coming here in early or late season, and camping away from the lakes can make your wilderness experience at Eagle Cap unexpectedly authentic. The area around Mirror Lake can absorb a lot of people, and if you take the time, you can find a camp that gives you a bit of solitude. Look in the granite outcrops surrounding the lake for hidden sites. Most hikers are drawn up here by the beauty of the lakes, so for a better experience find scenic benches and higher slopes for your tent. Carrying water a hundred yards is a small price to pay to have a patch of paradise to yourself.

The hike in to Mirror Lake is, surprisingly, not particularly strenuous, at just over 7 miles (12 km) and a couple of thousand feet elevation gain. While here, take at least one extra day to roam the meadows, basins, and lakes around Eagle Cap. Two days is better, as the terrain around Eagle Cap is conducive to rewarding explorations from base camp, encumbered only by your day pack. On day one, venture northeast into the heart of Lake Basin, to Douglas Lake, Crescent Lake, Horseshoe Lake, and back to Moccasin. With more time, think about getting up to nearby Glacier Pass, or Ivan Carver Pass. Bring your fly rod, as the signature alpine lakes of the Eagle Cap Wilderness offer pretty good fishing.

A complex system of trails around Eagle Cap allows for exploring. From this crossroads hikers can choose from the fascinating Lake Basin, to remote basins, to the summit of Eagle Cap itself.
PHOTO BY COOPER ATKINSON.

The classic route deep into the heart of the Eagle Cap Wilderness follows the East Fork of the Lostine River Trail from Two Pan Trailhead through broad meadows up to Mirror Lake.
PHOTO BY COOPER ATKINSON.

If you've got another day, use it for an ascent of Eagle Cap. From Mirror Lake, the trip to the summit covers 6 miles (10 km) and takes most of the day, especially with extra time spent on top taking in the surroundings. The route requires no technical climbing skills, and in fact is the only high peak in the Wallowas to have a trail to the summit. The view from the top makes sense of the entire range, and gives you the best possible perspective on the major drainages and high peaks. Sacajawea, the highest point in the Eagle Cap Wilderness, is clearly visible, as is the Matterhorn.

It comes down to personal preference, so make your own decision on priorities. But for me, the concentration of alpine lakes and their unique wilderness flavor is what separates the Wallowas from other hikes. So roaming Lake Basin to me makes the most sense, and gets top priority, for the single extra day spent up here in the high country. Save the climb of Eagle Cap for a second day here if you have it. Few vantage points this easy to get to are so rewarding.

Once back at Mirror Lake, it's only 7.5 miles (12 km) and a half day downhill on the East Fork of the Lostine back to the car. You could make it a loop by hiking over to Minam Lake on Trail 1661 and following the West Fork of the Lostine north back to the car.

HAZARDS

Bears are in the Eagle Cap, but seldom present problems. Still, it's important to practice safe camping procedures by cooking at a distance from your tent and hanging your food out of the reach of wildlife. Cougars, too, roam here, and are increasing in number faster than bears as hunting with dogs is now unlawful. Be aware of predators, and report sightings.

Mountain weather is perhaps the major concern in the Eagle Cap Wilderness, especially in the upper elevations. Sudden storms can strike in any month, with the potential for hypothermia. Make sure your gear and clothing can stand up to the elements. Bad weather with low visibility can roll in with alarming speed, presenting real navigational problems if the trails are obscured by snow, which can be the case even into July and August. Navigate carefully, and descend if sudden storms approach.

Significant use of pack animals in the wilderness means that it is imperative to treat or filter all drinking water thoroughly.

SEASON

Like other alpine areas, hiking in the Wallowas is dependent on the previous year's snowfall. Most years, the trails open up by late June, although the passes and higher routes may be under snow much longer. By July most routes are clear enough to hike. The fall season easily goes into October in the Eagle Cap Wilderness, weather permitting. Bugs are a problem in midsummer; late season is better.

ABOVE: *A lunch stop in the Eagle Cap Wilderness.*
PHOTO BY KEITH GUNNAR.

RIGHT: *The Eagle Cap Wilderness gives birth to multiple rivers, including the "Wild and Scenic" Lostine, here tumbling down into the meadow with late summer lupine still in bloom.* PHOTO BY COOPER ATKINSON.

Numerous alpine lakes near Eagle Cap offer some of the most interesting alpine exploration in the Wallowas. PHOTO BY KEITH GUNNAR.

ROUTE

From La Grande, Oregon, drive north on Highway 82, following signs for Enterprise and Wallowa Lake, reaching the town of Lostine in about 60 miles (97 km). From there, drive 17 miles (28 km) south on the Lostine River Road (called Lostine Canyon Road on some signs in town) to the Two Pan Campground at the end of the road. The Two Pan Trailhead (5,585 feet, 1,700 m elevation) is near the south end of the ample parking lot.

Take care to find the correct trail, as there is more than one trail leaving from Two Pan. Find the East Fork Lostine Trail, #1662, head up the trail into the wilderness area, and cross the East Fork on a log bridge about a mile from the trailhead. The trail ascends quickly, reaching the expansive meadows along the trail beside the East Fork of the Lostine River. A big pool along the way allows for fishing. Views of Eagle Cap open up as you climb higher. About halfway up the trail crosses the river on a bridge to work up on the east side of the creek. At about 5 miles (8 km), the trail steepens again and ascends on switchbacks up to an intersection

with Trail 1661, which leads right to Minam Lake. Mirror Lake is to the left a few hundred meters, about 7.5 miles (12 km) from the trailhead, at 7,600 feet (2,316 m).

Look around the lake for nooks and crannies on the benches and side meadows and rock outcrops to find a campsite suitable for a few days, and remember that regulations mandate that you camp at least 200 feet (60 m) from the shore, or from any lake. Some of the rocky ledges as far as a half mile from the lake make good camps. From your home at Mirror Lake, you are well positioned to climb Eagle Cap and explore Lake Basin.

To reach Lake Basin, follow Trail 1810 northeast deeper into Lake Basin and past Crescent, Craig, and Douglas lakes, and then via Trail 1821 see Lee and Horseshoe lakes. Spend most of the day here exploring the signature alpine lakes of the Eagle Cap area. Bring your fly rod, as most of these lakes offer pretty good fishing. By combining trails 1810 and 1810A, you can visit Moccasin Lake on the return, and if you have time, make the trip over steep Glacier Pass and down to Glacier Lake on Trail 1806. Another good excursion from Mirror Lake is to Ivan Carver Pass on the way to

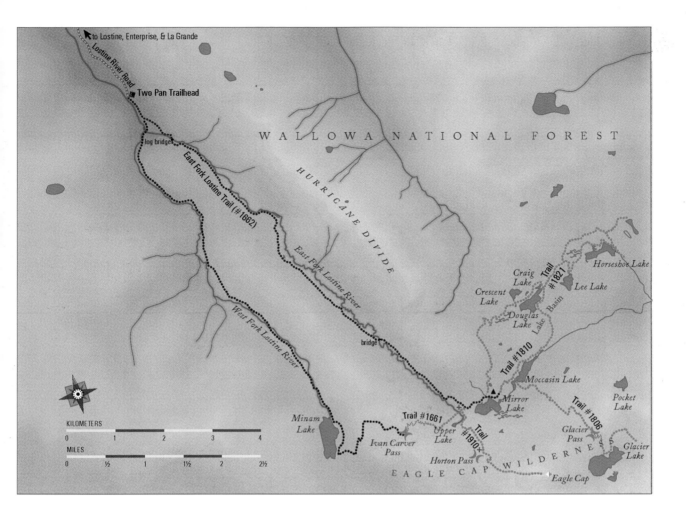

Minam Lake, on Trail 1661, with good views down into the West Fork drainage. A topo map makes exploration of Lake Basin easier and enables some off-trail roaming. The only decent map I could find for this area was the USGS quad named "Eagle Cap."

For the climb up Eagle Cap, expect a 6-mile (10-km) round trip from Mirror Lake with 2,000 feet (610 m) of elevation gain. Head west on Trail 1661 less than .5 mile (1 km), then turn left, south, on Trail 1910, skirting Upper Lake on its east side. Hike 1 mile (2 km) to the intersection where Trail 1910 turns right toward Horton Pass. Instead, bear left on Trail 1805. Soon the Eagle Cap Trail switchbacks up to the ridge. Turn left at the top of the ridge and follow the crest up toward the summit. The final few hundred feet to the top is a series of switchbacks, finally reaching the summit at 9,572 feet (2,917 m).

Once back at camp near Mirror Lake, it's just a half day down the East Fork of the Lostine and the trailhead. You could make it a loop by hiking over to Minam Lake on Trail 1661 and following the West Fork of the Lostine north back to the car at Two Pan Trailhead.

INFORMATION

A $5 Northwest Forest Pass can be purchased at a dispenser at the trailhead. Fill out a mandatory self-issue wilderness permit at the trailhead, and take one copy with you.

EAGLE CAP RANGER DISTRICT
Wallowa Mountains Office
201 East Second Street
P.O. Box 905
Joseph, OR 97846
541-426-5546 or 541-426-4978

WALLOWA-WHITMAN NATIONAL FOREST
1550 Dewey Ave
P.O. Box 907
Baker City, OR 97814
541-523-6391
www.fs.usda.gov/wallowa-whitman

RAE LAKES LOOP
High Sierra
Kings Canyon National Park
California, United States

DISTANCE: 46–53 miles (75–84 km) loop
TIME: 5–7 days
PHYSICAL CHALLENGE: 1 2 3 4 5
PSYCHOLOGICAL CHALLENGE: 1 2 3 4 5
STAGING: Fresno, California

The Rae Lakes Loop through Kings Canyon National Park shows you the rugged, wild side of the southern Sierra, peaks that radiate a totally different vibe from that of the mountain landscape farther north in Yosemite. Glacial-sculpted granite walls and impressively deep canyons—deeper even than the Grand Canyon—contrast with lovely sub-alpine meadows and a stunningly diverse conifer forest. What else would you expect from an ecosystem that harbors the giant sequoia trees in the famous groves of Kings Canyon and Sequoia national parks?

But it's the hiking that makes this week-long route irresistible. Here's a 50-mile (80-km) jaunt through the scenic heart of the Sierra that takes in roaring waterfalls, high mountain passes, and perhaps the most sublime alpine lakes in the range. The pilgrim gets all this in a loop that starts and returns to the same trailhead, virtually eliminating transportation hassles such as car shuttles.

Just be prepared to do a little work. You'll carry that pack up more than 7,000 feet (2,140 m) of elevation gain in just the first four days as the loop takes you from the 5,000-foot (1,525-m) trailhead to stunning Glenn Pass at 12,000 feet (3,650 m). But that's just the ante up, the effort applied to get into the sweet part of the trip: the eponymous Rae Lakes nestled in their wild basin. The hard work gives you in return three or four days of easy roaming in a magical mountain world, especially if you take the recom-

mended side trip into Sixty Lakes Basin. That detour changes the character of the route by taking you off the classic trails and into a remote and secluded basin that presents a hidden side to these epic southern Sierra Nevada mountains.

John Muir visited here in 1873 and 1875 and may rightly be credited with saving this part of the range from wanton exploitation. Luckily the big trees in the mind-blowing sequoia groves were voluntarily spared by logging interests before the park was established in 1890. Then known as General Grant National Park, only the fourth US park, it was expanded in 1940 when it was renamed Kings Canyon, and expanded yet again in 1960. Its 400,000 acres make it one of the United States's biggest western parks when combined with the adjacent Sequoia National Park, together setting aside more than 860,000 acres. The two parks' unparalleled expanses of pristine High Sierra backcountry is designated more than 90 percent wilderness, the most stringent protection it can have. This is a hiker's park if there ever was one.

The route itself comes with multiple route options, allowing you to go as you wish, a strenuous five nights or an easy seven nights. The Rae Lakes Loop gets you into the most scenic parts of the park by connecting two big drainages—Woods Creek and Bubbs Creek—with a section of the John Muir Trail. From a trailhead at the end of the spectacular Kings Canyon park road, Roads End, the route ascends the South Fork of the Kings River into its upper section, known as Paradise Valley, before joining up with the John Muir Trail where it crosses Woods Creek. The JMT turns south to reach the legendary Rae Lakes before climbing over Glenn Pass and descending steeply to Vidette Meadow for the route back to the trailhead along impressive Bubbs Creek. Add the two-day side trip into Sixty Lakes Basin and you've got a grand tour of the southern Sierra that is unrivalled.

Along the way you can stop for a glimpse of the resident giants of the Grant Grove of sequoias, and even the largest living thing on the planet (just think of that!), the General Sherman tree. You don't have to be a tree-hugger to appreciate the majesty of these groves, but it helps. In fact, trees turn out to be an unexpected highlight of this wilderness walk. The big sequoias grow at lower elevations, but even on the

OPPOSITE: *Hikers work up into Paradise Valley on day one of the Rae Lakes Loop.* PHOTO BY PETER POTTERFIELD.

Mighty Bubbs Creek slows its pace as it rumbles through a relatively flat section near a camp near Junction Meadow.
PHOTO BY PETER POTTERFIELD.

hike you'll pass towering red fir, white bark pine, ponderosa pine and the unmistakable twisted-bark beauty of western juniper. The Rae Lakes Loop shows you the most extensive, most diverse old-growth coniferous forest anywhere in the world, and that by itself is reason enough to come here.

LOGISTICS & STRATEGY

While the Rae Lakes Loop Trailhead in Kings Canyon National Park is about five hours from either Los Angeles or San Francisco, Fresno makes the better airport through which to stage the hike and rent a car. Just two and half hours from the trailhead, Fresno has everything you need. Even if you choose to arrive via Los Angeles or San Francisco, you'll probably want to stay overnight in Fresno, or in one of the motels or other accommodations on California Route 180 between Fresno and Cedar Grove Village.

As you prepare for the hike, besides the usual considerations of transport, food, and supplies, there's one more complication to the Rae Lakes Loop: you've got to pick up your hiking permit (even if reserved in advance) at the Roads End ranger station in Kings Canyon National Park by 9 a.m. of your first hiking day. That means a 6 a.m. start even from Fresno. (If you can't make it on time, be sure to call ahead that morning so the rangers don't give your permit away.)

The route to the trailhead follows Highway 180 from Fresno all the way to the park entrance, to the Grant Grove visitor center, and finally through Cedar Grove Village to the final half hour on the winding mountain road to its terminus at Roads End. The small, funky permit cabin at Roads End is both

the start and finish of this famous route, making this hike unusual among great Sierra routes in that a shuttle or a second car is not required.

Basically, the Rae Lakes Loop connects two epic rivers that converge in Kings Canyon—Woods Creek and Bubbs Creek—with a stretch of the John Muir Trail. The route can be done in either direction, but I recommend the clockwise version, and that's how the hike is described here. Starting via Paradise Valley and exiting via Bubbs Creek works best in terms of elevation gain, camps, and scenic climax.

Going clockwise, you start at Roads End, hike up beside the South Fork of the Kings River into its upper section, known as Paradise Valley, and in about 16 miles (26 km) join up with the John Muir Trail. The JMT crosses Woods Creek, turns south to travel to Rae Lakes, ascends Glenn Pass (almost 12,000 feet, 3,650 m), and descends steeply toward the intersection with the Bubbs Creek Trail near Vidette Meadow in about 21 miles (34 km) from Paradise Valley. From Vidette Meadow it's another 14 miles (22 km) downhill along Bubbs Creek back to the trailhead at Roads End.

If you make the side trip into Sixty Lakes Basin, as recommended here, you detour off the JMT at Arrowhead Lake and hike into Sixty Lakes Basin "through the back door" on an easy but off-trail route. After a night in the basin, you emerge to the south on a secondary trail system that exits the basin and descends to Rae Lakes. That side trip changes the nature of the hike in a major way by getting you off the classic route and into very pretty Sierra high country that is seldom visited. The Sixty Lakes Basin filigree is well worth the extra night and additional 8 miles (13 km) or so of hiking.

As the hiking route is straightforward, the primary logistical issue becomes strategy on where to camp, and that comes down to how much work you want to do. From the trailhead, it's about 23 miles (37 km) and 5,600 feet (1,725 m) of elevation gain into the sweet part of the hike, which is the Arrowhead Lake/Rae Lakes vicinity at about 10,400 feet (3,200 m). I chose to tackle the climb and the distance in two days of strenuous hiking, which enabled me to spend more days in the high country. If you don't want to work that hard, or if you have extra time, then take a more reasonable three days to reach the Arrowhead Lake/Rae Lakes area. Once you're up there, the hard labor is over and you can enjoy two or three days of high country roaming with only moderate daily mileage or minor elevation gain to contend with.

As for camp specifics: the park mandates that no camping is allowed between the trailhead at Roads End and the entrance to Paradise Valley, a distance of about 6.5 miles (10.5 km). And, in Paradise Valley, you *have* to camp in designated sites, there's no getting around the rules there. Three legal camps in Paradise Valley have five to eight tent sites each: Lower Paradise, at 6.5 miles (10.5 km), Middle Paradise at about 8 miles (13 km), and Upper Paradise at about 11 miles (17.5 km). So the distance you decide to do on day one pretty much decides where you will camp on the rest of the hike.

With a late-morning start from Roads End, 11 miles (17.5 km) and almost 2,000 feet (610 m) up to Upper Paradise Camp can be a bit of a grind, but it positions you to reach Arrowhead Lake or Rae Lakes by making an even more strenuous hike—12 to 14 miles (19–22 km) and 3,500 feet (1,060 m)—the next day. An easier option would be to choose an itinerary that goes from Roads End to Lower Paradise Camp, then an easy day to Woods Creek Camp, then an easy day to the Arrowhead Lakes–Rae Lakes area. Your decision will come down to personal preference and the days you have available for the hike.

Eventually, whether it's day two or day three, you'll reach pretty Dollar Lake (no camping allowed), right at 10,000 feet (3,050 m) and 22 miles (35 km) from the trailhead, and just beyond it Arrowhead Lake. That's another decision point. Almost everyone doing this hike walks right past Arrowhead and continues on the John Muir Trail 2 more miles (3 km) to camp at Rae Lakes. That's a good option. But the route recommended here includes a side trip into remote Sixty Lakes Basin, accessed by a short, easy, cross-country route from the outlet of Arrowhead Lake. That does two good things: it puts you at relatively uncrowded Arrowhead Lake instead of Rae Lakes for your camp, and it takes you into one of the prettiest high-country basins in this part of the Sierra, a tranquil place where few hikers venture.

If you eschew that option, then proceed with the classic loop hike and remain on the John Muir Trail. Camp at either Arrowhead or Rae Lakes, your preference (but remember there is a two-night maximum stay at Rae Lakes), and continue on over Glenn Pass toward the Bubbs Creek Trail and the exit to the trailhead. If you are game for a look at Sixty Lakes Basin, however, plan on taking one night and two days to experience it: After camping one night at Arrowhead Lake, climb into the basin the "back way," over Basin Notch, about an hour from Arrow-head Lake, and meander down into the basin to find a camp. There are no worries about getting lost, as there is a good way trail in the basin, or you can just follow the drainage up through the basin for the hike back down to Rae Lakes and the next night's camp. A couple of days in Sixty Lakes Basin is worth the time, and in fact will prove a highlight of your hike.

From midway in Sixty Lakes Basin, it's only a half a day and maybe 5 miles (8 km) down to Rae Lakes, a spectacular place surrounded by high mountains on all sides, including Fin Dome and Painted Lady. An evening at Rae Lakes after a night in Sixty Lakes Basin combines to make the true climax of this backcountry loop. From your camp at Rae Lakes, it's a steep 1,600 feet (490 m) up and over Glenn Pass at 11,978 feet (3,640 m), followed immediately by an equally steep descent down to the Charlotte Lake Trail intersection

Mount Clarence King rises above remote Sixty Lakes Basin, aglow in dawn light. PHOTO BY PETER POTTERFIELD.

ABOVE: *Hikers descend toward Vidette Meadow on the John Muir Trail.*
PHOTO BY PETER POTTERFIELD.

LEFT: *The basic tools of the backcountry traveler, map and compass, are never made obsolete by technology.*
PHOTO BY PETER POTTERFIELD.

and Vidette Meadow. Either of those places make a reasonable spot to camp, positioning you for a final—if long—day out to the trailhead. The option I recommend, however, is to continue past the Charlotte Lake turnoff down to the Bubbs Creek Trail intersection, and turn there for an easy descent another hour to Junction Meadow Camp. From there it is still more than 11 miles (17.5 km) to the trailhead, which is long enough for the last day, even though it's all downhill and goes pretty quickly.

Remember that backcountry permits are required for this hike through Kings Canyon National Park unless you go in extreme off-season. Between early October and early June (check with the park for exact dates) permits are free and can be self-issued at the Roads End permit station. For the rest of the year, park quotas limit the number of people entering on a single day, and a wilderness camping fee is applied. It is highly advised to reserve your permit in advance, otherwise you'll end up taking your chances on getting one of the first come, first served permits which are made available starting at 1 p.m. the day before the hike.

Reservations can be requested at least two weeks in advance of your hike. If you reserve a permit, the wilderness camping fee must be submitted with the reservation request. For each calendar year, reservation requests are accepted from March 1 to September 10 by fax or mail. One important note: even if you have reserved your permit in advance, you must pick it up at the Roads End permit station by 9 a.m. of the first day of your hike. You can't drive from Fresno to Roads End by then, so you have to call the Grant Grove wilderness office at the visitor center to let them know you'll be late.

On the Rae Lakes Loop, except for the first 6 miles (10 km) and the final 6 miles (10 km), you are free to camp in most places on the route, as long as you are 100 feet (30 m) from a trail and 100 feet (30 m) from any stream. You'll pass areas where camping is prohibited, but not as many as you would think. My view is that campsites are important, so I take the time to look for a good one, preferably with a view, running water nearby, and a modicum of privacy. Just where you camp will be influenced by multiple factors, including your own personal inclinations, available campsites, etc. Surprisingly, not the least of these factors is the location of bear boxes.

Bears are a big problem throughout the Sierra, and the Rae Lakes area has more reported black bear sightings and incidents than any other high country area. Bear-resistant food containers are required, and hefty fines are levied on those who don't comply. If you don't have a bear-proof container, you can rent one at Grant Grove on the way to the trailhead. The containers add a little weight (mine weighs in at 2.2 pounds empty) but they help keep the bears from becoming even more habituated to robbing hikers. Somehow, the bears seem to know they can't get into them. The use of lockers and canisters has greatly reduced bear incidents at Rae Lakes.

The bear boxes or lockers, a fairly recent development, are simply big metal boxes fixed in place onto a concrete slab. These are totally bomb-proof, and you can fit all your food and toiletries easily into these things. You'll grow to like them, even to the point where the presence of these boxes becomes a persuasive argument to camp in a well-used spot with boxes, rather than seek out a place with more solitude but no boxes. The relatively recent park requirement that all campers carry bear-proof canisters makes the boxes less crucial, as long as every odoriferous item in your pack fits inside your canister. As the parks continue their efforts to remove broken and unused lockers from the wilderness, previous locations of food storage lockers may not be guaranteed. So the canisters give you greater flexibility by obviating the need to camp near bear boxes, and, by regulation, you have to carry them anyway.

HAZARDS

Bears are troublesome and potentially dangerous on this loop. Some campgrounds have sturdy bear boxes in which to store food, and those can be helpful. A bear-resistant food container is required on this hike, which can make the bear boxes redundant. Treat or filter all water. If you are coming from low elevation, the altitude can present problems—Glenn Pass is almost 12,000 feet (3,650 m) high—so try to give yourself a few days to acclimatize. Consistent good weather, and hot conditions, makes sunburn and dehydration potential problems, so wear a big hat and use a hydration system.

SEASON

Summer in the Sierra is often gloriously sunny, especially this far south, with only thunderstorms or weak systems to cloud the blue skies. July to September is generally considered the best time to hike the JMT, but the season will vary depending on the previous winter's snowfall. Heavy snowfall in 2011, when I did the route, made late August the real start to the hiking season. Snow in the passes is the issue. Even in July—and sometimes August—expect to be hiking on snow at the higher passes. Hiking into October is sometimes feasible, but by then you're pressing your luck. July can be biblically buggy.

Regal Fin Dome and its trailing ridge draw the eye north across Rae Lakes. PHOTO BY PETER POTTERFIELD.

A hiker travels along the isthmus between the Rae Lakes as he makes his way southward on the John Muir Trail. PHOTO BY PETER POTTERFIELD.

ROUTE

Once you drive past the Grant Grove visitor center and Cedar Grove Village, the spectacular park road stops abruptly at Road's End, 8.5 miles (14 km) from the park entrance, in a large trailhead parking lot. A small cabin-like structure serves as a ranger station, called locally the permit station, where permits are picked up and the trail begins at 5,000 feet (1,524 m) elevation.

From the permit station, hike 1.9 miles (3 km) along the South Fork of the Kings River down the sandy, sunny trail through big, open timber toward the junction of the Bubbs Creek and Paradise Valley trails. The short section before the intersection is popular with day hikers. At the intersection, proceed up the Paradise Valley Trail, passing pretty Mist Falls in 2 miles (3 km). Above Mist Falls, the route climbs steeply up beside the river into the stretch of valley known as Paradise Valley. No camping is allowed for the first 6.5 miles (10.5 km) from the trailhead, until you reach the Lower Paradise Valley Camp at 6,500 feet (1,900 m). The

striking rock domes rising on the west side of the trail. Here the Paradise Valley Trail joins the storied John Muir Trail and soon crosses Woods Creek on an impressively large suspension bridge at 8,500 feet (2,590 m). This is one crossing not likely to wash away. A designated camp with fire rings lies immediately across the creek, but remember, above here you are not obligated to camp in designated sites so only need to follow park regulations in terms of being 100 feet (30 m) off the trail, and 100 feet (30 m) from water sources. Stamina and schedule will determine your strategy here.

Note that day two can be a long, tough one on the trail, particularly if you choose to push on to Arrowhead Lake, about 6 miles (10 km) from the Woods Creek bridge, or Rae Lakes, about 8 miles (13 km) from the bridge. On a hot day the moderate mileage but steep elevation gain (3,500 feet, 1,067 m from Paradise Valley), coupled with a heavy pack (as it's still early on in the trip), can present challenging hiking. I made the 12 miles (19 km) from Upper Paradise Camp to Arrowhead Lake in a long, hot eight-hour day. The route crosses the big bridge, then climbs steadily (steep in places) up the broadening, always rising valley past the confluence with Baxter Creek, eventually reaching scenic Dollar Lake about 4 miles (7 km) from the bridge. Arrowhead Lake is less than a mile (2 km) farther, at about 10,300 feet (3,140 m). I chose to camp there, but most hikers doing this loop proceed another 2.5 miles (4 km) from Dollar Lake to Rae Lakes on the John Muir Trail, the marquee destination for the hike.

I found that Arrowhead Lake has surprisingly pretty campsites, with Fin Dome dominating the scenery. Upper Paradise Camp to Arrowhead is a full day, but I stopped at Arrowhead for another reason: so I'd be in a position to explore Sixty Lakes Basin, a place revered by old Sierra hands. A two-day detour into that remote basin really changes the character of this classic hike, enhances the experience, and provides a glimpse into a rare pristine place in this otherwise well-traveled part of the Sierra. Directions follow for those so inclined, otherwise pick up the classic loop route description from Rae Lakes, farther below.

After a night at Arrowhead Lakes, retrace your steps a few hundred yards north to the lake's outlet stream, then travel cross-country to the southwest toward the obvious low pass in the Fin Dome Ridge. There's no trail, but the going is easy as you work your way up to the low pass, about 10,600 feet (3,230 m), so about 300 feet (100 m) above Arrowhead Lake. A way trail appears as you work up toward the broad crest of Basin Notch. From the notch, stroll downhill toward the big lake just below, which is approximately in the middle of Sixty Lakes Basin.

A pretty good way trail can be found on the west side of the string of lakes, all connected by a single drainage, and

Middle Camp (6,700 feet, 2,042 m) comes 1.5 miles (2.5 km) later; the Upper Camp (6,900 feet, 2,013 m) comes 2.2 miles (3.5 km) later at about 11 miles (17.5 km) from the trailhead. This is where Woods Creek flows into the Kings River. I opted to make the first two days long ones to quickly reach the high country, so I chose the upper camp, which put Arrowhead Lake in reach of a long second day. The upper camp meant six hours hiking from the trailhead.

From your camp in one of the Paradise Valley campsites, continue up valley, climbing steadily, finally reaching Castle Domes Meadow in about 6 miles (10 km), so named for the

Bubbs Creek rushes in staggering torrents as it descends to its confluence with the South Fork of the Kings River.
PHOTO BY PETER POTTERFIELD.

Not for nothing is this loop named after these beautiful alpine lakes.

I was pleasantly surprised to find yet more lovely camps at Rae Lakes, despite the popularity of these alpine landmarks, and even enjoyed a degree of solitude. From Rae Lakes, the John Muir Trail climbs past the southern end of the lakes and then steeply up 1,600 feet (490 m) to the crest of Glenn Pass at 11,978 feet (3,650 m). The trail here is well built, switchbacking up the mountainside, and the 2.7 miles (4.5 km) from Rae Lakes to the crest of the pass go quickly. My party required two and a half hours to reach the summit, and had to kick steps in a long final snow slope despite it being late August. From Glenn Pass enjoy the stunning views down to the Palisades, over to the Great Western Divide, and down toward Forester Pass. Glenn Pass is an extraordinary viewpoint in this part of the Sierra, and definitely a place to tarry.

From the pass, descend steeply through austere rocky basins via hundreds of switchbacks before catching the first glimpse of the oddly shaped Charlotte Dome rising above Charlotte Lake. In 2.5 miles (4 km) from the pass, reach the intersection with the 1.5-mile (2.5-km) side trail to Charlotte Lake, where many hikers doing the loop choose to camp. Others continue the descent another 2 miles (3 km) to the intersection with the Bubbs Creek Trail. At the intersection, you have the option of staying on the John Muir Trail another mile (2 km) or so to camp near the bear boxes in Vidette Meadow. (Note that "meadow" is a misnomer; the area apparently once was open, regularly burned by Native Americans, but it is now deep within a mature forest with only a remnant of open space remaining.)

dozens of good camps can be found nearby. Sixty Lakes Basin is an area of light use; good campsites abound, and we saw no one in the basin the two days my party was there. Take time to walk downstream to see the lower lakes; you'll see the upper lakes on the hike out. After a night in the basin, pick up the good way trail (now well marked on most maps) on the west side of the lakes, and hike out the 4 miles (7 km) from mid-basin to the surprisingly high (11,200 feet, 3,414 m) pass and its final lake before the fast, steep descent 2 more miles (3 km) to Rae Lakes. The impressively large twin lakes sprawl below as you descend past the wildflowers back down to the John Muir Trail and a camp at Rae Lakes, with stunning views of Painted Lady and Fin Dome.

Hikers ascend along the Paradise Valley Trail under the granite outcrops known as the Castle Domes. PHOTO BY PETER POTTERFIELD.

I find most of the well-used camps at Vidette Meadow unaesthetic and too close to one another. It's a bit off route anyway, so I chose to descend the Bubbs Creek Trail another 2 miles (3 km) from the intersection of the JMT and Bubbs Creek Trail to Junction Meadow. There I found a prettier camp along Bubbs Creek. Staying in Junction Meadow also shortened my final day by more than 2 miles (3 km). The final day of the loop follows the Bubbs Creek Trail 11 miles (17.5 km) from Junction Meadow back down to the trailhead.

The route descends the astoundingly robust and beautiful Bubbs Creek past several impressive waterfalls on a long, gradual downhill grade 6.5 miles (10 km) to a prominent rock formation known as the Sphinx, sitting high on a ridge south of the creek. (Sphinx Creek is the final legal campsite on Bubbs Creek.) From there the trail descends quite steeply for 2.5 miles (4 km) to the intersection with the Paradise Valley Trail. From the intersection, the familiar 1.9 miles (3 km) of broad, sandy trail leads past all the clean day hikers and back to the car at Roads End. A perfect beach on the Kings River, replete with white sand and a turquoise swimming hole, is just a hundred yards beyond the parking lot, the perfect place for a cooling dip after an epic hike.

INFORMATION

WILDERNESS MANAGEMENT OFFICE
Sequoia & Kings Canyon National Parks
47050 Generals Highway
Three Rivers, CA 93271
559-565-3766 or 559-565-3341
E-mail: SEKI_Wilderness_Office@nps.gov
www.nps.gov/seki

KINGS CANYON VISITOR CENTER (IN GRANT GROVE)
559-565-4307

CEDAR GROVE VISITOR CENTER
559-565-3793

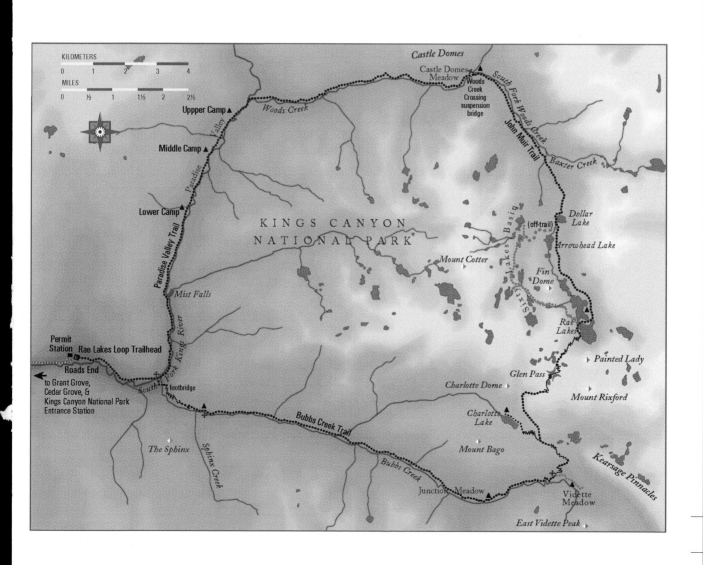

INDEX

Page numbers in *italics* refer to illustrations.

Sunset from Window View, Chisos Basin, Big Bend National Park.
PHOTO BY PETER POTTERFIELD.